John Lane spent 35 years serving worldwide with the Royal Navy in frigates, a guided missile destroyer, and in the Commando Carrier HMS *Albion*. He saw operational service in the Malayan Emergency with the 1st Loyals (North Lancashire Regiment), in Aden, and in North Borneo during Confrontation. He commanded naval establishments in Oman whilst on secondment to the Sultan's Armed Forces, and in Gibraltar, and also served on the NATO Staff in Malta and at the British High Commission in Canada. In 1972 he was evicted by Colonel Gaddafi from Tripoli following the departure of the British Naval Mission from Libya, and from 1975 to 1977 he served onboard the Royal Yacht *Britannia*. He was awarded the OBE in 1985.

After leaving the Navy John Lane was Senior Manager for the Armed Forces Hospitals Southern Region in Saudi Arabia during the Gulf War and in 1991/92 he was head of mission for the HALO Trust in Afghanistan. He has also worked for the Ryder Cheshire Foundation in Western Tanzania with Burundi refugees, and with Christian Solidarity International in Eritrea and Nagorno Karabagh. Humanitarian appointments with the International Red Cross, the European Commission, British Executive Service Overseas and VSO have included post-earthquake Armenia, Croatia during the Balkans War, post-genocide Goma, Hargeisa in Somaliland, Belize, Northern Bangladesh, Peru, Tanzania, Ethiopia, and what was then North West Frontier Province, Pakistan following the SE Asia Earthquake. John Lane now tends an allotment on the banks of the River Wandle in London and has a *chacra* smallholding near Iquitos on the banks of the River Amazon.

CHICKEN STREET

Afghanistan before the Taliban: Clearing the Deadly Remnants of War

John Lane

"Now all is done that could be done
And all is done in vain."

Helion & Company

G G Books UK

Co-published in 2013 by:

Helion & Company Limited
26 Willow Road
Solihull
West Midlands
B91 1UE
England
Tel. 0121 705 3393
Fax 0121 711 4075
Email: info@helion.co.uk
Website: www.helion.co.uk

and

GG Books UK
Rugby
Warwickshire
Tel. 07921 709307
Website: www.30degreessouth.co.uk

Designed and typeset by Farr out Publications, Wokingham, Berkshire
Cover designed by Euan Carter, Leicester (www.euancarter.com)
Printed by Henry Ling Ltd, Dorchester, Dorset

ISBN 978-1-909384-26-2

British Library Cataloguing-in-Publication Data.
A catalogue record for this book is available from the British Library.

For details of other military history titles published by Helion & Company Limited contact the above address, or visit our website: http://www.helion.co.uk.

We always welcome receiving book proposals from prospective authors.

For those who have gone on ahead

"May their souls rest peacefully on the wings of the Afghan winds"

Contents

List of maps and photographs

In colour section

FOREWORD

After a distinguished career in the Royal Navy, John Lane could have eased back and become a hospital administrator or school bursar, like so many of his kind. Instead he decided to save the world, or at least to have a go at it. The part of the world he decided to save was unsalvageable Afghanistan, in the turbulent period between the departure of the Russians and the rise of the Taliban.

He was head of mission (no capital letters, he insists) for a British-based de-mining charity under the direction of a controller known as 'the Colonel'. Neither the charity nor its controller is named, though their identities can easily be guessed. The Colonel's military exploits as a legendary battalion commander on active service had not endeared him to the High Command of the time – but he made an inspired choice with his head of mission in Kabul, a mariner whose previous mine experience was mainly with sea-mines, except for a tour of duty in Croatia. There were no sea-mines in Afghanistan, but it was a devil's garden of other sorts leading up to the later IEDs (improvised explosive devices).

Commander Lane RN learned quickly and he writes about it brilliantly. He has an ear for dialogue and irony and an eye for detail and history. He casts light on our present grim predicament by explaining what came before it.

Many of the best war memoirs arrive rather late on parade. This is one of them. It takes time to reflect and to draw conclusions from the chaos and anarchy of life on the front line. J.G. Ballard said of his own war time experiences, as an internee of the Japanese, that it took him twenty years to forget and another twenty to remember.

In John Lane's case it looks like ten to forget and ten to remember. His own front line in Afghanistan, then as now, was wherever the armed groups decided to fight – either in the capital, or where advantage might be gained from an ambush, a rocket attack or the laying of a minefield.

He has a rare ability to describe a fire-fight and the shock of the incoming. He is also acutely aware of the costs and casualties. And of the necessity, in a memorial stone (in a Christian cemetery in a Moslem country), of making the inscription as short as possible, so that it gives less offence and makes a smaller target. Such are the details that make his book a masterpiece of its kind.

If only our politicians had shared his understanding of the history of Britain's three Afghan wars, set out in the back-light of these pages, they might not have opted for our fourth. An Epilogue like rolling thunder gives a factual account of later events including the vacuous expressions of optimism from successive British Defence Secretaries, set against the rising death toll from our costliest and longest conflict of modern times. We have to ask, in opting for this fourth war, did they ever pause to wonder who won the other three?

The quotation on the title page says it all:

"Now all is done that could be done
And all is done in vain."

Martin Bell
Journalist, ex-MP

Key Events

1839-1841	1st Afghan War.
1878-1881	2nd Afghan War.
1919	3rd Afghan War (Treaty of Rawalpindi 8th August 1919)
14th January 1929	King Amanulla abdicates.
October 1929	Nadir Shah proclaimed King.
November 1933	King Nadir Shah assassinated. Crown passes to Zahir Shah.
1964	Constitutional Monarchy established.
17th July 1973	King Zahir Shah deposed; exiled in Italy (returned home in 2002, died aged 92 on 23 July 2007). Republic declared under Mohammed Daud Khan.
27th April 1978	President Daud murdered, together with 30 family members.
	Nur Moh'd Taraki declared President of the Democratic Republic of Afghanistan. Treaty of Friendship signed with Soviet Union.
September 1979	US Ambassador killed in Kabul. President Taraki killed. President Hafizulla Amin installed.
December 1979	President Amin executed. Babrak Karmal made President.

	USSR invades Afghanistan.
1985	President Babrak Karmal removed from office. Replaced by President Najibullah.
15th February 1989	Soviet withdrawal from Afghanistan.
15th April 1992	Mujahideen (resistance fighters) take Kabul. President Najibullah seeks refuge in UN compound.
May 1992	Interim President Mojahedi is followed by interim President Burhannudin Rabbani (*subsequently killed by the Taliban, Sept.2011*).
1992 onwards	Civil War – Kabul largely reduced to ruins.
1994	Emergence of the Taliban militia (originally US funded and supported). Rapid advances made against Rabbani's government.
27th September 1996	Taliban fighters enter Kabul. Ex-President Najibullah hung from a gantry.
August 1998	Taliban take Mazar-i-Sharif
October 1999	UN Resolution 1267 imposes sanctions against the Taliban.
December 2000	UN Resolution 1333 – further sanctions against the Taliban for 'their support of terrorism and narcotics cultivation'.
March 2001	Taliban destroy statues in Kabul Museum and historical sites in Ghazni, and bombard the giant 5th century Buddhas at Bamiyan.
April 2001	Ahmad Shah Masood ('Lion of Panshir' and former

	Defence Minister) visits Europe to gather support against the Taliban regime in Afghanistan.
9th September 2001	Ahmad Shah Masood killed by suicide bomber
11th September 2001	Attack on Twin Towers, New York. Subsequent US bombing of Afghanistan (as from 7th October); in-country military support against Taliban/Al Qaeda. Mazar-i-Sharif falls 9th November.
13th November 2001	Taliban garrison in Herat defeated. Northern Alliance forces enter Kabul; Taliban regime terminated.
End of 2001 onwards	Inception and consolidation of NATO's International Security Assistance Force (ISAF) – 11,000 military personnel (UK: 900)
22nd December 2001	Mr Hamed Karzai inaugurated as Chairman, Afghan Interim Authority (following meeting of Afghan leaders in Bonn, Germany)
June 2002	Nationwide Loya Jirga (Grand Assembly) convened.
	Transitional Islamic State of Afghanistan formed (President: Mr Karzai)

(*See Epilogue for subsequent events*)

Chapter I

IN THE MIDDLE

'And when the One Great Scorer comes
To write against your name,
He marks, not that you won or lost,
But how you played the game.'

Grantland Rice

The explosion came as no surprise. It had been a busy day in our part of the city.

As explosions go, it wasn't that big. Although it did knock the house down, or rather, up. Floatingly skywards it went, a swirling cloud of dust and debris, dirty yellow and reddish maroon with black specks mixed in, twisting and twirling.

I can see it now, gazing from the gutter, face up.

That trough of discarded, rotting rubbish with the black pools of fetid water was a sensible place of refuge at the time, quite the best on offer. I imagine I must have been blown there; it was not a spot you might opt for voluntarily, whatever the circumstances.

As for the vibrating, dancing stars, there was no question about those.

After the shattering, all-enveloping, wincing detonation of the too-close-for-comfort rocket, a myriad coloured lights hovered in front of my eyes like a cartoon knockout, ears pounding with the compression, the whirring projector somewhere towards the back of my head. That I can remember, head hunched deep into my shoulders like a threatened tortoise.

Then, as gravity took possession of the obliterated house, now hanging vengefully vacant above us in fragmented, suspenseful particles, I turned over in the roadside drain, quite forgetting about the old vegetables and the mud – and the detrimental effect on my almost-new bottle green corduroy trousers, tailor-made in fashionable Chicken Street downtown (once the Savile Row of Kabul), painstakingly hand-stitched by master-cutter Samir Babakar in return for 12,000 *Afghanis*, all of eight pounds. A bargain, if ever there was.

There followed a light pattering sound, like summer rain, punctuated by a few heavier, more threatening and decisive thuds, descending anonymously through the pall of enshrouding dust.

There's much to be said for low-tech rockets with pocket-sized warheads. And for houses built predominantly of clay.

How long we lounged around in the gutter, nobody can say with any accuracy. It's not important. The story of that memorable explosion is folklore now, oft recounted by the Project de-miners as after-supper entertainment following a hard day's work in the field. It has grown tenfold in the telling – 'each time the stirring tale is told anew, the embellishments and exaggerations being greater than the last' – so that on hearing the laughter, the cooks abandon their stoves and leave the dishes in the sink, and the guards and drivers likewise forsake their duties to gather round and vicariously re-live the drama. That's the Project house style: no point in whimpering about near misses, make the most of them. What's more, we had broken the golden advocation – 'May you never be in the wrong place' – so it served us right.

But we can't have remained at the side of that road for too long, because pieces of the house were still gently descending, ever more peacefully, when, with one accord, we were galvanised into action, bouncing back to our feet like rubber hoopla men on a fairground stall, briefly unsettled by events but ready for more, although of what, we weren't quite sure.

There were four of us in the group that day: happy Dr Rhubar, general practitioner, outwardly irrepressible Afghan adviser-cum-manager for our mine clearance Project; his brother Dr Nasseir, visiting from our clinic in the north with time on his hands and who had come along for the walk for no particular reason; rock-like Karimullah, enthusiastic handyman and general factotum who had tagged on out of curiosity. And me – whose idea (now revealed to be questionable) it had been to take some air, and to try to find some lunch (my recently-assumed duties and responsibilities in my capacity as head of mission for the Project were elastic and wide-ranging, adjusted on the hoof to contend with all contingencies).

Bizarrely, I was still clutching a packet of biscuits bought barely five minutes earlier. They were probably stale anyway, and now definitely included a few freshly broken ones (unrelated to moisture content at the moment of baking). I recall conjecturing how high the house must have gone if only now the pieces were falling back to earth. I suppose they would have swirled about a bit at the apogee, but even so, it seemed it was taking an awfully long time to come down.

Anyway, up we bounced like a formation gymnastics team and in unison down the road we started to run. It was involuntarily: our feet did the running and we followed.

I was last at this point, trailing, but that was a detail really because, even though it felt like one, it wasn't supposed to be a race and thankfully, I still had the biscuits.

Passing the smoking hole where the house had been (pre-rocket) and looking in over the low front wall, the way one does, I saw (paradoxically speaking) that everything had vanished. Except for the front door, which curiously was still standing, more or less, although at a funny angle. There was loud banging coming from the far side of that door, frantic banging, as the surviving occupants, old and young, until very recently the residing family of the now demolished house, tried to escape. In their panic and distress they were overlooking the opportunity, newly presented, of fleeing around the jammed door without impediment. And in turn, our shameful running feet omitted to stop.

Along the pavement we sped, colleagues and passers-by inter-mingled, newly-joined by the dishevelled survivors, all swept up and herded together in the confusion of the moment.

'Back!' I shouted. 'Back! Go the other way!'

There was no demonstrable logic for this, simply a sudden sensation that we were moving in the wrong direction, into the path of the next incoming missile. It just happened, the directive coming with conviction and authority. Obediently, everybody about-turned, and off we all shot in the opposite direction, which put me and the biscuits now nicely in the lead of my companions and the burgeoning group. Breathlessly we reached the far end of the dusty, pot-holed street and slowed uncertainly. Whereupon there was a further unexpected development.

A bright yellow Kabul taxi hurtled into sight round the intersection, practically on two wheels like a Keystone Cops fugitive. With an embarrassed sideways lurch it recovered its perpendicular composure and skidded to a stop amidst the panting throng. All four doors flew open simultaneously and out leapt a two-man and one-girl TV camera crew, followed nano-seconds later by the black bearded Afghan driver, his *kolah* hat – the ubiquitous collapsed-soufflé *chapan* – askew on his head, anxious not to lose his fare.

'No!' we cried to the new arrivals. 'Back! There's another rocket coming in!'

Everyone had taken up the mantra. As it happened, it wasn't true but it seemed that way at the time. At least, the confident forecast was not immediately borne out by events; no more rockets came whilst we were there – maybe later, although we didn't stay to find out.

On receipt of this re-echoing and unsettling prediction the compliant camera crew tried desperately but unsuccessfully to get back into their taxi as the driver engaged in a gear-grinding emergency three-point turn. At that juncture, for no obvious reason aside from the lull in the firing, the sense of urgency ebbed away from the adrenalin-charged gathering as rapidly as it had been provoked, to be replaced by a corporate sense of self-conscious aimlessness, a loss of direction and purpose.

Perhaps it was the absence of police cars, fire engines and ambulances responding to the attack, sirens wailing. Kabul wasn't like that. In the late summer of 1992 there were no emergency services coming to the rescue. Not that day, not any day. After all, it was just another explosion. Just another rogue rocket. As for the injured, the lucky ones – sticky with blood – were pushed into the back of a yellow cab, any yellow cab, by anxious relatives; the rest travelled by wheelbarrow or on a rickety wooden trolley, sooner or later.

The displaced householders, the bedraggled survivors, would gather up what possessions they could, putting the tattered remnants of their disordered lives on to a hand cart, precariously piled, and wander off to who knows where to find somewhere else to live. Perhaps they might move in with friends in town, perhaps they could squeeze in with the extended family in a distant village. Maybe life – devoid of hope, and after a fashion – would continue under a sacking shelter in a far-away refugee camp, anonymous and far from home across the border in Pakistan.

The streets of Kabul were forever peopled with families on the move, and not just ones and twos: mute and impassive recipients of the injustices of life. It was a daily ritual: the familiar trundle of the wooden-wheeled hand carts, stacked high with pots and pans, brightly coloured plastic buckets, faded rugs and stained blankets. Sometimes there was a bicycle in the retreating column, being pushed by the head of the household and bearing a sack of lentils, rice or chickpeas across the handlebars with a small child perched on the saddle; the mother walking to the side with the remaining children, all wide-eyed, her dress billowing in the sharp, cutting wind that swoops down on the city from the surrounding mountains. And we were the silent observers.

'What kind of rocket was that?' I enquired. It is academic really, but it shows interest and fills the ruptured void. We don't feel any particular animosity against the artillerymen who sent that missile on its way so that it chanced to land almost at our feet. After all, we have never met, it wasn't really aimed at us, and such attacks were part of the daily routine of city life. Not really accepted – or acceptable – except that no one could do anything about it.

Roused from his trance, Dr Nasseir looks surprised and then considers thoughtfully. 'Sakar,' he decides, staring at the ground, shaking his head and half speaking to himself. 'Must have been a Sakar.'

Looking round invitingly, first at the TV people who are seeming slightly discomfited, and then at the two doctors and stoical Karrimullah, I suggest we all go home and have a nice cup of tea, it being past three in the afternoon and therefore both too early and too late to embark on any new adventures that day. 'I've got some biscuits,' I add enticingly, glancing at the newcomers and trying to compensate for the abruptness of our initial salutation.

This pronouncement furthers the calming process, and the camera crew nod in agreement, readily prepared to be easily diverted from the repetitious and irksome task of filming footage of exploding and imploding houses.

'We live in Shar-i-Naw, just a few streets away,' I explain, clinching things.

In the crumbling, volatile atmosphere of Kabul, addresses never came more precisely than that – after all, it was not as though we were residing in the sedate comfort of Bath or Cheltenham, or the Royal Borough of Kensington and Chelsea. Anything further would have been out of place, a fanciful refinement. Like our PO Box number for mail, redundantly allocated even though the local Post Office had been blown up months ago and postmen were long extinct. What's more, we lived on Lucky Five Street; some personal details should stay that way.

Thus, for want of anything better, the TV people came back to Shar-i-Naw.

In the unusual absence of Abdul-the-reliable-cook, unversed Karrimullah searches noisily for an un-chipped plate for the chipped biscuits, lights the gas at the fifth attempt in a singeing plume of flame and red-hot finger-wringing imprecations, puts the kettle on and prepares to do the rounds with a pot of green tea.

As for absent Abdul Ahmed, the five foot two *chef de cuisine extraordinaire*, his normally regular attendance was a staunch loyalty born of economic necessity. Except that he lived distantly and remotely on the other side of town and just occasionally, and when the intervening street fighting was particularly fierce, his rusty old bicycle (itself free of the obligation to feed a family) baulked at the prospect of running the gauntlet. Whereupon eager Karrimullah would seize the moment with clumsy gusto.

The tea party flickers with faltering animation until dusk. It is almost time for Prayers and the rocketing has stopped for the day. The small-arms fire is both distant and reassuringly sporadic now, and for some reason makes me think of bells across the meadows and hurrying for evensong.

'Now is coming six o'clock and still the people they are here,' observes Karrimullah in an informative monotone, not-so-sotto-voce, centre stage and shaking his head with theatrical concern to make his point.

The desired effect is achieved: the guests consult their watches and with darkness falling hurriedly abandon the unending discussion on the future of Afghanistan, coupled with the never-ending analysis of the complex internal tangle of warring factions arrayed against the president of the day, President Rabbani. They drain their cups and take their leave, anxious to be away before the hour of that relic of the Russian occupation, the quirky curfew, nebulous and idiosyncratic though it had become since the enforcers had fled.

The on-site review of the civil war, and the abstract and circular debate of the relative merits and political prospects of radical Gulbuddin Hekmatyar, the sagacious 'Lion of Panshir' Ahmad Shah Masood (whose assassination by a suicide bomber linked to Osama bin Laden was still nine years distant), powerful General Dostum from the north, and all the other factional warlords will have to be continued another time.

Meanwhile, there are more immediate, down-to-earth and pressing pre-occupations demanding attention nearer to home. Not least being resumption of the day-to-day running of the Project – latterly abruptly interrupted by the intervention of *force majeure* – devoted as it was to the extraction and neutralisation of as many as possible of the lethally dangerous detritus of abandoned anti-personnel mines that lay scattered the length and breadth of Afghanistan, seemingly the land of eternal conflict. And the land where no one wins.

****

Chapter II

IN CONTINUATION

'Good judgement comes from experience; experience comes from poor judgement.'

Anon

Quite aside from such a rare and notable social event as the post-explosion impromptu tea party, the day in question had already taken several unexpected turns following a briefly humdrum dawn, deceptively docile.

The Project head of mission, relatively newly arrived and still finding his feet, had stirred, as usual, at first light – not that there was ever an abundance of light in my room, whatever the time of day. The protective sandbags judiciously stacked to the ceiling on the east-facing window sill saw to that. Just the faintest chink remained along the top of the dusty sacks, sufficient to reveal the capacious double bed, full of unfilled promise. Its welcoming expanse lay spread-eagled invitingly, thickly covered by eight blankets, dank and heavy, piled high in an attempt, futile, to exclude the invasive pre-dawn chill. Or more accurately, to prevent ingress of the nightly frost that seized exposed and elevated Kabul, more than a mile above sea level, with such visceral intensity.

Normally I would hear the symphony of Abdul-the-reliable-cook-Ahmed's arrival: I had become accustomed to the squeaking churn of his un-oiled ancient bicycle in the passage beyond the window – that rusty old bike of his that so aptly mirrored the run-down functionality of its surroundings – followed by his unvarying, unanswered muttered catechism of cursing as he busied himself collecting the copious mouse droppings in the kitchen. These he harvested and arranged tidily, ordering them into a neat pile on the bread board before carelessly clanking the sonorous kettle into the sink and grumpily grappling with the bad-tempered stove.

But on that particular day, silence. All quiet on the kitchen front.

Outside in the street were the beginnings of a different story. The dawn chorus – an alien concept in these parts and difficult to believe it had ever existed – had long since been banished and replaced by a regular, if intermittent, serenade of stuttering small-arms fire. With no advance notice, it ricocheted and rippled chatteringly through the city, lacking form, balance or discernible rhythm, the unorchestrated asymmetrical cadenzas rising and falling without apparent reason, punctuated by the percussion of rocket-propelled grenades and the occasional thumping resonance of heavier ordnance.

Customarily, the sound of fighting was a distant backdrop, like the whisper of breaking waves, or motorway traffic, borne on the wind, more often than not coming from the north western margins of the city, now predominantly pulverised. But today the epicentre appeared to have shifted to Shar-i-Naw in general. And to our backyard in particular.

Street-fighting: '*jang*' they called it in the vernacular, somehow appropriately and semi-onomatopoeically. 'Serious *jang* today!' observers would exclaim to each other on occasions, eyebrows lifted. 'Mmmm,' we would concur, pausing reflectively and listening semi-abstractedly to the din, as though it stemmed from a world apart. 'Lots of *jang* out there.' Those were days for assumed detachment, days for adoption of the no-longer-fashionable stiff upper lip.

To stoical Karimullah, former stonemason of immense strength and he of the legendary, surely apocryphal, doubtful dalliances with donkeys (a disgraceful product of idle and febrile imaginations, but nevertheless oft-told, perpetuated and much debated from a clinical perspective by cherubic-faced Dr Rhubar in his managerial advisory capacity), fell responsibility for collection of our daily bread. On the morning in question, unable to perceive any good reasons for doing otherwise (notwithstanding sundry indications to the contrary), he, Karimullah, slipped out through the wicket door set in the big metal security gates of the compound and headed off down the street, leather-thonged sandals slapping on the dirty road, in accordance with his habitual routine. Only to return just minutes later, short of breath and empty-handed, with the unsurprising news that the bakery was not only shut but shuttered, as indeed were all the neighbourhood stalls and shops. Furthermore, as he made tracks to the kitchen to fill the calming kettle, he firmly advised against any further shopping sorties in the immediate future. And, come to think of it (an afterthought, flung forcefully over his shoulder), in the foreseeable future as well.

'This is not a right place for living,' he declares unequivocally as he lights the beard-singeing gas, and leaves the world to ponder his pronouncement. But I remain in denial; it is not convenient to agree. Particularly as I had been in Kabul for hardly half a dog watch – a mere matter of weeks – and the Controller in the London office was rather hoping I might fill the breach and steady the ship after the severe setback suffered by the Project occasioned by the loss of three men.

It is a moment for displacement activities. Clearly, in view of such tidings as had been brought by intrepid Karrimullah, the established civility of taking an early breakfast on the terrace to the rear of the house – peacefully overlooking the rose garden and overseeing the sprawling vine with late-summer wasps at the grapes and the bordering magenta geraniums clinging to life amidst the hysterical lavender round the much abused square of lawn – was unlikely to occur that morning. No fresh *nan*, unsullied by the attentions of the elusive mice (or mouse), and no Abdul Ahmed bearing happy fried eggs and the pot of steaming green tea.

'My oven she is very fine,' Abdul would regularly remark to the world in general and *á propos* of nothing, contentedly placing the plates. Followed by: 'But sorry for my English. She is not so fine.'

Dear, endearing Abdul. Of course, nothing could be permitted to impinge on professional detachment, but secretly it worried me when he couldn't make it to work, and I imagined all kinds of unfortunate setbacks and possibilities. And I hoped his bicycle was all right.

So be it. The rise and fall of the now extremely adjacent *jang* was evidence enough that nothing was particularly fine that day. Continued compilation of the outstanding monthly report on our mine clearance activities was the only alternative diversion that sprung to mind. No breakfast was but a transient disappointment; if the periodic report was not timely – or in this instance, was yet further delayed – it could mean a moratorium on our European Union and UN programme funding. No money, no Project. I set to.

By mid-morning Dr Rhubar had somehow reached the house, picking his way through the troubled and noisy situation in the surrounding streets – and the accumulating rubble – with astute caution, borne of what must have seemed a lifetime's experience of civil strife. And probably assisted in no small measure by personal acquaintanceship with many of the protagonists.

'Muj: big beards, small brains,' was the only comment clean-shaven Rhubar had to offer, calmly pulling up a chair as though he were about to partake of a convivial glass of sherry or a gin and tonic before indulging in a spot of luncheon. 'Mujahideen: They lead a hard life and generally die with great suddenness,' he might have added, had he elected to quote Kipling.

Together, heads bowed over the blur of statistics and other data submitted by our field workers, we sat side by side at the dining-room table, requisitioned as office desk and also home for the HF radio, our long range high frequency communications set. Why was it that those people in Brussels insisted on making their reporting forms so absurdly convoluted?

As the assorted close-to-hand gunfire continued, markedly increasing in intensity, it was difficult to concentrate on compiling the maze of figures. I found myself wondering about Wilfred, Isabel, Dan and Dan, the dedicated band of missionaries we had met arriving at the airport a few weeks earlier, unaccountably (to the uninitiated and unenlightened, that is) opting to conduct their ministry in Kabul. Not a good day for missionaries, I would have thought; difficult conditions. Not easy for mine clearance, either.

Notwithstanding, and returning to the slog of the papers laid and sprayed out in front of us, the overall situation was reasonably clear. Since starting operations earlier that season – on a date dictated by the warm spring sunshine melting the snow and coaxing the frost out of the ground – about 1,000 mines had been cleared, similarly coaxed out of the earth. Meantime, the lives of three men had been lost.

But good work had been done by Trotter and McScumble with their 60 trained Afghans based at Pol-i-Khumri way to the north of the country, apprehensively advancing step by step with their super-sensitive Vallon mine detectors to the fore, sweeping in wide arcs to the right and left, their legs, even their lives, dependent on methodical and painstaking panning. Good work too by isolated Walduck and his 30 locally recruited helpers at the newly-opened operation at Jebal Seraj at the mouth of the Panshir Valley, this end of the Salang Pass, lying flat on their stomachs, feeling ahead with their finger-tips, searching the ground with their eyes intent on spotting any abnormalities and signs of soil disturbance, cautiously probing and sifting through the dirt to determine the identity of suspicious contacts. Tinnie ring-pull? A small coin? Or something considerably more potent? The firing pin in a detonator, for example …

{The detectors are designed to respond to less than half a gram of metal content – one sixteenth of a five pence piece. Ultra-sensitivity – a reassurance for the operators – inevitably results in a host of false alarms, in spite of increasing sophistication giving an improved capability to sift clutter.

The operating principle behind hand-held monitors (similarly used by enthusiasts seeking medieval treasure) is unchanged from World War II – as originally conceived by

Lieutenant Josef Stanislaw Kosacki of the Polish army whilst stationed in exile in Great Britain in defence of the Fife coastline against possible invasion: two induction coils in the head of the device producing a local magnetic field. Anomalies and variations to this field are identified and in turn are reflected via the visible flickering of a dial or audibly through headphones. Power comes from two small batteries, such as might serve in a bicycle lamp, re-charged overnight at the end of the day's activity. Highly sensitive and responsive suspended locators that make direct use of the earth's magnetic field – and, importantly, changes thereto – are also employed, but generally in static situations, such as bomb disposal}.

Theoretically, every mine detected and destroyed represented a life or a limb saved. Hearsay suggested that Afghan civilian casualties perhaps ran as high as 300 in some months. An unverifiable statistic; unreported because it had become un-newsworthy.

Pessimistic upper estimates put the total number of mines awaiting clearance in Afghanistan to be as high as 50 million. That indicated, mathematically, that unless things speeded up, another 50,000 years would be needed to complete the job. Possibly, in accord with more conservative estimates, there were only 10 million mines, unexploded bombs and discarded shells lying around. Or even only a million. That might reduce the work to just 1,000 years. The debris of war, they called it. The little bombs, many yet to detonate, were termed 'bomblets' – as though they were more recipient-friendly.

Clearly, if 2,000 mines could be swept before the onset of winter … and of course, our Project was not the only organisation actively engaged on clearing land mines … moreover, not all of the live ordnance and mines lay in high-risk, populated areas … The positive outlook was that if the work continued apace, then normal life could be restored to most villages in perhaps three to five years – assuming, that is, the land was not mined again …

But with the ever-increasing ambient noise level invading our office it is becoming ever-more difficult to focus on the figures … and the future. Amiable Dr Rhubar gives an uncharacteristic sigh of exasperation, pushes back his chair across the stone-tiled floor and leads the way up the stairs to the elevated terrace – the one used for breakfast in quieter times. On this particular morning, however, it was as if we had the builders in, or, preposterously, almost as if someone had established a machine gun post directly over the table where we were trying to concentrate. One can only tolerate so much.

On reaching the top of our building, things were exactly as we had thought. The two Afghans manning the newly-sited machine gun greeted us politely, smiling bashfully as behoves trespassers. *Salaam aleikum*, peace be on us, plus a resigned shrug of the shoulders to indicate, unfortunate though things appeared, the circumstances were not of their choosing. Only, perhaps, of their making.

For our part Dr Rhubar replies in patient Afghan Dari, explaining the disturbing inconvenience of the situation as we saw it. Especially as we were trying to write our monthly report, which was now seriously overdue, as the person who had been going to write it was no longer with us. It was all a question of perspective.

The Afghan fighters considerately conduct a respectful consultation, taking this fresh intelligence into account but concluding inconclusively, and still clearly undecided as to their best course of action, tactically speaking.

'Tell them this is private property, please, and that we are a neutral, non-profit making, non-governmental international humanitarian de-mining organisation,' I suggest, trying a new tack. My efforts at not coming across as an antediluvial throwback are not always entirely one hundred per cent successful. Even before I had finished speaking, I could picture the intruder telling his family about the incident that evening over supper when he got home from work. 'There I was, like, stood on this roof firing away at all and sundry when up pops this old geezer going on about as how we was making too much inconsiderate noise and this and that and all sorts of how's-your-father. Well, I was like, blimey and thinking to myself, this bloke is *weird*.'

'Oh, just tell them to bugger off!' I eventually exclaim impatiently. 'And anyway, why can't they use someone else's roof? They all look the same to me.'

This last observation strikes a responsive chord. The machine gunners survey the neighbourhood expanse of sun-baked roofs thoughtfully and converse further before turning back to Rhubar.

'Is that a "yes" or a "no"?' I ask, expectantly.

'They say they have finished their business here for the moment, as it happens, so they will take a break. First though, they want you to take their photograph. Then they can leave. *Insh'allah*.' Hopefully. If Allah agrees, or rather, decrees.

Down to my sand-bagged room I hurry, returning with my camera. The machine gunners pose, obligingly pack their kit and the tools of their trade, and bid a formal farewell – dippy-dip half-bow, hand across the heart – quite forgetting to leave a forwarding address for the snap.

I still have their picture, enlarged: the sky gentian blue behind them, vacation weather; the drab yellow roofs of the houses contrasting with the occasional dark green of lone pine trees, rising from nearby gardens, soughing softly in the wind with the pain of the people, and thus far spared the axe; the snow on the distant mountains largely obscured by the mid-morning mist (and the technical limitations of the photographer and the camera); the two proud warriors gazing fearlessly into the lens. Where are they now, I wonder? What became of those two Mujahideen fighters, aliens who came that day and visited my house but briefly from another world of which I know nothing? They of that fraternity who lead a hard life and generally die with great suddenness.

We return to the Project statistics. It is definitely quieter following the departure of our guests, easier to work; even so, even with a doubling of productivity it still seems it will take at least another 500 years to remove all the mines. Assuming, once again, that there are no further hostilities.

****

Abdul Ahmed-the-dependable-cook's unavoidable absence on account of the prevailing *jang* was not the only problem that day. At the same time, and just to compound the confusion, it soon transpired that not only was Abdul out of the kitchen, the kitchen was out of food.

Not long after midday, prompted by the rumbling stirrings of starvation and the beginnings of boredom in unequal measure, we opted to venture out, with the added pretext of checking on the welfare of our acquaintance, the head of the Red Cross, occupant of offices in a similarly rented house nearby. The tide of simmering, rippling unrest in the neighbourhood, though apparently incapable of subsiding permanently, seemed to have ebbed and passed on for the time being, and the moment appeared opportune for a touch of furtive foraging. In that considerately carefree way of his, Dr Rhubar invited his brother, Dr Nasseir, from our adjacent primary healthcare clinic to join us for the foray. Then Karimullah, who was curious as well as bored, elected to come along, just in case. So we were four. Four field mice, venturing forth.

On setting out, the sky was as blue as only a Kabul sky can be, the early autumn air was as a fragile flute of the finest champagne, and the small boys in the street had their red and yellow kites – those infallible barometers of danger – tugging and swooping overhead in the katabatic breeze. Kite flying: that ubiquitous and seemingly peaceful pastime yet to be prohibited by Taliban decree, on account of its previously largely unsuspected 'wicked consequences, such as gambling, death amongst children and truancy'.

Meanwhile, at street level, the itinerant vendors of cheap cigarettes and doubtful packets of sweets were plying their trade, their wares arranged on trays hung from frayed string looped around their necks. That's how we came by the biscuits.

On our arrival at the protective gates barring the way to the Red Cross offices, a viewing hatch flips open in response to our summoning knocks – a square port scarcely sufficient for one eye and half a nose. The suspicious optic scans us with rapid movements and then relaxes on recognition.

'*Bisyaar tashakor.* Thank you very much,' confirms the caretaker contentedly, talking through the hatch so that all we can see are the undulations of his ululating tonsils. 'We are just fine. For when the rockets come we have a bonker under the house.'

The wily Red Cross man wisely not being at home, we pause to pass the time of day with a group of idling street fighters, lazing around their improvised pill boxes and barricades at one of the crossroads. Things look promising for a cup of tea. But hardly have greetings been exchanged, and even before a forecast on the likelihood of further skirmishing has been sought and obtained, the atmosphere changes. Adversely.

The street falls silent, oppressively silent; the innocent kites come down, mothers reach out to pull children inside and doors close, gates click surreptitiously shut. No birds pass; the biscuit seller and his companions disappear. The fighters reach out for their AK-47s, their eyes elsewhere. It is time to make ourselves scarce, time to be somewhere else. Anywhere else.

It is not the time for tea.

The first rocket explodes several streets away, somewhere over to our right. It is almost incidental, apart from being a juddering prelude of things to come. The smoke from the second rocket rises black and thick less than 100 metres away, again on our right. The closer proximity increases the psychological impact of the detonation. It is nothing personal, surely, but as it happens, elementary geometry, unaided by prisms or a theodolite, shows the trajectory of the salvo to be running exactly through the spot where we happen to be standing.

Which is why the arrival of the third missile was predictable, and the explosion itself came as no surprise. Certainly we were startled to find ourselves in the gutter. That was quite unexpected.

****

Chapter III

IN THE BEGINNING

'Hope … an anchor of the soul, both sure and steadfast'

Hebrews 6.19

To reach Afghanistan, once a part of the ancient Persian Empire, I travelled through India. The Imperial route, you might say. The highway of history, even. Over-imaginatively I wondered if perhaps I was following in the footsteps of Alexander the Great, conqueror of the country in the year 328 BC.

More prosaically, the Controller ordained a pre-departure rendezvous at Heathrow airport. There he slipped across US $60,000 to be taken to Kabul – 'for Project expenses' – plus an elastic-banded bundle of dog-eared letters for the handful of Project expatriates. Followed, incongruously and awkwardly, by four cumbersome, bulky replacement wing mirrors for the Land Rovers, urgently required in the field. Something to reflect on.

In passing, and incidentally, the Controller wished me well. He looked at me thoughtfully for a moment, gave an authoritative parting nod in my direction and then made to leave the departure lounge, heading back to HQ, his command post in central London.

I watched him go, equally thoughtfully. Then, as I gazed after him, he took me by surprise. He had hardly gone half a dozen strides when he hesitated and half turned.

'We're most grateful to you,' he said quietly over his shoulder.

I hadn't thought of it that way. He was gone before I could reply. Nothing is always a good thing to say.

****

It was nearly midnight when the Air India flight landed at Delhi, air traffic control having suspended us mid-air for an additional hour and a half along the way in traditional manner as a character-building exercise. The delay gave opportunity to review the comforting aura of my meticulous injection inventory, everything primly recorded in accordance with International Regulations. Smallpox, Cholera and Gamma Globulin had been discarded, and the Kabul climate gave no call for malarial prophylaxis. But Rabies, three variants of Hepatitis, Typhoid, Meningitis, Tetanus, Diphtheria, Yellow Fever, Polio, Measles, Mumps and Rubella all remained. A list of such conscientious magnitude was surely sufficient for fast-track passage across any border in the world.

Not so, and nothing so illogical. Rightly unmoved by the extent and scope of the 'Health Passport', Delhi Immigration searched for the non-existent entry visa that their counterparts in London had confirmed was unnecessary, while the night grew longer and shorter simultaneously. Airports being primarily for coming and going rather than sleeping, at length a diplomatic compromise was found and it was decided that as the traveller was 'Head of Mission linked to UN funds', all indeed was in order. What was it the Controller – fearsome military man that he was – had said about taking post at the double? And that flapping feebly like a hooked haddock created a poor impression? Whatever, no one could disagree with the general thrust. Who would dare?

Six o'clock the following morning, and back at Delhi Airport, I made new friends: Wilfred and Isabel, also with their immediate earthly aspirations centred on the Ariana Afghan national airline twice-weekly flight to Kabul, indicated for 0800. *Insh'allah.*

Wilfred ('we're from Sydney') and Isabel ('I'm seventy') were missionaries. Missionaries? Afghanistan? Certainly three score and ten was the age of purple indiscretion, but surely … Isabel had looped a shawl over her head out of respect for local sensibilities at our destination. Paradoxical, that. Wilfred made no such concessions. He wore a flat cap of the sort described as homespun, a fluffy green bobble sewn loosely on top so that it wobbled when he moved, like a jaunty cooking apple in an equinoctial gale. He looked like an off-track Celtic supporter.

Apart from the three of us, the terminal was wholly deserted; plenty of opportunity to explore the mysteries of the missionary business, the nuances of proselytising in Moslem Afghanistan (and even the rationale of de-mining in that country, when I came to think of it). Except those confrontational 'why?' questions might seem like a criticism, even a reproach. Wilfred and vulnerable Isabel looked as though they had enough worries without seeking to explain the well-intentioned inexplicable.

'And you?' enquired Isabel with a flick of her shawl and with down-under directness.

Who? Me? What about me? Well, now that you ask, and if you really want to know, I'm saving the world, as it happens. Nothing more complicated than that. A few short months ago I was set to become a bursar. Then suddenly I woke up. It would have been forever. Predictable; institutional; pensionable: a life sentence, a 'second career' preceding dishonourable retirement. At the eleventh hour I upset the applecart and ran away. Not to sea this time. I'd already done that. To Kabul. A perfectly normal behavioural pattern. Nothing complex, such as a mid-life crisis. Just the belief that as we are here only once – or so it seems – it's best to make the most of it, keep right on to the end of the road and keep the circus turning. All in all, quite inexplicable.

Isabel was waiting, watching. 'Oh, I'm just helping out,' I replied, casually. 'You know how it is.' No point in tying myself in knots with involved explanations about things which I thought I didn't need to understand. And Wilfred's bobble wobbled as he listened, giving metronomic encouragement and indicating that he didn't understand either but it was quite alright by him and that he knew how it was. Probably quite a good missionary was Wilfred, I decided. Just needed to select his parish with a bit more care and discernment. When the call comes, it must be mighty powerful. I could see that, although in truth it was more than I could grasp. But I could think it. And it struck a familiar and resounding chord.

Isabel was still hovering at my elbow, unconvinced, keen to probe. 'Head of Mission …' she ruminated. 'That sounds very important …'

'I'm only a lower case head of mission,' I explained, effectively confusing her. 'The de-miners are important. I'm just a cog; like a lot of cogs I help to make the wheels go round.' The long-awaited announcement of the flight saved further puzzlement, further sinking in the swamp.

For no evident reason we took off for Kabul at eleven o'clock – 1100 hours bang on. Ariana, 'one of the great eccentric airlines of the world', providers of the occasional thrill, the moustachioed pilots masquerading as born-again Biggles. Perhaps the missionaries had a prayer about safe journeys and punctuality in their repertoire …

The other passengers, experienced locals, had shuffled up nonchalantly, flip flop, some time after ten, cool and unhurried, robes and baggy pants flapping unconcernedly. I gave a backward thought to my almost-comfortable hotel room in downtown Delhi, precipitately abandoned before sunrise. Embarkation was Third World: smooth, efficient, well-ordered and courteously conducted. Like the planet, the plane was crowded, almost to excess, standing room only; mine was the last seat in the last row, the one without the armrest and with half the seat belt missing. On the credit side, half the seat belt remained. Perhaps a previous occupant had suffered a problem with his trousers.

Scheduled flying time was only a couple of hours. Perhaps less – that was the worry. Squares of bread and cheese were passed down the rows of passengers. Conceivably all would be well; especially now I had fallen in with the missionaries.

Arriving high above the Kabul landing strip it was possible to identify remains of wrecked aircraft littering the ground either side of the runaway, including the huge skeleton of a burnt-out Russian cargo plane. Biggles dropped us dramatically from 20,000 feet, like a planeload of trainee Stuka pilots, outwitting the malicious intentions of any chance ground-to-air missiles. Then, having bumped down safely, not once but thrice, we taxied past the symbolic bones of the control tower. This had long since been shot away, with only the perforated concrete of the Swiss cheese silhouette and a few heat-twisted window frames remaining to mark the spot, as stark as a winter gravestone in a cemetery. Around the perimeter of the airport, groups of Mujahideen strolled importantly, pausing in twos and threes for a social cigarette and a chat, their badges of office – Kalashnikovs and rocket-propelled grenade launchers – slung casually over their shoulders.

For some reason my mind replayed my recent interview at HQ, London. 'We recruit orphans,' the Controller had stated matter-of-factly on completion of the preliminary interrogation, in that staccato, one-way conversational style of his, like a Bren gun with the catch set to 'short bursts'. I inadvertently blinked, just as he had intended. 'Only orphans,' he confirmed. 'Orphans under thirty, unmarried, with a military background.'

'I'm not scoring too highly here,' I had suggested helpfully, in case he had got my details confused with someone else, someone more suitably qualified. 'Not many ticks in the profile boxes.'

'No,' agreed the Controller readily and with soldierly directness, as he snapped the firing catch from 'short burst' to 'single shot' and back again with practised precision. 'But you'll do.'

The Controller – alias the Colonel – was not an advocate of the psychometric-testing school of personnel selection. The 'Seat-Of-One's-Pants' was good enough for him – the straightforward, no frills proven SOOP system. 'We've had a slight hiatus on the personnel side in Afghanistan and need to get back on an even keel,' came the added non-explanation. 'You'll find things there a little different to your work with disabled refugees in Africa, and your Gulf War time running a Saudi hospital. But not entirely. As well as the de-mining activities, we also run some clinics. And you can still spend your nights with a hurricane lamp if you want, as there's no electricity, by and large. Anyway, after 30-odd years in the Navy, I expect you'll manage.'

That was that, and as a result, here I was, disembarking at Kabul airport. Or at least, what remained of it.

Wilfred and Isabel were met by two more missionaries, Dan and Dan. Dan had glasses and Dan had a beard: that way you could tell them apart. Also, Dan came from Seattle and played the trumpet – a revelation that boded well for the trombone I happened to have in my luggage. Now I was pleased I had not asked too many discordant missionary questions in Delhi whilst waiting for the flight.

Under the welcoming aegis of Dr Rhubar, I bought an instant entry visa from a man with a tray of handy rubber stamps and an array of inkpads in a box-like booth in the echoing vastness of the reception hall. No fuss, no queue; all smiles. In fact, the job must have been something of a sinecure. Demand for entry visas did not appear to be excessive. The warm sunshine beamed in pleasantly through the spaces where the windows used to be, before they were blown out, but the visa man was in the shade and in need of a thick overcoat and a pair of those contrary gloves with no fingers. Chilly work: cold mornings and, no doubt, long waits for Ariana. As for Rhubar, he was immaculately clad in a dark blue pinstripe suit, complete with matching waistcoat. He caught my appraising eye.

'Oxfam,' he said, disarmingly. 'I bought ten suits for ten pounds from a charity shop in Yorkshire. They gave me a discount when I said where I lived. One for every day of the week. And three spare, in case.'

'Amazing. Yorkshire!' The inescapable sartorial thread of existence was once again spinning on the loom.

'I could have stayed in England, of course,' declared Rhubar, over-riding the perceived non-sequitur and just in case I was wondering, which I was. 'But Afghanistan is my country and this is my home.' He laughed. 'So here I am.' He had the uncertain air of a man trying to convince himself of something, and who had recited that explanation many times before.

The missionaries held an animated re-union, Isabel adjusting her shawl nervously after the long journey from eastern Australia, Wilfred's bright woolly bobble bouncing and bounding like a ball booted loosely upfield at Celtic Park. Together we breezed through Customs – no problems with the wing mirrors, nor the trombone and the VHF hand-held Motorola radios which had been pushed into the handy case along with the collapsible music stand at the last moment; no need to mention the $60,000 for Project expenses (keep things simple, never confuse; don't ask questions, questions beg questions). We vowed to keep in touch, missionaries all, come what may. And off they went, steadfastly, to spread the Word.

As the missionaries receded I made a further mental note of the existence of Seattle Dan's trumpet, visualising imminent soirées of melodic brass. Rather overlooking the dark shadow of the curfew and one or two other realities.

I was introduced to Zahir: long-distance driver and mechanic. Zahir gave a soft smile and a softer handshake, rolling his eyes distractedly in welcome. We were destined to spend much time together, undertaking those long-haul journeys. I hoped I might get to know him. That was for the future; today's trip was a mere 20-minute short haul to the Project office, the rented 'villa'.

But first came the roadblock – my first Afghan roadblock. The first of a hundred – no, a thousand – such barriers to be negotiated in the coming weeks and months. Roadblocks that ranged from the temporarily inactive and dormant, through to thieving, through to murderous. There are no innocuous roadblocks in this world, the intent is invariably perverse. The thickness of the dirty yellow tape, the suspended knotted rope, the peeling painted pole, the unravelled track from a dead tank that lies across one's chosen path – all these give no reliable indication, no sure hint of what lies behind and beyond, or what is likely to befall in the coming moments. But innocent and benign it will not be.

As it happened, my initiation was not life-threatening. The sub-species manning the barricade were in playful mood that lunchtime, business was slack. Zahir smiled back, but too readily, unknowingly allowing his eyes to roll: faulty roadblock protocol.

'We cannot go,' he whispered. He knew; it was his country. 'First some small chattings. If you do not stop, they fire warning shoots. Or worse.'

This time, however, the sun shone and the presence of smartly-suited Dr Rhubar and my freshly minted visa were sufficient to see us through.

'Just one thing before you go,' grinned the cat-and-mouse, self-appointed guards, looking to Dr Rhubar for entertainment. 'Why has your friend tied himself to the car?'

All eyes swivelled to look at my neatly clipped and adjusted seat belt, correctly fastened in the style of another world, and I wished I hadn't.

'*Burra bikheir*!' laughed the guards. 'Go in peace!'

So saying, they let fly with a duet of shattering shots directly above my open window. Whereupon I obligingly jumped out of my skin and in turn they collapsed to the ground with merriment. Uncharitably, I half-wished they had promptly split their sides and died of laughter. I had never seen that done before.

'They just wanted to welcome you to Afghanistan,' said Dr Rhubar apologetically, as Zahir let out the clutch and rolled his eyes.

'Whose side are they on?' I asked.

'Their own,' replied Rhubar, astonished by the naivety of the question.

Back in London the Controller had asked which I preferred – a posting to Afghanistan or to Cambodia? 'The Great Game or the flesh pots?' he questioned. 'Be shot by a boy soldier practising with a rocket-propelled grenade or catch a dose? Our Kabul office could use reinforcements,' he said, guiding gently. 'In fact it's unmanned at present. There's a vacancy. Of course, the work is unsalaried, but you would receive an honorarium. Modest, naturally.'

Rose Cottage? That overcrowded clinic for clap-happy cases and crabby crabs? No thank you. It was not a difficult decision; I knew the answer in advance. Cambodia was a long way away; perhaps another time.

'Afghanistan will be fine,' I had replied. 'I'll take my chance with the RPGs.' Like anyone and everyone else who has ever ventured vaguely into harm's way, I was quite secure behind the imaginary, illusory shield of knowing that nothing would ever happen to me. Of that I was sure.

At which point the Controller had exchanged quick glances with the Assistant Controller – the latter hitherto sitting quietly in the corner, but now moved to speak.

'Afghanistan is bigger than France,' explained the Assistant Controller helpfully, leaning forward in his chair and consolidating my decision. 'Although not as big as Burma. Kabul is about the size of Birmingham.' I inclined my head to indicate I was following – or trying to – the way one does at interviews; I hadn't been to Burma, nor to Birmingham, but I had been to France. 'There are about one and a half million people in Kabul,' continued my new mentor.

'Well, considerably less these days because of the refugees leaving,' he amplified, pausing for thought and giving me the chance to read between the lines, before proffering as a sudden explanatory afterthought: 'The ethnic breakdown, rather than any particular tribal groupings, is the key to understanding the country – forty per cent Pashtun; twenty five per cent Tajik, give or take; ten per cent Hazara, although some say twice that; seven or eight per cent Uzbek. An assortment of minorities make up the balance. Minority ethnics, I should say. It's a pretty complicated patchwork – that's more than half the problem. Aside from the principal groups which I've mentioned, you've got Turkmen, Baloch, Pashay, Nuristani, Aymaq, Arab, Kyrgyz, Qizilbash, Gujar, Brahui, and a few others. Colourful but complex.'

At which point the Assistant Controller paused to see if I was keeping up, before he continued. 'The total population of Afghanistan is coming up to 25 million. The life expectancy is 45, give or take – you know how it is.'

And with that he subsided and resumed the watchful quiet of his corner.

'It's only fair to warn you of one or two things,' intervened the Controller gravely, re-assuming command. 'Aside from the random rockets and the RPGs, and the skirmishing on the outskirts, you might find life in Kabul a bit tedious. There are hardly any expatriates left there these days; you'll be thrown back on your own resources. But we really do need a Head of Mission in Afghanistan as our Project representative. On occasions you will find yourself meeting with Government Ministers, the next day it will be a question of fiddling around with insurance claims, stores and accounts and visas. A bit balls-aching and routine, but it can't be helped. That's the way it is with HQ staff. It's the same for me here, if that's any comfort to you. We could employ an army of clerks, but as a charity it doesn't read well on the pie chart, so we don't. Instead we roll up our sleeves and do these things ourselves. A thousand things without a name.'

And whilst the luxury of a sigh was beyond his reach, the Colonel's eyes clouded and flickered as his mind went to past glories, distinguished soldier that he was. 'Of course, on-site liaison with the donors is imperative,' he continued, almost seamlessly. 'No funding, no de-mining operations. It won't leave as much time as you would like for visiting our teams in the field, but that can't be helped and anyway we have that side well covered. It's in Kabul that we urgently need someone. Landlocked, but that can't be helped either. It's a good spot for a sailor,' declared the Colonel, noticeably without elaboration. 'Minefields are not the Royal Navy's natural habitat,' he consoled drily and paternally, brightening briefly.

When last seconded to work with the Army I had found them equally caring: As we headed out into the jungle around Ipoh during the Malayan Emergency, the section Sergeant insisted on Senior Service first; everyone was unanimous on that, right down to the lowliest Private. So it was, wetter than wet behind the ears, I fronted the patrol. Fortunately the world was young in those days, and no one jumped out from behind a tree to spoil the party as we squelched along for the best part of a fortnight. The only shot fired was when the Corporal tripped over a log – fuck, fuck, fuck, so many of those like ducks in a row that they ran together and formed an intelligible expression of his sentiments, so eloquent that they echoed our feelings exactly. According to the weighty tenets of the unfamiliar Army Discipline Act, I was told this was a court martial offence (not the offending log or the language, just the rogue shot), except as no one referred to the accidental discharge ever again, proceedings are still pending and that was in 1958.

Back to the present, here I was finding myself going against the tide of refugees just a few weeks after my induction at HQ London, and arriving in Kabul. Still trying to recollect those all-important ethnic percentages the Assistant Controller had mentioned.

Dr Rhubar took up the burden of continuing my induction as Zahir drove us along the expansive, tree-lined avenues of the city, grandiose buildings to either side, once finely architectured but now reduced to piles of rubble, generally, so the vista was less fine and more like Britain after the Blitz.

'You may not remember all of this,' said Rhubar, portentously, 'but to the monarchy that followed the 3rd Afghan War against the British in 1919 goes credit for the construction of our city. Of course, the subsequent destruction is another matter. After King Amanullah abdicated on 14th January 1929, as a result of the unpopularity of his modernising reforms, Nadir Shah was proclaimed King of Afghanistan. Regrettably, he was assassinated in November 1933, which is what happens here sometimes, and the Crown passed to Zahir Shah. He ruled for almost 40 years, creating these wide thoroughfares and planting the white flowering acacia trees that you see. By the way, I am telling you all this just in case you might be interested in understanding how things have been here, historically speaking. Don't worry if it seems a bit complicated. I can write it down for you in the office and then you can refer to it whenever you need.'

'Anyway, in 1964 a constitutional monarchy was established. King Zahir

Shah was deposed in July 1973, once again regrettably. At least the coup, on that occasion, was bloodless, and the King went to live in exile. In Italy, I think, so things didn't turn out too badly for him and, so far as I know, he's still alive. A Republic was proclaimed, under Muhammed Daud Khan. On 27th April 1978 we suffered another coup, led by the Armed Forces Revolutionary Council. President Daud was murdered, together with 30 members of his family.'

Dr Rhubar emitted a little laugh before continuing.

'Presidency of the Democratic Republic of Afghanistan was then assumed by Nur Muhammed Taraki, who was killed in September 1979, just 17 months later. It was an internal dispute, but the outcome was the same. Anyway, President Taraki was succeeded by President Hafizulla Amin. I probably don't have to mention that he was killed at the time of the Soviet invasion of Afghanistan in December 1979, which was just three months later. The Russians immediately installed President Barbrak Karmal. That was about the 29th December 1979, I think. He survived in office until 1986 when the Russians removed him into exile in Moscow. At some point after that he was returned to Afghanistan. I suppose the Russians just got fed up with having him around. Anyway, back he came, but as a house-prisoner, or so I believe. They say the conditions were very bad and that he died of ill-health in 1989 or 1990. Something like that.'

'People talk about the lessons of history; you will have spotted the common thread in my story. Becoming President of this country is not one of my aspirations. I can tell you more about Barbrak Karmal's successor, President Najibullah, another day. Of course, he is the ex-President now, since April 1992 when the Mujahideen took Kabul and he went into hiding. He is a near-neighbour of ours, actually. It's good that you should know some of these things if you are going to live here for a while, helping us with the de-mining and the Project.'

'What's that noise?' I asked, interrupting. 'Like thunder.'

'Just *jang*,' said Dr Rhubar. 'My little boy – he's just had his first birthday, you can meet him – is called *Bachai Jang*. It means "Son of Battle" or "Son of War". Even "Son of a Gun" if you want.' He gave another short laugh.

Two tanks, turrets twitching, rumble past in the opposite direction. They are moving with intent, the heavy tracks glinting, throwing up the dust in a whirl of cogs and wheels, vibrating the tarmac under our vehicle. Reacting anxiously, Rhubar hurriedly motions Zahir to the side of the road; the pedestrians in the street shrink back defensively against the walls of the broken buildings. Tanks have that effect.

'T57s,' announces Rhubar. 'Russian made, Mujahideen manned. Dangerous. Have you ever seen a tank run over a taxi? I have. They said there were four passengers inside, but of course, no one could be sure. And the driver.'

I waited for the little laugh. I could afford to be the silent observer. Not deliberately, but then I didn't have to live here; not permanently. More to the point, just at that moment I couldn't think of anything to say. When the laugh came, escaping from Rhubar's being in that curiously detached manner, it might equally well have been a cry.

****

Zahir guided the white Land Rover to arrive at the Project house in Shar-i-Naw – the smart end of town, once upon a time. Karimullah clanged the big metal gates closed behind us, drawing the long bolts tight, shutting out the turmoil of the city, but not the rumble of the *jang.*

'Abdul Ahmed is your cook,' explained Dr Rhubar, moving on, 'except he is away with Walduck in Jebel Seraj at the moment, helping out. So Karimullah will cook. He does meatballs.' Rhubar hesitated, enjoying the moment. 'You will have noticed that on the way here we passed a few camels, some donkeys and lots of spare dogs.' And Rhubar paused again. 'Don't worry, we also have goats and sheep. Anyway, Abdul should be back soon, *insh'allah.* He cooks apple pies. Tarts! Together with the meatballs!'

It seemed Dr Rhubar would choke with the hilarity of his devastating humour, just like the guardians of the roadblock, but he recovered.

'Normally we don't have any electricity provided, that's why we have a generator. Two actually. But only Karimullah is strong enough to turn the big one. Also, we don't have any water these days, but fortunately for us and unlike most people, we have a pump and a well. So we run the generator for half an hour in the morning and fill the water tank in the roof, which should be enough for the day. In normal circumstances. Also we can run the generator in the evening after dark, if you want to read or perhaps heat some water. Karrimullah has an old coil from an electric fire on a bit of flex which you can drop in a bucket and which seems to work fine. Only, just be sure to remember to turn the coil off before you use the water or try to move the bucket.

'Anyway, don't have the motor running for too long because the noise of the engine and the lights are a temptation. To outsiders, that is. There should be some oil lamps somewhere about. Now that the weather is getting colder we can use our *bukhari*, our heater. I'm not sure, but I think it is a unique Afghan invention, very ingenious, just a little ticklish. The diesel fuel is heated and somehow falls drop by drop to the flame. Occasionally they explode, it is true. Don't get confused. Sometimes you may hear a bang and think that perhaps it is one of Gulbuddin Hekmatyar's rockets – possibly a Sakar – when actually it is just the *bukhari* stove of one of our neighbours over-reacting. The sound is different – you will learn.

'I expect everything is no doubt quite confusing at the moment and I should probably remind you that Mr Hekmatyar is the leader of the *Hezb-i-Islami* party, or HIH, in opposition to President Rabbani, who is JIA or the *Jamiat-i-Islami* party. So at the moment it is Hekmatyar who is attacking and rocketing the city. I hope that explanation helps. In a way it doesn't matter whose rockets they are, the effect is the same. Oh, yes, this is Hajji the houseman, he is the *bukhari* expert, except he is not always here. Nobody knows where he goes.'

And elusive disappearing Hajji, the shrinking, ageing five foot houseman, veteran of the arduous pilgrimage to Mecca, gives me a lingering double-handed handshake of profound welcome, looking mystically upwards, deep into my eyes as though seeking the second coming. He waggles his wispy grey beard reassuringly. Fear not for the *bukhari*, that's what he's telling me.

Through the house into the garden we walked. The gaily blooming roses were thriving in the Kabul climate, vigorous growth, total absence of greenfly infestation, not a hint of black spot fungi on the shining foliage. Definitely no spraying necessary. Nevertheless, ever the perfectionist in an imperfect world, I resolved to find time to do some overdue pruning.

'This lawn we use for Mine Awareness instruction,' explained Dr Rhubar, shunting my horticultural train into a siding. 'We have a big box of mines in the tool shed over there. All the usual ones: you know, POMZ – the Russian stick mine, PMNs and PMN2s – the pressure blast mines, of course, and then the inverted MS3 that activates when the pressure is released rather than applied, good for booby traps. The East German PPM2 anti-personnel mine is not so common here but we have lots of Butterfly mines which the Russians just scattered from helicopters, like sweets, really, and which the children like to play with – well, until they go off. The repatriated refugees are most at risk because they are unfamiliar with these things. That's why Mine Awareness courses are an important part of the work of all the de-mining agencies. And as I'm sure you know, you can also use shell fire as a random means of delivery for mines. The mines are supposed to have a self-destruct capability after a set period, so everyone feels better about that. Except it doesn't always work.'

'What else have we got here? Oh yes, what they call the 'shampoo' bottle, the green Russian mine, the PGMDM, which is anti-tank, and the Italian TC6 with the plastic ribs which looks like a cog wheel, also for anti-tank use. The Italians make a lot of mines; well, so do other countries. It's big money. Anyway, the Russian TM57 and TM62 are both common, with the handy handle for carrying the tin and the big hole for the fuze. There used to be a Pakistani P2 somewhere in the box, unless someone has borrowed it – I'll have a rummage around later – and also we have a British Mk 7. I think that's all the anti-tank ones. From memory, that is.

'And Claymores?'

'Oh, yes. Directional fragmentation mines for perimeter defence; excellent, very effective. We have US and British Claymores and then three Russian examples, the MON50, the 90 and the 100/200. Also I didn't mention the anti-personnel PMD6 in the little wooden box which we come across quite a lot, and also the bounding mines, which as you know, jump up when triggered to give improved damage capability.'

Dr Rhubar gives that reluctant laugh of his at the thought of the improved damage capability. His hollow laugh of sadness, his apologetic laugh of despair.

'The Czech bounder is the PPSIMH and there should be other bounding mines in the box, like the OZM3 and the OZM4. The type 72 that we have is the anti-personnel blast mine. The other Chinese type 72 is for anti-tank work. I forgot to say that. Nobody really knows if we have 300 civilian casualties a week in Afghanistan, or just 300 in a month. It's difficult to say. Anyway, I expect they told you that in London before you came. It's not news anymore. It's normal. Now I have something else to show you.'

Rhubar leads the way back from the garden, through the former dining room that has now become the office, and into the sitting room – which was called the drawing room before the house was rented – and which now perforce doubles as the dining area.

'In this cupboard we have some Pear Liqueurs for you. The Brandy has all gone – well, it was drunk, actually – but these Liqueurs also came from the cellar of the French Embassy after the Russians finished their occupation of our country in 1989. Did you know that in ten years the Russians lost 14,000 men, killed? There's another lesson of history for you in that statistic, which you might care to remember. Although it is true that we lost maybe one million of our own people over the same period.

'Anyway, most of the foreign diplomatic staffs, including the French – and incidentally, the British – decided it was wisest to leave at around the same time as the Russians. Certainly the majority had packed and gone by the time the Mujahideen entered Kabul in April 1992 and ousted President Najibullah. That's how it became possible to liberate these nice bottles from the French cellar. Now I will show you your room before lunch, then, after we have eaten you can rest on the terrace in the sun.'

Rhubar again leads the way. He eyes the enormous, libidinous double bed.

'It would be fun if beds could talk, don't you think?' he muses dreamily. 'As for the sandbags blocking your window, well, if the situation changes, and it will only change one way, then we can fill some more and build a bit higher, if you like. There are lots more Hessian sacks spare under the stairs. This wardrobe is for whatever you have in that big suitcase of yours, the one with all the colourful labels saying where you have been. And for your trombone, which I couldn't help noticing. You may find a few things left in the drawers, perhaps a jersey and some old socks. They were your predecessor's, but you can use them if you want. He won't be needing them any more. Obviously, as he's dead.'

I waited expectantly for the little laugh and was not disappointed.

We had lunch. Meatballs, provenance unverifiable. No apple pie. No tasty tarts. We ate off a low table in the sitting room, bent forward uncomfortably. Clearly it was a cultural thing, the Afghan way. Don't ask questions on your first day. Look and listen. Be grateful for the knife and fork. Only weeks later came the realisation that the true dining room table had been hijacked for the radio and by then there was no point in changing things round. My back had gone.

On the terrace afterwards the sun was hot; no doubt about it, the roses definitely needed pruning. But first I needed to get to grips with the Project admin. A mid-afternoon UN transport prop aircraft took off from the airport, circled lazily in the azure sky to get on a safe south easterly heading and droned evocatively into the distance; shrewd not to spend the night hereabouts. 'I'm off,' said the fast-disappearing black speck. 'Take care.'

Daily aircraft movements were limited in number, each one sub-consciously logged (especially in default, in absentia) by those left on the ground, the leaden-footed lookers. Ariana returned to Delhi on Mondays and Saturdays; sometimes flying to Peshawar, possibly to Dubai, on Sundays. Or so it was rumoured, depending on their mood. It all hinged on circumstances. Indian Airlines ran twice a week. But not any more. There were occasional UN and Red Cross flights. Variable, but not so frequent since the UN expatriate staff were evacuated, and the Red Cross hospital closed. That was after armed Mujahideen fell into the habit of taking their casualties directly into the operating theatre, bursting in and at gunpoint ordering the doctors to carry out whatever restorative treatment was necessary for their wounded comrades, there and then, regardless of the needs of other patients. That included whoever had the misfortune to be recumbent on the operating table and under the surgeon's knife at the time.

As for the situation at the airport, Dr Rhubar claimed that if the pilots parked their aircraft on the apron for too long, shadowy figures appeared under the wings with buckets and pails, funnels and jerry cans, and siphoned off the fuel. Half to be re-cycled for home use; the remainder for re-sale in the bazaar. I had a lot to learn.

High, high overhead an anonymous vapour trail crossed the sky; the thread of cloud drifting gently 40,000 feet above Karrimullah, who was furiously waging war on the clattering lunch plates in the kitchen. Illusory or real, the physical properties of the frost-filled mountain air seemed to promote an unequalled crystalline clarity of sound and light.

Half a century ago I would perch with the seagulls on the tired wooden boards of the Town Pier at Gravesend, the waterlogged supporting timbers hung with seaweed and barnacles, to watch the Sun and Watkins tugboats across the River Thames at Tilbury ushering the ocean-going liners on their romantic way, and, legs dangling over the muddy waters, I would dream of accompanying them on the ebb tide to unknown far away places. Now I was sitting on the fringe of the mountains of the Hindu Kush, within touching distance of those 'intensely-tangled cloud-capped peaks and summits', looking skywards at passing airliners, indulging similar travelogical fantasies.

Maybe, way up there in the glinting strato-cruiser, it was time for tea in Business Class. 'Lapsang Souchong? Rose Pouchong? Orange Pekoe? Ceylon Dimbula? Gunpowder Green? One lump or two?' But possibly there were no passengers in the payload that day. Just a few, fat, well-primed bombs in the hold, heading sleekly for some exotic destination. Together with a cluster of user-friendly bomblets.

Which prompted my thoughts to return to the abandoned grey jersey and the two comfy pairs of dark green socks, no longer required – 'not wanted on voyage' – lying in the wardrobe of my room.

When I left the Controller's HQ in London, the Colonel had accompanied me to the landing to see me on my way. Later he was to tell me that he obtained his best information, the most revealing confidences, while the ancient lift, caged in brass, was making its ponderous way from the ground floor.

It was psychological, he said. Having departed the influential boundaries of HQ, visitors felt divested of the burden of gravitas; as the creaking lift slowly ascended, the relief – and more – gushed forth. However, in this instance the flow of intelligence was reversed.

The Assistant Controller had slipped back into the shadows. I was left alone with the Controller. He released the advisory safety catch on his machine gun and put his finger smoothly to the trigger. He fired two short informatory bursts.

'We've just lost three men in Kabul,' came the first bulletin.

There was silence, an extreme silence, broken only by the continuing creak of that labouring lift. I knew I had missed a trick. The interview had followed the standard pattern. More or less. 'Is there anything you would like to ask us?' my interrogators had enquired solicitously. 'No, thank you,' I had responded, green as grass and forgetting the drill. 'That all sounds very nice.'

Quite wrong. Always enquire as to how the vacancy had arisen. Basic. Retirement? Re-location? Resignation? Promotion? Hanky panky? Fingers in the till?

As the inquisitive lift ground to a halt on the landing, the Controller fired again. And out of the silence came the second bulletin.

'More exactly, we have one dead and two dying.'

****

Chapter IV

INTERRUPTIONS TO THE DAILY ROUND

'Oh, don't the days seem lank and long
When all goes right and nothing goes wrong'

Princess Ida

Afghanistan in general – Kabul in particular – is without respect for daily routines. Dark forces and mischievous caprice delight in thwarting plans and pre-arranged programmes. Always have a plan, insisted the Controller. Then he would complete the military maxim: 'That way you can change it when things go wrong.'

In Asia, as in Africa, better by far to let the road unfold, and never bless the day before the setting of the sun.

Notwithstanding, effective and smooth continuance of the Project de-mining operation demanded that certain administrative procedures – those unavoidable shackles of management – be completed as efficiently as possible. This in spite of the sundry spanners-in-the-works – sporadic Sakar rockets, the menace-charged roadblocks, hyperactive AK-47s and RPGs in the hands of boy soldiers and hardened hooligans, the intermittent absence of water and electricity, those thundering tanks – that cropped up from time to time, or rather, at every turn. As the Controller might have pronounced (in the unlikely event that anyone was foolish enough to raise the subject with him): 'Difficulties are there to be overcome'. Motherhood and apple pie; obstacles are merely hurdles.

Thus it was with our daily round. There were bills to be paid (even electricity bills – to my surprise – for non-existent supplies, but borne of bureaucratic habit); no speedy direct debits or standing orders here, each payment involved a swag bag of notes and a drive across town. Diverting, but time consuming. There were stores to be bought, drums of fuel and cylinders of gas to be sought, personnel visas to be procured, vehicles to be maintained and repaired, reports to be rendered – particularly for impatient donors – radio schedules to be observed, facilitating honorariums to be slid across to various backhanded friends. Insurance nominal lists had to be prepared and checked (forever changing, forever out-of-date, forever thus) – mind-numbing but vital; unfamiliar three part names, no Gordon Bennetts, Joe Bloggs or Fred Spoons hereabouts. Get it right or else cruel fate would ensure that the very de-miner who had mischanced to activate a mine and was missing a limb would be the very man missing from the records.

There were governmental and other liaisons to be greased and furthered, ditto with the few Non-Governmental Organisations that still remained (not to mention the missionaries – Wilfred and Isabel and bearded Dan, and especially short-sighted musical Dan with his trumpet from Seattle); sundry squeaky wheels to keep well oiled, accounts to be penned, and disappearing money transfers to be traced.

The Controller had been right. Bothersome it was, this 'silent work of uneventful days'. But if we didn't do it – Rhubar and me – no one else would. And then things would grind to a halt. Not least the funding. Followed by the de-mining.

Above all, and whenever time and *jang* permitted, there were regular field visits to undertake to see the de-miners on the frontline. Trips to get the operational picture first hand, and to cheer isolated Walduck battling alone at Jebel Seraj 75 kilometres northwards. Likewise to independent Trotter and McScumble a further 150 kilometres beyond that at Pol-i-Khumri on the far side of the Salang Pass.

Not least on the agenda were the imperious summonses to attend cerebral mine clearance conferences in Islamabad, scenically but perilously reached down the Kabul Gorge. Thence onwards via the beguiling scarlet sea of the unchecked opium-producing poppy fields; swiftly through festering, fermenting Jalalabad; slip across the border at swarming Torkham; drive on past the heterogeneous bazaars of Landi Kotal, into and down the fabled Khyber Pass, where the regimental emblems of the former British North West Frontier garrison are emblazoned proudly, high on the rock face. And finally into turbulent, jostling Peshawar. There, a brief halt in the calmer back-waters of the pink-painted Pearl-Continental Hotel to partake gratefully of five-star strawberries and cream – a symbolic thanksgiving feast for safe deliverance from the 'dangers of the way and the violence of the enemy' – before confronting the high-speed hazards of the Grand Trunk Road on the ultimate leg of the journey leading to the green spaces of Pakistan's well-ordered capital. Failure to attend these meetings inevitably left the donors wondering if all was well with our Project – and their investment.

These, then, were the quotidian mundanities of existence, the routine administrative paraphernalia fettering our lives, those thousand things without a name. Inescapable chores, the execution of which an unsympathetic, granite-hearted Afghanistan obstinately and obdurately declined to facilitate or assist. Such was the way of our daily fare in the Kabul office – a readily recognisable round of activity, familiar to back-room staff the world over. Balls-aching, the Colonel had said, in that succinct, crisply descriptive and colourful way of his, and balls-aching it was. We could have employed an army of clerks; instead we did it ourselves. More people, more problems; bigger payroll. Ergo, said our leader, NYBTTB. And no one was ever brave enough to ask what he meant.

'Don't I know you, Guv?' the archetypal taxi driver had asked, en route to Heathrow and simultaneously en route to summing up the way things were.

'Don't think so,' said I, similarly unoriginal and matchingly lacking in creativity.

'There – it's the voice! You're that what's 'isname, the one in the what-you-call-it, surely?'

'No. I'm nobody. Mr Nobody. Just a cog.' But onwards he pressed, until inadvertently, I tripped. Eureka!

'Blimey! Bomb disposal and mine clearance! Nerves of steel and dead steady 'ands! You a bit loopy, then?'

'No, no and not really. I'm just a sort of fixer. You know, helping out. We also serve, so they say, and anyway, someone's got to do it. Not so much "hands on", more like "hands off".'

'Hands off! Ha! Nice one, Guv! Nice!' The thought of which kept him entertained and chuckling all the way to the airport without recourse to further conversation. Nice indeed.

It was the office terrace overlooking the garden that became central to our role as Project fixers, the focal point and hub of our activities. It was more agreeable than the gloom of the house – and, after all, any fool can be uncomfortable. I expect the Controller said that. We couldn't spend our entire day tearing round Kabul in a sea of mud and humanity, confusing movement with action

– or thumping up and down the Kabul Gorge in a cloud of dust.

Time spent in reconnaissance is never wasted – I remained readily and increasingly receptive to military maxims, especially those so well-suited to the circumstances. Thus it was that in the calm – relatively speaking – of that sylvan oasis hidden behind the Project villa we unconsciously established the planning wing of our operations room, the nub and launch pad of our endeavours. Those endeavours that admittedly were not invariably fruitful but which were always of earnest intent and predictably (almost without exception), prolonged. The Controller had his HQ and command post in London; ditto for us, Dr Rhubar and me, on the sun-blessed terrace in one-time up-market Shar-i-Naw (Lucky Five Street). And bleak indeed were those days when rain, and even snow, kept us locked below, trapped in the cold, grey confines of the sand-bagged sitting room.

Breakfast at 0645 was timed to coincide with the first rays of the sun banishing the hoarfrost from the balcony. This signalled the moment for beaming Abdul Ahmed in his off-white apron to make his tripping entry from the opposite point of the compass, bearing the joyful eggs sharing space on the tray with the daily bread (Karrimullah's freshly garnered *nan*), and the precariously balanced teapot memorably painted with purple pansies; totally un-chipped, just the gold banding a touch distressed. So much steam surged from the spout of that freshly filled pot that I imagined if you lifted the lid and peered inside, there you would find the fat lady herself, seated within *au natural* and taking a frolicking good bath.

At that time of morning Shar-i-Naw was already quietly active: skyward smoke rising straight from backyard cookers; the tinkle of a purposeful bell from a cyclist, or a scavenging goat, from somewhere down in the street; our neighbours' shutters on the far side of the grape vine stirring surreptitiously as unseen eyes confirmed and observed our presence. Breakfast down below in the sombre shaded sitting room, the bunker, was but a sad and cheerless alternative.

However, before the al fresco meal could commence, the established drill was to complete the radio schedules. Dial up Trotter and McScumble, callsign Whisky Papa, in the far north; do it first, so as not to interrupt the 0630 morning parade of their 60-odd de-miners. If Pol-i-Khumri were slow answering, spend a few envious minutes eaves-dropping on the unknown UN man driving to his humanitarian work, somewhere over the mountains in this country that is not quite as big as Burma, whispering shortwave radio inducements to one of the enchanted secretaries in Mazar-i-Sharif. Sloppy radio discipline and poor lack of technical appreciation by Lothario, imagining that if he whispered then no one would hear. Trust not the incapable. Probably the whole world tuned in every morning to get an update on his nefarious affair. Well, except his wife, that is. Didn't he know that the penalties for such transgressions tended to be extreme in these parts? Skinning alive, for example. Even (according to enthusiastic Dr Rhubar) a barbed and thorny inverted rose twig pushed up his peripatetic penis, and then withdrawn, slowly. Never again would I wield the secateurs amidst the hybrid teas and the carefree floribundas without a passing pang of concern for the fate of that deprived and careless UN man in the mountains.

Anyway, all well with can-do will-do Trotter and McScumble, the endangering minehunting sweat, toil and toll of the previous day laconically reduced to just two key indicators: square metres of terrain surveyed and painstakingly checked, and the number of lethal devices located and cleared. Possibly ten mines removed, more probably five, or two, or perhaps only one to show for the day's labours. Maybe even none. But most importantly of all: no mishaps.

Now pass on to Jebel Seraj to see how Walduck was faring. Similar drill, just a routine arithmetical courtesy, garnering the stats. Except that Afghanistan does not respond to routines.

'Tango Yankee Papa Hotel Oscar India Delta,' radioed gallant Walduck faintly from afar.

'Oscar Zulu, say again your last,' said I, twiddling the knob and adjusting the volume.

'Typhoid,' crackle, crackle, sob. 'I am suffering from typhoid. Acute. Over.'

Oh, t-y-p-h-o-i-d. That was inconvenient. Acute, too. Directly overhead I heard Abdul Ahmed, bang on cue, advancing uncertainly with the eggs. I looked up at the ceiling in exasperation, but to no effect; he would be wondering where I was. The trouble with Walduck is that he travels with a thermometer. Pity he never met my Grandmother, although it's too late now. Never travel with a thermometer was her brisk advice; more trouble than they are worth. Again I think upwardly to the eggs, fast congealing on the frosty platter.

'Roger, Oscar Zulu. Typhoid. Acute. Understood. Wait. Out.' Good, pithy radio procedure. I flick the switch to 'Off', successfully precluding a prolongation of the interruption and hurry upstairs to rendezvous with my breakfast. Abdul has remembered to cut the *nan* into soldiers to go with the eggs, and as I dip them into the yellow yokes, quite unforgiveably I picture Walduck stretched out on his *charpoy*, that flimsy trestle bed of his held together with string, up there in the wilderness of the Shomali Valley. The saddest of scenarios, redolent of Empire. Alone in the outpost, as life ebbs away.

One of Walduck's favourite possessions was his Stetson hat (history and *raison d'être* undeclared – there are strict unwritten rules and rigid invisible boundaries limiting the exchange of confidences between comrades-in-arms). They were inseparable, Walduck and that big, flamboyant Wild West hat. Probably he was wearing it in these final moments. Or, perhaps, in the manner of a fallen hero's cap adorning the end of the coffin, he had placed it at the foot of his bed. It scarcely bore thinking about, and I poured myself another cup from the pansy pot, pending developments.

I discussed the situation with Dr Rhubar later that morning, almost as soon as he arrived in the office, in fact. In consequence we sent a fax to the Controller, informing HQ of Walduck's imminent demise, at the same time trying to avoid over-dramatising things. No point in provoking London and exacerbating the situation. 'Noted your last,' replied the Controller, seemingly unconvinced and not overtly impressed. Maybe he had met my Grandmother.

But wait, there is more: 'Dr Boggis-Battie, newly recruited medical cover for the Pol-i-Khumri minefields operation, will arrive next Thursday', writes the Controller in his second paragraph. 'Please meet and despatch northwards. He will hand-carry two more replacement Land Rover wing mirrors.' I look at Rhubar quizzically.

'Only two?' he queries, pensively. 'We never seem to have enough. Anyway, are we supposed to call him Boggis or Battie?'

The trouble with Walduck – aside from the thermometer and the Stetson – was that he had taken to eating his solitary breakfast, indeed all his meals, in his Land Rover so that he could tune in to the BBC World Service the whilst for company. This cramped posture behind the wheel was undoubtedly not conducive to smooth digestion. Although not a Land Rover driver herself, Granny could have told him that too.

Mercifully, Walduck radioed a medical 'all-clear' later the same day.

'This is Oscar Zulu. Typhoid alert cancelled. Out.' Brief with relief. He sounded less faint, too. Yet the incident had clearly unsettled him: almost immediately he followed up with a request for enhanced sanitary facilities at his newly established camp. In other words, please purchase and deliver a bathroom suite to his location. Asap (if not sooner). Always ready to oblige, we conjectured as to what his colour preferences might be. Emolient Avocado or perhaps stentorian Shocking Pink? I deferred to Dr Rhubar to ascertain his medical opinion.

'Only one?' he queried, tangentially. 'With or without bidet?' He was so taken with his lavatory humour that the conversation foundered.

Ever willing, back we radioed to Oscar Zulu a swift and supportive 'Roger your last. Wait. Out.' We didn't know how long Walduck could wait, but we would address the issue forthwith.

Breakfast, and sundry other minor excitements concluded, there was normally opportunity for a few moments of reflection on the terrace before finalising the battle plan for the day with Rhubar. Memories of 'the long ago and far away', quiet time for a touch of cloudless contemplation against the tailor-made, indigo void of the Kabul autumnal sky.

At times I even fantasised that it might be possible to orchestrate our entire ministrations in support of the Project without the need to move from that sun-filled, elevated command post. Until, that is, the diurnal, early-morning churning arrival of super-charged Dr Rhubar brought me back to earth with energetic reminders that we needed to call on the President – of our vehicle insurance company – and the other President – of Banke Millie (sic), who had lost our money – with whom we felt we ought to open a dialogue. Such as: 'Where's the money, then?'

Then there was the President himself – the real one (or his representative) – to wait on, to enumerate our activities, hypothesize on our progress, and hypothecate continued support (in both directions). Important, that. Obtaining the audience was not the problem; since the withdrawal of almost all diplomatic and agency expatriate staff, parking in the city and arranging official appointments at the highest level had become miraculously elementary. It was just a question of telephoning; that was the tricky part.

After all of which, if there was still time before lunch, we could go and see Mr Bhaksheesh, reputedly the sole survivor at the Pakistan Embassy, who, presciently, was hardly ever in his consular office to help us with visas. However, as luck would have it, there was a first-rate table-tennis table (Olympic one-size-fits-all – had to be – possibly even bigger) in the basement of the building, which made waiting for Mr Bhaksheesh no real penance. On the contrary, it was a pleasure. So much so that we tried to see him at least twice a week to maintain the momentum of our inaugural international ping pong tournament, Great Britain v Afghanistan. Management is all about handling pressure: so much to do, so little time.

Quite apart from the vortex of Dr Rhubar's daily arrival in the office, once in a while my terrace reverie would be interrupted (rudely) by a resounding hammering on the big metal gates of our compound. I knew what caused it, even without opening my eyes. The Press. They didn't mean to be intrusive, naturally; they just didn't fully appreciate the percussive properties of those stern portals, and, into the bargain, they probably assumed the lodger was deaf. Not entirely, as it happens, just on the one side.

The first instinct was to dismiss the unscheduled intruders, to send impassable Karrimullah to invite them to make a proper appointment. But then again, and after all, they were the Fourth Estate. And this was Kabul. And with that came the recurring problem of the telephones. Hence, the Press were graciously admitted (they generally descended in pairs, like carrion crows). Chairs were drawn up in the sunshine. Business cards were proffered: The Washington Post, The Independent, Pink Times, Reuters, Associated Press, so forth – in dribs and drabs they all came.

Ever alert to events, Abdul, the genie's brother, would promptly appear, his head cocked to one side like an inquisitive sparrow, the gold-spouted pansy pot brimming, billowing steam like the fat Duchess in her bath.

'Sorry for my English,' he would begin, confidently, 'she is not so fine ...' After which he would run out of words and tail off back to the galley to continue with his menu planning (meatballs or meatballs?), larding the baking tin and rolling the pastry on the mousey bread board in readiness for the apple pie (if we were lucky), the lunchtime shot of sugary tart.

In principle, he was spot-on to offer himself for interview; who better than he, who daily pedalled the length of the city? There was just the language barrier, the linguistic roadblock. So it fell to me to pontificate, by default.

Yes, I would tell the reporters knowledgeably, the fighting was continuing. The situation was confused. Interim President Burhanuddin Rabbani of the JIA party, *Jamiat-i-Islami*, remained in power; fanatical Gulbuddin Hekmatyar, leader of the HIH, *Hezb-i-Islami*, was threatening the city from without, engaging in random rocketing. Well, it felt that way because it seemed pretty hit and miss. Yes, it was sporadic; a question of logistics rather than goodwill, presumably. Sluggardly supply trailing demand. He, Mr Hekmatyar, controlled the south-eastern region and therefore the generation of hydro-electric power.

A useful lever. Well, for instance, he had switched it off. More or less, he also controlled the road through to Pakistan, on and off, so stocks of diesel fuel were dwindling. Hard on the *bukharis*, those temperamental indigenous heaters, and winter was fast coming on. No, thankfully, there were no in-bound air strikes. Not at that time. Rabbani still held Bagram, the former Russian air base. Defence Minister Ahmed Shah Masood? The so-called Lion of Panshir, he was quietly biding his moment, while General Rashid Dostum's Uzbeks (or Tajiks) still occupied certain parts of the city – down by the Zoo, for example – thereby bolstering Rabbani. Or could it be they were Hazaras, with those Mongoloid features? Unclear and difficult to tell sometimes. Well, yes, as mentioned earlier, the entire situation was confusing.

The reporters would make busy notes in their curly-edged pocket books. At which point Abdul usually re-appeared, ever hopeful of getting a mention. 'Your tea she is well?' he would enquire of the visitors.

I would suggest to them they might like to visit the Zoo, if they had time, in case it hadn't crossed their minds. It never had. They would look up in slow motion from their scribbling, curious, stubby pencils poised. Amazing, I would tell them: Bears, lions, an elephant, wolves, yak, deer, wild boar, an eagle, umm … a pelican or two … er, mountain goats, vultures … but above all, three magnificent Siberian tigers. The visitors would ask if I was positive with my identification, and question that these endangered animals still existed. I would obfuscate, telling them that the Hazaras – or the Uzbeks – reportedly keep their prisoners in the cages at the Zoo (a gross calumny, no doubt) and that when last seen, the three tigers were purringly fat and glossy-coated. Although, disturbingly, there had also been rumours that the other captive creatures, such as the rainbow-coloured pheasants (the Tibetan Goldens, the rare Scintillating Coppers and even the brace of Lady Amhert's) were themselves gradually – or even rapidly – being eaten by the jailors (assuredly yet more of the same, grosser calumny still).

In fact, rumours abounded: now it was said that with poetic justice the elephant had been Sakar-ed – hit by a rogue rocket – and that the fornicating monkeys had escaped, rambling and roaming their wanton way through the ravaged city.

Anyway, returning to the fighting, yes, the situation was slowly getting worse. Well, quite quickly, actually. The west of the city was now totally destroyed. Gone. It was like Dresden. Even the Inter-Continental Hotel (devoid of guests) had been rocketed out of existence, the water in the swimming pool had all but disappeared, drained out through the cracks, the goldfish in the ornamental pool surrounding the fountain had long since vanished through the fissures. Anyone hoping to book into the Khyber Suite had missed the boat, or rather, the camel train. It seemed that the struggle would go on and on until there was nothing remaining, and then whoever was left would be King of the Ruins.

The reporters licked their pencils and wrote it all down as fast as they knew how, dropped by at the Zoo (admittance fee waived in those dire days in the absence of the attendant) on the way to the airport and filed their copy when they got home. Weeks – or months – later we would read erudite analyses of the Quandary in Afghanistan, headed 'Geneva Convention Flaunted in Kabul Menagerie', 'Monarch of the Rubble', or similar.

Sometimes the visitors asked about the future. The future? Oh, everything has a future, we take that for granted; up until now, that is. The notion of better times to come was implicit in the reporters' questions. Accepting the premise and running with the concept on the basis that the alternative could not be countenanced, together we would explore and adumbrate the touristic possibilities, once all this had been sorted out, naturally. And the anti-personnel mines, those too.

Kabul, heavy with history, had much of it encapsulated in its world-renowned Museum. That was before it was looted and the greater part of one of the finest collections of antiquities in Asia flung, mah-jongg style, to the four winds, a dress-rehearsal for Baghdad 2003. A field day for the moneyed mafia, the private collectors. History may repeat itself, the curator had said, but it is rarely recoverable.

Then there's Bala Hissar, Dost Muhammed Khan's old citadel at the onset of the First Afghan War, although best to delay visiting until all the unexploded ordnance embedded in the crumbling battlements of the 'High Wall' Fort has been cleared. The once famed Gardens of Babur – 'that cool retreat, Baghe Babur' – were now an arid wasteland, where President Rabbani's local *Jamiat* commander had set his tanks to overlook the sewer that is the Kabul River. Yet, I would tell the reporters, for the price of the avionics of one stealth bomber, all could be re-planted and the former tranquil beauty restored – and then maintained by a hundred gardeners for a hundred years. The same budget could also include provision of a replacement carriage for The Noon Cannon, that peculiarly British relic, still identifiable high above Kabul, but, as we spoke, lying sadly on its side in the sand.

As the post-war concept gathered momentum, the listeners would be reminded that not much further afield there was white water canoeing and rafting to be had in the Kabul Gorge, where the tumbling waters plummet over the rocks on their way to join the headwaters of the mighty Indus beyond the border, across the Pathan patrolled frontier. Skiing holidays could be taken from mountain chalets, divested of butterfly mines; bus tours might visit the sad remains of the Great Buddhas of Bamiyan and to see the deceptively innocent vista of the hallucinatory mauve and stunning purple poppy fields that stretched away from the Jalalabad road; the endless vineyards could be revitalised, the resultant reds and whites marketed worldwide as in former times: 'explosively heady and aromatically spiced with intrigue', suggested one creative copywriter.

Warming to the hypothesis, the possibilities appeared to be many and varied. The only flaw being that everything envisaged came from a western perspective. Shades of sacrilege.

'There's one thing we've overlooked,' I said.

'What's that?' enquired the journalists, their notebooks growing weary.

'Embroidery.'

'Come again?'

'You might not think it's central, but it's the obverse side of the coin. Just an example, you understand. In every valley here the women have a priceless and unmatched heritage of needlework, handed down across the centuries. Exquisite patterns and geometric motifs, romantic flowers and stylised leaves, the designs worked in gold and silver threads, coloured silks and dyed wools. The ladies devote their talents to the decoration of woollen coats and dresses in velvet; cushions, curtains, door hangings and adorned bands for the house; trousseaux for young brides, handkerchiefs embellished with love poems in classical Persian, even reins for the horses, bodice fronts, shawls, waistcoats, bed linen, table and bread cloths. They still use hand woven fabrics, you know.'

'So?'

'So this is a glorious treasure trove. It paves the way for coach loads – plane loads – of stitchers, sewing enthusiasts, needle-artists, to arrive from Europe and the United States on educational excursions, staying in the homes of the Afghan ladies and picking up rather more than just a few new needlework techniques.'

Silence.

'Well, it's just an idea, an illustrative suggestion. It might lead to a better understanding and appreciation, more of a two-way thing. Something of an eye-opener, actually. Of course, foreigners – that's us – will always be foreigners. We should never make the mistake of thinking otherwise. But this kind of thing might help.'

The important point – the point perhaps being made rather too obliquely – was what did the Afghans want for *their* country? It was just a thought, but perhaps they would quite like to be left alone, instead of being someone else's adventure playground. The 'let history take its course' approach. In all events, the prospects were indeed varied. Including (my diatribe faltering and the shared optimism evaporating as the shadow of a small cloud brushed across the terrace), the unspoken and unthinkable fear of the ever-downward spiral of this majestic land into long-term oblivion, terminally contaminated by the debris of war and internecine venom, coupled with the de-stabilising corruption of the drugs trade. The failed state that declined to be rescued from history.

****

Infrequently, reporters came who wished to travel into the hinterland, to see things for themselves. Unfortunately, in this hazardous world, journalists increasingly share with aviators the common denominator that in the professional execution of their duties, 'boldness' and 'oldness' are qualities but rarely permitted by the deities to enjoin. Nevertheless, ever helpful, we saw one youthful pair boldly on their way north, to Pol-i-Khumri to pass a few days with our Project de-miners.

Once there, they were favoured with an invitation from a local warlord to witness a game of Buz Kashi, the traditional Afghan recreation involving whirling tribesmen on horseback, tussling for possession of the carcass of a dead sheep. The singular and colourful spectacle was too good to miss; the hospitality even included generous provision of a transporting helicopter to the not-so-distant town of Khayan, and then home for supper.

Sadly, the visitors never arrived at their destination.

The radio call came mid-afternoon. Our new friends were overdue. Their helicopter was missing. The fuel would surely have been expended by now. Time to alert their parent press agency in Islamabad.

In another place, at another time, making a not entirely dissimilar flight from Stepanakert back to Yerevan, Armenia in a Russian-built MI-8, returning after completing an overnight overland delivery via the Latchin corridor to Nagorno

Karabakh, I remembered how our pilot and co-pilot had sat chatting in the cab whilst everyone, including livestock, had piled aboard regardless. When we were chock-a-block with passengers and chattels, some 40-strong, or so it seemed, the doors were squeezed shut, as on a rush-hour commuter train.

Flicking his cigarette out of the cockpit window, the pilot had eased back empirically on the collective to see if he could achieve lift-off. Just then, a belated stretcher case arrived at the helipad and the doors were re-opened. The wounded soldier was loaded; a pig and an elderly couple were booted out by way of brutal compensation. Peasants. Turning and burning, up we climbed; the pilot put the nose down and we were on our way.

My place, or rather, where I had ended up, was right forward, squashed between the aircrew in the see-through cockpit bubble, perched thermostatically on what seemed to be the gearbox. This gave an excellent view of the jagged mountain tops beneath my feet as the pilot delighted in keeping low, following the contours of the land, and then yanking back on the stick at the ultimate moment of moments, so that everyone held their breath or gasped in terror, buttocks clenched.

Conceivably, things were not too different on the flight the intrepid journalists took on their way to see the game of Buz Kashi. Perhaps that day the pilot over-egged his flying display, under-estimating the altitudinal pull of his payload. Maybe an undetected, unsuspected mechanical defect degraded the aircraft's performance at a critical juncture. The upshot was the same. The scurrying helicopter clipped the crest of a mountain en route and, on contact with the unyielding wall of rock, shattered and burst into flaming shreds. And likewise disintegrated all the souls on board.

Early evening brought confirmation of the disaster. The wreckage had been found. But not before looters had done their work and picked their inhumane way through the remains: the pieces, the wallets and the scattered remnants. Shapeless plastic bags containing the two reporters were taken by roof rack to Mazar-i-Sharif the following day, 200 kilometres by road. It was another 36 hours before the UN transport plane made it up from Pakistan. The weather was hot and sunny, and there were no refrigeration facilities.

At the memorial gathering in Islamabad, two enlarged pictures of those smiling young adventurers stood in front of the chancel steps, whilst the officiating minister reminded us of 'the brevity – and fragility – of our lives on earth'. The service was informal; members of the congregation – old friends, colleagues, new friends – came forward to express their tributes, to pay their respects. Fifteen lives were lost in that crash. Engine failure was the official finding. One year on, and correspondence with the bereaved parents of the reporters was still unfinished.

'Blessed are those who have died in the Lord,' intoned the minister. 'Let them rest from their labours for their good deeds go with them. Go forth Christian souls from this world. May light perpetual shine upon them. God grant to the living, grace, and to the departed, peace.'

****

'There's another fax just arrived from London,' said Dr Rhubar in passing, on my return from the service in Islamabad, in that offhand informative way of his. 'More reinforcements are coming. I can't remember if I told you how we blew the windows out of the front of the Red Cross offices by mistake? It was a while ago now, in your predecessor's time. Well, anyway, the Controller's sending a munitions expert to work with us. Someone called O'Deere. And by the way, I think we had better order some more body bags. Always useful.'

****

Chapter V

IN CIRCLES

'...the relentless quest for a better way, the daily pursuit of perfection ...'

October was fast giving way to November. Dr Boggis-Battie, medical cover for the Pol-i-Khumri mine clearance operations, arrived at Kabul airport in accordance with the Controller's prognostication and was duly despatched northwards. O'Deere, expert in all things explosive, arrived two days later than the Controller's forecast, having inadvertently missed his flight. He told us that he'd rung the Controller from Heathrow to advise him of his chronological misadventure. We gazed at him in wonder: this man was truly fearless.

O'Deere was welcomed to the Project team in Kabul, bedded down in Lucky Five Street and settled to his destructive duties. It was also at this time that Suzi, intrepid resident BBC correspondent in Afghanistan, and one of the very few expatriates remaining in the circuit, introduced me to Lady Sale.

****

Weather permitting, the all-purpose ops-room terrace of our office villa also served as language laboratory in the continuing quest for some degree of modest mastery of Afghan Dari, the Afghan dialect of Persian. Functional Dari, roadblock Dari, survival Dari – uncomplicated aims, limited but pertinent first-step ambitions. Leading, perhaps – and I hoped – to a modicum of under-the-skin Dari.

Each day, as we fulfilled our urban medley of rounds and errands in furtherance of the upward fortunes of our de-mining Project, a mental note was made of words and phrases that would have come in handy, had they in fact been to hand. 'Drive faster!' 'Take cover!' 'Another cup would be delightful.' 'Faster!' 'Meatballs?'

Helpful and ever-willing Dr Rhubar would then write the Dari equivalent – first in Arabic and then transliterating to the Roman alphabet – in the vocabulary book, especially purchased for the very purpose in the multi-faceted mall that was Chicken Street. That same evening, in the glow of the flickering hurricane lamps, I would prepare pocket-sized, miniature 'flash cards', faithfully copying Rhubar's Arabic script, the wiggly characters – all 96 of them – previously learnt during sojourns in Libya, Oman and Saudi Arabia. The ever-growing packs of cards were then secured with sturdy elastic bands, available for further study and memorising in whatever moment of calm, or stress. And likewise, ready for instant use in whatever circumstances that might arise, dire or otherwise.

'*Shutor didi*? – Have you seen the camel?' 'No, I haven't – *Na didi*.' 'Have you seen the mouse? – *Mosh didi*?' 'I am a poor man – *Marde gharib hastam*.' 'Bad luck – *Chans-e-bad*.' (Easy, that one). 'Don't shoot! – *Fair nakon*!' (Handy). 'I am English – *Man Englis hastam*!' 'Bugger off! – *Gom sho*!'

Simple, except Rhubar obtusely and steadfastly declined to accept the brilliance of the concept.

'I don't understand,' he would say, first straight-faced and deadpan, then frowning heavily and screwing up his features theatrically. 'What if you can't find the right card at the right moment? You might end up telling Abdul not to shoot when all he wanted to do was offer you a tart, and you might ask the roadblock donkeys for more tea when all they wanted to do was shoot you.' And Rhubar would shake his head to simulate total mystification. And to provoke.

'I've told you before it doesn't work like that. This system is proven. It was used during the First World War. Probably even before. Maybe even in the First Afghan War. Certainly during the Third. I still have my father's pack of semaphore cards from 1917.' Rhubar's expression revealed that I was hindering, not helping. 'Anyway, some of the roadblocks make quite good tea.'

Rhubar would nod non-committally, avoiding eye contact. Enough fun for now; lots more opportunities to be perverse.

'What shall we do today?' he would ask blandly, smoothly changing tack and at the same time putting paid to any unworkable schemes and dreams of orchestrating events exclusively from the relative comfort of the terrace. Fanciful and impracticable and inadvisable indeed, yet time spent with the Afghan Dari books was the blue chip investment of the day. Language, language, language: that was the way to lifting the veil that lay over this impenetrable country. Even a glimmer of light and understanding would be a seven-league stride …

Stay emotionally detached, keep your distance; become emotionally involved and you become a secondary casualty of the situation. So much for the received wisdom. I wasn't going to argue, but I did want to know what made Abdul tick. In Africa, armed with fluent Kiswahili, it had seemed easy to reach under the skin. Here it was harder, and not just the intricacies of the Afghan Dari; there was a yawning chasm of incomprehension. Which of the ethnic groupings beloved of analysts was perky Abdul? He was not a twenty five per cent Tajik, that I knew; and certainly not a twenty per cent Hazara; probably not a forty per Pashtun either. So he must be a five or six per cent Uzbek, or one of the balancing assortment of minorities. Except that it didn't matter that much, particularly to Abdul; survival was his motivator. Survival for him and his family – the family I supposed (rightly) I would never be invited to meet.

And Zahir? Like Abdul, he too needed the salary. And he too was a gentle, peaceful man. Happiness for him was cuddling up in the workshop with six or eight cylinders of well-oiled and smooth purring machinery, touching the glistening tappets and titillating the timing with those soft hands of his.

Gung-ho Karimullah was rather different; wholly unabashed by Dr Rhubar's merrily slanderous and ribald chatter, he was a true disciple and adherent of the Project ethos and house style: maintenance of the objective and press on regardless, come what may.

What about Will-o-the-Wisp Hajji, revered pilgrim and performer of Haj, esteemed traveller to Mecca? A closed book for ever, of that I was sure. I think he only came to the house each day to tend the *bukhari* stove through curiosity of what made me tick. And if he ever found out, then without the language I would never be enlightened.

And highly intelligent, educated Dr Rhubar himself, ever the optimist, blessed with that rare quality of absolute integrity? He surely wanted the best for his family, and that meant the best for his country. Peace and security for Najia his wife and for *Bachai Jang*, his 'Son of a Gun' little boy – and for Afghanistan, so that he might practise as a doctor without being blown up or shot on the way to work. Surely not too much to ask.

Which brought me to the men on the roof. What was their motivation? No mastery of Afghan Dari needed there – it's quite fun firing a machine gun, isn't it? Following in their fathers' footsteps – and those of their grandfathers. Like going down the pit, a generation game unless the cycle is stopped.

Aside from Dr Rhubar, perhaps my best line of investigation lay with Abdul. That English of his was a starting point, and he was quick on the uptake. '*Hujambo, Mzee*,' I would say to him in Kiswahili, '*habari za chai*?', or even '*Buenos dias, Señor. Hay té, por favor*?' Without missing a beat, back would come his unfailing response: 'My cooker she is very fine. Tea is coming!'

Language, language, language. That was the key to getting to getting involved. And that was the key to understanding.

****

Off in the Land Rover we would go, scarcely out of second gear, picking our way through the poverty and squalor of the muddy streets, a mêlée of bicycles, assorted livestock, heedless pedestrians, and those over-loaded, trundling, straining hand carts. The women draped in *chadar* and *chadari*, their *abbeya*-like, canary cage covering of veils and head dresses; the men in flapping *pirahan tonban* – Afghan pyjamas – less frequently wearing the *lungi*, the turban and robe.

Our first call was usually on the President. Mr Amir Maqsudi, President of oxymoronic Universal Afghan Insurance. His un-palatial presidential office could be reached via rickety stairs at the back of a low building, also rickety. Not only decrepit but dirty too – no dutiful cleaners of common parts hereabout, only an abundance of Third World third party cover. The Project de-miners were insured through Lloyds; for better or for worse the vehicles were insured through Mr Maqsudi. Money changed hands. The room undulated with hills and dales of yellowing documents; in a quiet valley in the furthest corner an elderly clerk of distinguished mien was attacking an antique, handraulic Imperial two-fingered typewriter (coincidentally and simultaneously declaring ditto to Mr Hekmatyar's power cuts). In all probability he was the company Vice President, fervently hoping that a Sakar rocket might pass this way. *Insh'allah*. Should God so wish. Best not to dwell too deeply on how things might fare if ever we had cause to make a claim.

Business concluded, such as it was, we drive further downtown to see the next President. Mr Zia Qadir, President of Banke Millie, the national bank. We wondered where our money was … Bolivia? The President was looking into it. Except that the President had just slipped out. I study my flash cards. '*Khosh boshi*! Be happy!'

Dr Rhubar studies the rows of bank clerks, serried, predominantly female, seated in the hall beyond the customer grilles, flanked by dark green marble columns, Corinthian in form. I follow his gaze, if not his line of thought:

definitely Corinthian rather than Doric; certainly not Ionic.

'Do you think they are looking for our transfer,' I ask, purely to while away the time.

Rhubar starts visibly, colours and considers. 'No,' he says after a lengthy pause. 'I understand that they are engaged on a study of The Kama Sutra, which involves in-depth personal validation of all therein followed by publication of a detailed, illustrated addendum.'

As Rhubar warms to his theme it is clear that the conversation is taking a familiar turn. I hurriedly suggest we might return another day, thus forestalling the grand entrance of much maligned Karrimullah and the unfortunate donkey into the expanding thesis.

The route back to our compound leads past the house-cum-office of ubiquitous Médecins sans Frontières. Claude the logistician, one-time landscape architect, answers our call. Everyone else is working up at Charikar, he declares, 30 kilometres north of the city. But everything is OK, thanks, more or less.

When they return, we tell him, bring your MSF group and come and watch our video with us. We only had one. Hopefully they hadn't seen it.

Claude is happy for that. *Merçi beaucoup.* Then, before giving us the address of the trader who could supply bargain Afghan leather waistcoats, he shows us the fresh bullet that had lodged in the window frame in the hall of the MSF house that morning.

Just another stray bullet. Just a rogue malcontent and another acute case of Kabul sudden death syndrome narrowly averted. Humanitarian tenacity is an admirable quality, but where to draw the line? On with the good work or *gom sho*? That was the question.

Don't forget to come and watch the video with us one evening, we remind Claude, anxious to enliven our social round, non-existent as it was. There's room for everyone.

****

It could be postponed no longer. That same afternoon we headed back to the centre of town to cross the Kabul River, the once picturesque waterway that gives double service to the citizens of Kabul: communal latrine and a convenient place where the farmers from the surrounding countryside can wash the mud and dust off their lettuces, tomatoes and other succulent in-season produce before selling it in the market.

'Boil it, peel it or leave it' was never a truer adage than in Kabul. That, and ingesting a de-worming pill on departure. Or half a dozen, a box full.

Our purpose in crossing the river was to reach the side where the money-changers operated, the labyrinthine financial quarter. Hustling alleys and dark passages devoid of sunlight crowded with traders, every man a seeming specialist in sleight of hand. Plus a resourceful sprinkling of those ready with even sharper techniques.

Our dollars could have been exchanged at the kerbside, through the window of the car, but Rhubar, averse to unwanted publicity, had his preferred contacts, well hidden traders tucked into discreet cubby holes more suited to the substantial scale of our transaction. The threat of ambush, the loss of Project funds – and more – had in the past been only narrowly avoided.

At 1,000 *Afghanis* to the dollar, a couple of pillow cases were needed as well as a travelling bag in which to accommodate the heap of notes. O'Deere the destroyer, six foot plus in his demolition socks, obligingly abandoned blowing things up for the afternoon and lent his comforting presence to the party. Karrimullah shouldered the bulging bedware and we made it back to base without incident. No following vehicles detected in the rear-view mirror that day, no cause for abrupt detours, violent lefts and rights.

All done for another month, the loot stashed in the safe and Dr Rhubar, following the mores of his profession, was keen to be away to his private clinic. I was equally bent on catching the final rays of the afternoon sun, following the taxing rigours of the day. Accordingly, word was passed to Abdul in the galley to make good with the kettle and I ascended to the terrace to investigate whatever delights Lady Sale might have in store.

Such was the non-routine routine. Invariably a sprinkling of surprises and always those many-layered liaisons – a thousand things without a name that served to see us through the day.

Except that on that particular day, nothing being routine, things took a novel twist. Hardly had I settled in my chair, and with Rhubar still somewhere down below in the house fiddling and fussing around before leaving for his clinic, a rocket sailed past.

I stared vacantly after the departing missile, much in the manner of a dumbfounded fly fisherman, peacefully mid-river in his water-logged waders, mind on matters piscatorial and what might be for dinner, only to be taken aback by the unpredicated passing of a Great White Shark. Incredible. I hadn't realised they flew so slowly. Rockets, that is.

'I say, Rhubar!' I called down urgently. 'Just come and look at this!'

But it was too late. The rocket, already travelling tiredly, gave a final wobble and was lost from sight beyond our neighbour's unsuspecting patient pine tree. Dr Rhubar's obedient and breathless arrival on the terrace coincided with a plume of smoke rising just two streets away.

'Gosh!' we remarked in unison – or words to that effect – responding to events in general and the shoulder-flinching bang in particular.

'What kind was it?' wondered Rhubar.

'It wasn't that close. I couldn't read the writing. Anyway, it was in Cyrillic.'

'Well, luckily it seems it had someone else's name on it.'

'We'd better go and see if we can help.'

So saying, off we shot to assuage our guilty consciences from an earlier date, deserting the terrace and abandoning Lady Sale to her own devices.

Arriving at the recently rocketed house of our extended neighbours the scene was sadly familiar, although this time the missile had landed in the back garden, rather than in the front room. Hence the destruction was incomplete, in so much that most of the building was at least still standing. Even so, it seemed that a typhoon of maximum malevolence had passed through the house, blowing and sweeping everything in its path out into the street, including the occupying family, now huddled together in the road, dusty and dazed, uncertain and confused. Silent, the tears yet to flow. The dark blood that ran freely from the head of one of the youngest children contrasted reproachfully with his golden brown skin and strawberry cheeks.

Entering the house, we found that here the devastation and domestic desolation was comprehensive. Pitifully comprehensive. When starting with so little, is the blow greater or smaller when everything is lost?

The raggedy red curtains were hanging dejectedly out through the pane-less windows, the shiny-topped three-legged stools in the kitchen had over-turned in all directions, sharing the floor with a scattered turmoil of pots, kitchen implements, rolling rice and chickpeas. No supper tonight.

We took the mother, the trembling grandmother and the injured child to the Project Clinic. There they did what they could for them, whilst we stayed with the other children, seven in all, that had emerged from that blasted house. Avoiding emotional entanglement, of course. Except that we felt we needed to be involved right up to our elbows, otherwise there was not much point in being there.

Of the men of that family there was no trace.

****

'By the way,' observed Dr Rhubar slyly, when he returned from his first aid activities and things were a bit quieter, 'the neighbours say that whenever there is rocketing or local *jang*, they don't see you reading on the terrace.' He paused for the certain reaction, as guaranteed as a prankster's tin tack.

I was about to say something futile about prudence, then changed horses in mid-air, bewildered my metaphors and claimed it was a question of preserving the stream of concentration. 'Anyway,' I told him, 'I am not alone in this world.' Pause for Rhubar's interrogative glance. 'It would be irresponsible to endanger the edifying flash cards in such disturbed circumstances. And the enchanting Lady Sale. What's more,' I added stuffily, 'the Controller specifically advised me before I left London that he would not take kindly to being burdened unnecessarily with the necessity to fill any sudden vacancies that might arise as the result of lack of attention to detail.'

Rhubar looked disappointed but recovered well; lots more provoking opportunities would arise.

****

The fact was, in non-routine, war-torn Kabul, post-prandial prime time was forever prone to interruption.

I was on the terrace one afternoon, the sun on my back, heavily engaged as usual with Lady Sale, when unexpectedly, enigmatic O'Deere appeared at the top of the stairs.

'Everything's ready,' he announced, popping his head round the door frame at an angle and throwing me his wide-eyed look.

'Good show,' I replied calmly, not letting on.

'We can go and watch, if you like.'

So, yet again, off we shot, as was the way. Right across to the far side of town, the badlands, where groups of idling Muj raised interrogatory beards in the direction of the Land Rover as we passed, weapons loosely at the ready. Reassuringly, O'Deere seemed to know what he was about, casually exchanging the odd precautionary wave with the watching bandits as he drove, eventually heaving on the handbrake and bringing the vehicle to a halt in no man's land. He led the way to the centre of an expanse of desolate waste ground and jumped down into a deep pit. There he stood, balancing on a generous helping of discarded ordnance: old shells, bent bombs, rusty rockets past their sell-date, and undoubtedly a handful of bomblets littering the bottom of the hole to boot.

'Took a while to gather these up,' said O'Deere, his head just above ground level as he stood on the unstable pile, beaming up at me in that sunny way of his.

'I bet,' said I. 'Warm work.'

'I'll just wire up,' continued O'Deere, conversationally, 'backfill, and then we'll be ready for the off.'

'Rightee-ho,' said I.

When it came, the off was quite impressive.

'Must have been about 2,000 kilograms,' explained O'Deere. 'There were 442 different items in the hole. I counted them.'

I mentally logged the stat for our next report.

Another sunny beam came my way as the explosion reverberated for miles around and the yellow and black smoke swirled heavenwards, ever higher. And even higher. Expert that he was, O'Deere had carefully calculated the fallout radius, positioning us accordingly at a supposedly safe range. Even so, I became aware of a familiar pattering sound, as of light rain.

'Could have done with a few more yards,' observed O'Deere, brow furrowed thoughtfully, his turn for mental arithmetic, and re-checking his mathematics. But it in no way detracted from the grandeur and majesty of the spectacle, and we stood there united by the enormity of the occasion, silently watching the giant pillar of smoke rising and billowing imperiously and listening to the detonation echoing its way progressively through the city suburbs. Until, that is, we became aware of the shooting. We looked at each other curiously.

On reflection, it was obvious what had transpired. Hearing O'Deere's detonation of atomic dimensions, plumb in the heart of the mid-afternoon 'quiet-period' (local rules), black-bearded Mujahideen all over the city, startled from sleep, had reached out as one for their trusty AK-47s and were at that very moment blazing away at the opposition. O'Deere indeed.

It was not the first time that the Project had encountered unforeseen and unintended consequences of this nature. It merely confirmed that the disposal of UXO, unexploded ordnance, was an art, rather that a precise science.

High in the folkloric annals of our humanitarian de-mining efforts in Afghanistan was the occasion when a northern farmer had been given assistance to rid his acres of a fat scattering of the 'debris of war'. Everything was gathered into a highly satisfactory heap and all the necessary preparations for disposal were made. Except that the late September warmth of the weather somewhat impeded and limited the enthusiasm of those charged with digging the necessary safety pit. When it came, the demolition was indeed in all respects totally decisive and professionally fulfilling, aside from the fact that it also happened to set fire to the surrounding harvest. In consequence, the clearance was considerably more widespread and extensive than had been intended, or indeed, anticipated. Throughout the remainder of the day the farmer's crops crackled lustily and all goodwill hitherto engendered was discouragingly dissipated in a towering pall of smoke. That was pre-O'Deere, naturally.

Also pre-O'Deere were the first and second defective rockets to fall in the Red Cross compound in the city, adjacent to the vehicle park in front of their offices. Actually, they were rocket-assisted tank shells; ingenious, but a point of semi-abstract technical detail for the layman, as the effect was the same.

On discovery of the first unexploded missile, just the tail fin remaining above ground to indicate its menacing whereabouts, a request for assistance was passed to the Project. No problem – consider it done; precautionary excavations were made and the requisite charges laid. Three, two, one! Bingo! No problem at all, except that correspondence on the files attested to the fact that at the very moment of detonation all the Red Cross front office windows co-incidentally and inexplicably splintered to smithereens and inconveniently fell to the ground. The Project expressed profuse and profound apologies for this rare (albeit spectacular) oversight; the Red Cross Head of Delegation expressed restrained gratitude for the invaluable service rendered.

Three months later the second rocket, once again with a fortuitously faulty fuze, proceeded down the same flight path (the bored artillerymen at the launch point clearly unable to raise sufficient energy even to turn the ranging wheel on their weapon to alter the trajectory and their point of aim). Whereupon the Red Cross offices proceeded to pass a second urgent request for early assistance down the same channel of communication. This time we were taking no chances. Reputations were at stake. A call was made to Pol-I-Khumri by the head of mission, eager to excel, and forthwith came McScumble to our aid.

The necessary excavations were made, and then the depth of the pit was doubled, just in case. The requisite charges were laid. No problem – consider it a pleasure. McScumble, rigorously observing procedures unchanged since the time of Guy Fawkes, struck his match and applied it to the touch paper (yes, blue). Ten, nine, eight ... (longer fuze this time) ... three, two, one! Bingo! Well, nothing actually.

I looked at McScumble. McScumble looked the other way. Several minutes passed. McScumble looked at his watch balefully and picked up his box of matches. I noted they were safety matches but was far from re-assured. It wasn't the moment to say anything, but could it be that herein lay the snag?

'You stay here,' muttered McScumble, which tied in nicely with what I had in mind. This was clearly a 'hands on' situation, even though it was fast acquiring decidedly 'hands off' overtones. He raised himself from the security of our trench, cleared the parapet and inched forward to re-light.

Second time lucky, no problems. Not a cracked window in sight. Just the Red Cross Head of Delegation with a presentation bottle of whisky and back went heroic McScumble to Pol-I-Khumri in the north, heartily relieved. Not a precise science, indeed an art.

****

Thursday dawned and things were quietish in the city; on the morrow a day of mosque and rest was looming. Dr Rhubar arrived at the office more or less on time. Well, rather later than usual.

'"House first, Mosque second",' recited Rhubar, not altogether relevantly but by way of diverting any possibility of incoming flak. 'It's an Afghan saying, for Fridays and, well, in general. Here's another one: "Don't kill a poor man. Take his bread".'

'It's Thursday,' I said, accusingly, declining to be diverted.

'I know that,' he confirmed (wisely refraining from pointing out that yesterday was Wednesday).

'But that's not Thursday's suit.'

'Don't you like it?' Rhubar looked down innocently at his extravagant Prince of Wales check. From the looms of Yorkshire. What appeared to be a herd of antelope horn buttons were charging down the front of the waistcoat. Those were probably imported.

'What do you think?' Rhubar asked again, turning side-on like a tailor's dummy. He looked back at me, expectantly. If he'd had a tail he would have wagged it.

'*Faukulada*! Tremendous!' I declared, more or less truthfully, and at the same time confounding Rhubar with my apt and effortless flash card selection as he swivelled on his heels to reveal the other profile. *Faukulada* was right. I was transfixed by the bookmaker's yellow, red and black squared overlays. We could only hope that we wouldn't bump into too many acquaintances as we did our rounds of the downtown offices. Clearly the step from being an unsuccessful punter at York races to the Oxfam charity shop was but a short one.

'This is one of the reserve suits I was telling you about,' explained Rhubar, not the least bit disconcerted. 'Are you sure you like it? I chose it for our appointment with the Minister of Foreign Affairs today, Sayed Salman Gailani. He's also the Deputy Prime Minister, so if it happen, it will be doubly important.'

'What are the odds?' I asked, unsuccessfully aiming to pay back a couple of old scores.

But see Mr Gailani we did. Approaching the stately government offices, the surrounding formal gardens – undoubtedly dating from the not-so-distant days of the monarchy just two decades earlier – were well filled with roses, but were not well tended. I regretted not having brought my secateurs. Pruning was turning out to be a weak suit in the Afghan armoury.

We were ushered into the august presence without delay. There was no queue of waiting postulants – most had possessed the good sense to leave Kabul long ago.

The new head of mission was introduced and welcomed. This was an important meeting; regardless of the universal acceptance of our work we nevertheless were operating as guests in Afghanistan. We reported on Project progress; the Deputy Prime Minister expressed deep appreciation of the contribution being made to the de-mining task, a problem of national priority. He was sitting composed behind his perfectly empty desk in a heavy overcoat buttoned to the neck, but otherwise maintaining all the manifestations of normality. The year was drawing on; notwithstanding the jaded display of scarlet and yellow flowers in the beds below, a cold wind blew through the tall windows of the once-ornate office – that cold wind that comes swooping down on Kabul from the mountains of the Hindu Kush.

We sat stiffly through the audience in our best suits – Chicken Street chic and Rhubar's from the races – both of us well wound in long woollen scarves wisely bought from the Mumtaz Knitwear Industries Store in adjacent Flower

Street at the onset of Autumn. The glass window panes behind us, without exception, had long since been blown away, the wooden frames looted for firewood. The prime-ministerial office was thus freely exposed to the elements, giving an original and surreal twist to the open-door concept of management. The carpet, soaked from recent rain, too heavy and awkward to pinch, had oozed underfoot as we made formal entrance in our freshly-shined shoes.

As we asked for further assistance from the Ministry of Defence in making available vital charts of known minefields, Mr Hekmatyar's incoming rockets exploded at intervals nearby, well-targeted that day, as most days, on the seat of power. The proper drill – or rather, what was obviously the correct etiquette by extrapolation – was to ignore the noises off-stage: no nervous blinking, no faltering or change of pace mid-sentence. Much in the same way as you might be expected to treat the occurrence with contempt if, for instance, a Brussels sprout, a roast parsnip or a chicken leg happened to whiz past your ear during a weekend dinner party in Gloucestershire.

The Foreign Minister graciously concurred with our request for maps; Colonel Sharook from the Ministry would be pleased to assist. On the face of it, this was a positive advance; under the Geneva Convention combatants had an obligation to maintain a record of the whereabouts of barrier minefields. Except that in the heat of battle rigid observance and adherence to the rules sometimes proved difficult and precluded compliance – even by the right-minded and the willing. In reality, better no map than an inaccurate one … We knew that in the field our de-mining teams would continue to follow their rigorous standard operating procedures – their safety SOPs – with or without the maps: cautiously establishing an initial swept channel through the suspect area, well marked with tape, and then, step by step, expanding the safe path and broadening out from there, the secure base. Easily said, except that the contours of the land, the intervening scrub, fresh and former vegetation, abandoned buildings, and a generous scattering of rubbish, rocks and other impediments meant that it wasn't easy at all. Not all the mines were buried; be wary of the trip wires and the stick mines. And the booby traps. It was all a long way from the Deputy Prime Minister's office where we were sitting, oiling the machinery, helping the wheels go round.

With the business of the day transacted, the continued existence and importance of the Project firmly re-established at the highest level of pre-occupied Government, we were about to paddle from the presence when the smokey tea that had been brewing on the kerosene stove outside in the corridor was belatedly served on a silver tray by a faithful retainer, five feet tall, wispy beard. Assuredly it was the twin brother of our very own Hajji (yes, diminutive Hajji of our office villa, the *bukhari* ace, except that he was often absent), those familiar mystical dark eyes of unsettling profundity searing into my soul with the same smouldering intensity. One lump or two? Shades of Empire: always the authoritative sugar in the tea.

Work done, and now prey to a transient but compelling aberration, I was just wondering how it might be possible to turn the saucer unobserved to check the maker's name on the fine bone china (praying for the romantic and extravagant oddity of encountering an English potter so many miles from Stoke-on-Trent), when another rocket landed close nearby, setting the teaspoons on the tea tray rattling in concert. Thankfully, the silver lining to the ensuing cloud of smoke and dust brought me sharply to my social senses, thereby narrowly averting a serious solecism. Consequently, tea was sipped and taken without further incident, and all the formalities of normality having been correctly observed through to the end of the audience, we took our slippery leave across the soggy carpet and filed out through the empty door frame – even though it would have been just as simple to have exited via any of the yawning windows.

In retrospect, I realised that in a curious way, Dr Rhubar's eccentric suit selection had been the correct one in the circumstances. My own dark blue bespoke three-piece (slanting pockets, real buttonholes on the cuffs), fastidiously made in exchange for 40,000 *Afghanis* by master cutter Mr Samir (he of the bottle-green corduroys and one of the few survivors of that ever-dwindling and modish band, the Chicken Street tailors), had just about passed the test, although in a more conservative manner. I can still remember entering Samir's modest little shop to place the order for that suit, the traditional bell on the door sounding its summoning *tinkle ring! Tingaling!*

'*Salaam aleikum.*' Samir had offered respectful greetings, himself emerging slantwise through a rack of work-in-progress skirts and smoking jackets for the ghosts of goodness-knows-who, tape measure at the ready. 'You is well?'

'*Tashakor. Bisyaar khub astam.* Thank you. I is very – I mean – I am very well. I should like to buy a suit, *lutfan*, please.'

'For all over the body?'

One of life's minor-key memories. A few years later that forty dollar Afghan suit was absent-mindedly overlooked and left hanging in an Armenian wardrobe while passing through Yerevan and it was like a mini-bereavement. Tailor-made garments for all over the body from Kabul should be cherished.

'That was a good meeting,' observed Rhubar. 'The Minister was clearly very interested to hear our news, very supportive. Now the word will filter down the line, which can only help but give us better security and co-operation. Except those rockets were very loud,' he added ruminatively as we drove away, adding the little laugh.

Probably very loud, I thought to myself. I hadn't the heart to tell him that, every cloud having a silver lining, they were, in the main, on my deaf side.

****

All work and no play: the Project non-routine routine was almost so. Particularly as the Kabul society scene was defunct and in abeyance for the duration of hostilities. The invitation – albeit addressed to my predecessor – to attend at the Turkish Embassy on 29th October to assist with their National Day rejoicing came as a welcome exception in those grey days of social vacuum, devoid of music, sport, big screens and little screens. Even though, regrettably (for reasons entirely within our control) it was an invitation that was never to be repeated. But at the time, although it was not so much a 100-watt light at the end of the tunnel and more of a 25-*bukhari* glimmer in the gloom, it gave rise to a frisson of excitement.

We lost no time in confirming our acceptance to the Turkish Chargé d'Affaires, in town for the celebratory occasion, and Karrimullah immediately set to and removed most of the mud from our best Land Rover in readiness.

On the appointed day I drove punctually the short distance to the Turkish Embassy. By my side was O'Deere, brushed and scrubbed, pressed and neatly presented for the occasion.

Access to the Turkish diplomatic compound, and to the Embassy gardens that lay beyond, was through an arch, a brief ceremonial arcade, that penetrated the protecting walls. There, gathered at the far end of the tunnel for our arrival at the tea party, and radiating the warmest of welcomes, were the merry Turks. Smiling warmly in return, I was advancing with diplomatic decorum, driving sedately at about five miles an hour, when I became conscious that the whip aerial of our radio, a tall and striking antenna of robust construction, had failed to clear the ceiling of the arch and that even as it attracted my attention it had become caught behind the tube of a transverse fluorescent light illuminating the approach. Even as, too late, I applied the brakes, the whipped, wedged whip aerial quivered threateningly, as stressed as an English longbow on the field of Agincourt. Then, as I gazed upwards in awe, the inevitable happened and the mighty bow released its projectile. The tortured fluorescent tube had given up the unequal struggle, surrendering unconditionally and abruptly ceasing its illuminative role.

Wha-a-a-ang! Away flew the tube into the middle distance, twirling and whirling past the electrified expressions of the once-welcoming, blithesome Turks, mercifully missing their now frozen smiles.

'Goodness gracious,' I remarked to O'Deere, as it shattered dramatically on the trellis work of the far shrubbery. 'Did you see that?'

'Strange,' he observed, with that now familiar furrowed brow, eyes on the point of crossing. 'I would have thought it might have gone further.' And, unknown to me, he proceeded to ponder on some abstruse calculations involving muzzle velocity, trajectory angles of elevation, whipped wedged whips and the like. 'Pretend nothing happened,' he advised.

But there are some things I just can't do. I wound down the window and peered out.

'So sorry,' I shrugged bashfully at our shaken hosts. I couldn't bring myself to do otherwise.

The Turks manfully recovered their composure, accepted my profuse apologies for the unfortunate oversight, and sent for a ladder.

The National Day party itself – not very numerously attended (thinly supported, it might be said) – was something of an anti-climax. We dutifully strolled the gardens, sipped our tea to the limit of O'Deere's endurance and, expressing our profound appreciation for our privileged participation, took our leave.

What happened next as we drove out through the tunnel was so unthinkable that it doesn't bear recounting. All I would say is that at the critical moment my mind was on some rather fine burgundy coloured cosmos that happened to be flowering unseasonably late in the long border of the Embassy gardens, and that my thoughts had further meandered to fond recollections of buying seeds for similar annuals, together with clarkia and godetia, scarlet flax and larkspur for tuppence a packet from Cuthberts and Bees Ltd, in what must have been an unrelated life.

'Incredible!' I exclaimed, as the freshly repaired fluorescent tube whirled and twirled on its way, once again impelled by our virile antenna.

Wha-a-a-ang!

The only difference was that this time the projectile went in the opposite direction, down through the tunnel and out into the street, narrowly missing a vacant vagrant before shattering noisily against the far wall.

'I don't believe it,' sighed O'Deere heavily.

'No,' I echoed. 'Quite unbelievable.'

O'Deere, master of ballistics, pursed his lips and widened his eyes. 'Awesome,' he commented, before adding wonderingly: 'But I still think it should have gone further than that.' And he set to once again, mentally re-checking his arcane computations of muzzle exit speed and associated whipped data.

Just then I happened to glance in the rear-view mirror, only to observe that one of the diplomatic Turks was employing the olde English traditional archers' salute to bid us farewell – a truly astonishing demonstration of an impressively wide span of international culture and learning.

'Give him one back,' advised O'Deere.

Good suggestion. O'Deere was well read. It mattered not whether the Turks were inside the tent or outside; they hardly noticed which was which. Just keep them on-side, that was the point. At all costs. O'Deere knew his history. So I did as bid, and as we turned the corner and our new friends disappeared from view, my right hand index finger and the adjacent bowstring digit were lofted in a veritable vee of good will and good fellowship, in the manner pioneered by England's finest in 1415. Leave taking is not a precise science – but there are some things that get easier with practice.

On our return to the office, Dr Rhubar had news.

'Battie's coming back,' he announced, relishing the moment.

'You mean Dr Boggis-Battie? Back from Pol-i-Khumri? So soon?'

'Well, Boggis or Battie. Apparently there's only half of him left, metaphorically speaking. I'm just not sure which half. Perhaps things are even worse than we think – could be there's only a quarter of him coming. Imagine that: Bat or Bog!' At which thoroughly diverting prospect Rhubar came close to suffering a terminal seizure, precluding further clarification.

'Well, don't forget that I have to go to the De-mining Conference in Pakistan,' I reminded him. 'That's imperative for our funding, whether we like it or not. So I hope he doesn't delay me. Not even fractionally.'

****

Chapter VI

INTER ALIA

'Life passes, with us all, a day at a time; … so well is the harp of human feeling strung, that nothing but a crash that breaks every string can wholly mar its harmony; …'

Uncle Tom's Cabin

The incidence of *jang* in Kabul was on the up. There was no doubt about that.

Returning from Banke Millie one lunch time – chasing our money – we passed an intersection recently in receipt of a rocket. The strike had occurred but moments before our arrival. There were casualties.

The satanic setting was now all too familiar: the blood-covered injured were being shoved into the backs of taxis. A donkey was standing patiently in the shafts of a water cart, eyes fluttering nervously, its ears twitching as water ran on to the road from holes in the freshly punctured tank. All that was lacking was the blown-away driver.

We did what we could to assist. Someone questioningly proffered the mangled remains of a severed hand. Oh … we hesitated, mesmerised by the glistening patterns on the scarlet fingers but not wishing to be found wanting … oh, just put it on the side, over there, would you. Like a lost glove in the park, just stick it on the railings, maybe someone will be back for it.

That hand was like a chicken's claw hanging from a hook in the butchers. But in this instance, the owner was absent. At the time it was best not to dwell on it – there were other things to be getting on with. But images like that have an unpleasant way of sticking, an unwelcome habit of returning. It was a right hand, and I can see it now. And when it appears, that leads to thinking of how that hand used to be of service, greeting friends, lifting cups of green tea and doing a hundred other helpful things.

Anyway, we did our best and we left it on the railings, just in case. To its anonymous owner, the loss of that hand was indescribable; but, in truth, and against the wider sweep of things, it was but a microscopic part of the problem – or rather, the effect of the cause.

On occasions the rockets landed in the busy market place. Headless bodies lying between the stalls and people going about their shopping. Mercifully, the scale of the obscenity was practically beyond comprehension. It was in the days before collateral damage had been invented. No apologies. Bull's eye. If the score was upwards of 20 casualties, the hit was mentioned on the World Service the following day. Anything under didn't rate.

In simplistic (or perhaps non-simplistic) terms, the heart of the labyrinthine, tangled situation was thus. Professor Burhanuddin Rabbani of *Jamiat-i-Islami*, the JIA party, had been installed as the second interim President (the first was Professor Mojadeddi with a two-month government) after the Mujahideen had taken Kabul in April 1992. This had followed the 1989 Russian retreat, thereby depriving Najibullah – the previous President, reduced to hiding in one of the UN compounds – of support and protection.

The position had now been reached where he, Rabbani, was uneasily clinging to power in Kabul as his initially allotted six-month term of office drew to a close. This uncertain continuance was being achieved largely by means of a tenuous tactical alliance of convenience with warlords Ahmad Shah Masood and General Abdul Rasheed Dostum. The first of these (the Lion of Panshir and also a member of the JIA party) had been nominated in the key position of Minister of Defence; however, his seat of power lay in the Panshir Valley and his long-standing personal aspiration to occupy the presidential palace was an open secret. As for General Dostum and his Uzbek militiamen with headquarters in Mazar-i-Sharif in northern Afghanistan (whose withdrawal of support from the two previous regimes had prompted the downfall of both Najibullah and Mojadeddi), his continuing pledge in favour of Rabbani was even less assured and equivocal. Ever keen to extend their power base, Dostum's commanders continually jockeyed for territorial gains within Kabul, which periodically resulted in open conflict – street fighting – with Ahmad Shah Masood's government forces, ostensibly allies.

As if the internal skirmishing between the factions in Kabul was insufficiently de-stabilising (and confusing) – Shia Hazaras fighting ethnic Tajik troops fighting Uzbek militia, for example – outside the boundaries of the city were the forces of the fundamentalist Pashtun nationalist party, Gulbuddin Hekmatyar's *Hezbi-i-Islami*, or HIH. It was these government-opposed forces that were engaging in the rocketing of the capital and who controlled much of the strategic supply route from Pakistan together with the vital hydro-electric dams to the east. (Bizarrely, Mr Hekmatyar was shortly to be nominated by Rabbani as Prime Minister, in a final forlorn and wholly unsuccessful attempt to draw him into the governing fold).

In turn, and further to that brimming medley of martial discord, the following groups were also to be added to the competing miscellany: Islamic Unity (Mr Sayyaf's SAY party); the Liberation Front of Afghanistan (Prof Mojadeddi's MOJ party); the National Islamic Front of Afghanistan (Mr Gailani's NIF); *Harakat-i-Inqelab* (Mr Nabi Mohammedi's HAR); and a second *Hezb-i-Islami* (Mr Mawlawi Khales's HIK). Plus of course, all the lesser warlords, the countrywide groups of bandits and brigands, minor and not so minor.

In fact, there was (and is) nothing simplistic about the situation in Afghanistan. Not then. Not now. And not tomorrow. Probably not ever.

All we wanted to do was to get on with the business of de-mining. Politics were nothing to do with us. But they were; like the civilian population we were trying to assist, we were caught up in events. Try as we might to be on the sidelines, we were in the middle of things, especially in Kabul.

'Here's another Afghan proverb for you,' offered Dr Rhubar. 'We say: "Two kings can never rule in one island". Of course, here things are ten times more complicated than that. It's worse than trying to weigh a tray of frogs.'

'Peace Making' declared *The Times* of London in early December 1992, optimistically quoting Reuters with the text: 'Peace efforts began in Kabul yesterday as doctors reported at least 30 people dead and hundreds wounded in two days of fighting between two groups in Afghanistan's interim rule'. That was followed just a week later with the headline '100 killed as Afghan troops clash with militia'. On the same day, The News of Islamabad reported: 'Kabul tense amid reports of Dostum's bid for power'. In addition to talk of 'the latest battles to dislodge the Rabbani government and replace it with an anti-Islamic regime', the communiqué also declared that 'only 15 per cent of Ahmad Shah Masood's war machine was left intact in the wake of losses inflicted on it by the militias' – a claim immediately dismissed as 'baseless' by his supporters in Peshawar.

Not long afterwards, *The Times* followed with the announcement: 'Stranglehold on Kabul tightens', saying 'fuel for the winter now costs four times an annual wage'. It was reported that on the road from the Afghan capital to Jalalabad (some 78 miles to the south east) there were up to 40 roadblocks. Yes, that seemed about right. 'Some are manned by nothing more threatening than stuffed dummies, but others mean business,' read the account. 'Even the United Nations has had lorry loads of grain and vehicles seized.' Yes, even them. 'Apartment dwellers go to the wells for water and huddle over campfires to cook ... administration consists of laying sandbags and digging gun emplacements'. Good idea; with Karrimullah's help I added another couple of reassuringly bulky layers to the buttressed bulwarks of my baggy battlements.

Up at Jebel Seraj, solitary Walduck was robbed at gunpoint twice within a week. Regardless, he stuck unflinchingly at his lonely post. Rhubar remarked that the robberies would make packing easier for him when he went home for Christmas. If that was not enough, Walduck was also having increasing difficulties with the roadblocks in his area; one of the shock-haired Muj had taken a shine to the Stetson. *Marde divanaa* they called him, 'the madman – the mad Muj'. Somehow, presumably by sheer willpower, unarmed Walduck managed to retain possession of that Wild West hat. It had become a symbol to him; a sort of unlucky charm causing him long delays and the expenditure of much adrenalin.

Sometimes we could hear bobbly Wilfred and the distant Dans on the VHF hand-held radios, talking faintly to thinly veiled Isabel, unreachable, somewhere in the suburbs. Perforce, they were spending much of their time holed up; these were difficult days for missionaries, those well-intentioned, myopic allegorical evangelicals spreading the alien word in an alien land.

We monitored the radio waves as we went about our business on behalf of the Project: long wave for the distant calls to Jebel Seraj and Pol-i-Khumri to gather the de-mining stats, shortwave for the in-town chatter – greetings, banter, fuel and stores, movements, the civil transaction of daily office trade. Such as: 'When you finish your amusement there at home, please could you drop yourself down to my office. I think your agenda is very over-saturated but I am awaiting your kindness.' English (in all its forms) was the lingua franca. 'If I am not in the home, then you may give the massage to my wife,' declared one hospitable team player.

On occasions the traffic abruptly assumed a more serious tone. 'My house has been hit!' came the sudden transmission. 'A direct hit on my house,' reiterated the terse report from the unseen voice. Unknown colleagues, UN local staff guarding the empty offices vacated by the repatriated expatriates, answered over the airwaves. 'Do you require assistance?' they asked, the solicitous enquiry unintentionally superfluous. There was a pause before the radio came back to life and the freshly bereaved victim spoke again.

'Just three coffins for my family,' intoned the tired voice, now alone in this world. 'No, wait. I am wrong. I need four graves please. My wife, two relatives and one son.'

'That man,' said sad Zahir softly, 'that man I know; he is the family toast winner.'

We heard of one family whose house was occupied by thieves when they were out attending a funeral. On their return, the mourners were charged a premium for re-possession of their premises. On another occasion it was said that when the fire brigade attended a blaze, one fireman held the dribbling hose and the remainder did the looting.

Dr Rhubar, Najia his wife, and his little son – bright-eyed *Bachai Jang*, heir to the future – lived in an apartment block in Kabul. It was a joyless, barrack-like construction of Soviet origin, a couple of miles or so from the Project compound. It was home. They too were not immune from the fighting. The city rocketing was random, a lottery. One grey and wintry morning of mean snow flurries and drizzle, instead of arriving at the office, Rhubar called on the radio.

'Problems,' he reported, voice raised, breathless. 'Now our area has been attacked. I need help. I must move my family into the Clinic.'

'On our way,' I radioed in reply. 'Stand by.'

Prescient Hajji threw open the compound gates, wispy beard jiggling with the urgency of the situation; Abdul came out of the kitchen to cluck anxious and concerned encouragement. Karrimullah leapt into the passenger seat without words and took post alongside me in the Land Rover. Without delay we were off, winding our way through the chaos of Kabul, as always not knowing what was round the next corner or at the next checkpoint.

On arrival at Rhubar's address it was clear that the missile had struck neatly through the main entrance of the building. It was the usual scene: all the windows of the block had been blown out, the shredded curtains fluttering waywardly in the breeze, the ground littered with broken glass and general debris. The only difference was that this time, we – the Project family – were at the heart of things.

Practically central to the devastation was Rhubar's car, a possession of great pride. Now it had become the reluctant and shambolic *pièce de résistance* of the spectacle: the windscreen gone, the paintwork flaking and curling, the pock-marked bodywork bent and perforated like a giant colander, all four tyres blown out, shredded and terminally deflated, the wheels resting despondently on the rims. But it was only an old car; I hardly gave it a second thought.

As for desolate Family Rhubar, there they were waiting for us, standing tidily and silently on the kerb, uncomplaining, no tears, bundles and bags in hand, ready to take up their new residence in the Clinic. That was the one just across the road from our offices – our villa – an increasingly fanciful description that was becoming more surreal by the day.

The mini-rescue mission passed off without further ado. Leaving Family Rhubar, now uprooted, to unpack and settle in – squeeze in, more like – I went back to my bedroom and briskly filled yet a further two-dozen sandbags which Karrimullah helpfully popped atop the now towering fortifications protecting my nightly slumbers. Short of having an army of Karimullahs move my mighty bed into the Bala Hissar fortress, all had been done that could be done and I hoped it was not in vain. The last rays of light disappeared forever from the bedchamber, and then, in like manner, from the sitting room, and from this point on I was condemned to dwell in eternal Stygian gloom, like Gollum. No point in getting over-involved in events, and inadvertently becoming a secondary casualty of the situation. That was not the object of the exercise; not only would it dent the Project get-well programme, it would add to the paperwork and upset the Controller's plans – and pulse rate.

As for O'Deere, he continued come what may to commune with the stars, living upstairs in a perilous glass-walled pre-fab that had all the appearance of having been tossed absent-mindedly onto the roof of our house as an afterthought to the main design, like a discarded packing-case. He had a Survival Theory concerning his chosen domestic arrangements, although I never made the error of asking him to expound. He might have told me that he preferred to perish in peace under the Milky Way rather than endure the nightly cacophony of his colleague snoring like a chainsaw following the now established distribution of plentiful after-dinner *liqueur de poire.*

Be that as it may, I was standing shoulder to shoulder with broad-backed Karrimullah in comradely fellowship, shovel in hand and admiring our robust and self-satisfied handiwork stretching imposingly from the floor to the lofty ceiling, when I became conscious of Dr Rhubar fidgeting morosely behind us.

It was clear that he was uncharacteristically cast down.

'I'm really sorry about your house,' I said.

'It was only an apartment,' he muttered, contrarily.

'Yes, but still … '

'Trotter is a very brave man,' opined Rhubar, in his now familiar tangential-mode.

'I know. McScumble, Walduck, O'Deere, Trotter, they all are. Exceptional. No praise too high.'

'The last time my car was damaged, Trotter helped tow it back.'

It seems I may have been a bit slow on the uptake. But never let it be said that I can't recognise a thrown gauntlet when it socks me on the nose.

Hajji threw open the compound gates, Abdul clucked encouragement and Karrimullah jumped up alongside me in the Land Rover.

'You can leave the shovel,' I told him. 'Just bring the tow rope.'

Dr Rhubar's car was something called a Muscovitch. On bad days of particular exasperation he settled for Moscowbitch. Conceivably it was the only one of its kind in all Afghanistan (or even in the entire world): on our travels we never encountered anything remotely similar. Rumour was that it had been left behind by the retreating Soviet forces; gladly, I imagined, as a devious form of enduring mobile booby trap. Outstanding amongst its abnormalities was the uniquely engineered, or non-engineered, gearbox. Mechanical deviations apart, the front-seat stuffing had long since abandoned all pretence of providing any form of support, with the result that at roadblocks the Muj muzzles were disconcertingly directly at mouth level. In turn, this periodically provoked Rhubar's creative faculties into embarking on elaborate analogies, which I quickly learnt were best smartly curtailed.

'All yours, Dr Rhubar,' said I, as we regained home and safety with our cargo of scrap metal. Karrimullah cast off the tow rope and the wrecked Moscowbitch once again settled dispiritedly on its four bent rims.

Rhubar looked fondly at the reunited residue of his car, now languishing in the semi-security of the compound. No laughter today. This was a serious affront.

'It will be restored,' he vowed stoutly. 'That car will run again.' His faith was humbling; I had never heard a braver declaration of intent.

Then he judiciously added the convenient caveat: '*Insh'allah*' (just in case it proved impossible). Thine will be done.

****

Islamabad and the De-mining Conference were calling. Dr Boggis-Battie, wending his way infirmly southwards over the coldly impassive mountains of the Hindu Kush, had suffered unforeseen delays to his heartfelt desire to re-unite with friends and admirers in Surrey. But I could brook no delay and must away.

We left at first light, travelling fast, the long wheelbase Land Rover suspension equal to the challenge. Zahir said we had 440 kilometres to go; I said yes, about 273 miles; Zahir looked blank and said nothing. The chances of taking a wrong turn were minimal – far less than the prospect of getting lost when (for instance) moving between neighbouring pubs in rural England (Surrey, for example). Here, there was just the one road, more or less.

Down the Kabul Gorge we flew: I looked at the rushing white water and thought of canoes, then at the rugged scenery, the commanding peaks, and thought of Lady Sale. She would have relished this trip: so many memories, so many nostalgic moments to share.

As I drove ever faster, I glanced at Zahir. He sat there braced against the bouncing jolts that juddered through the springs at maximum compression and the inimical lurches occasioned as we swerved to avoid minor pitfalls in our path. He was gripping the roof through the half-open window, declining to use the seat belt, his eyes shut tight to stop them rolling. He spoke but once on the journey.

'This road is full of crumbling,' he observed, and then returned to his cocoon.

With the whip aerial oscillating ever more wildly from the front of the Land Rover, I fiddled with the radio, marvelling that with this dashboard mounted device the size of a ploughman's sandwich box, it was possible to range from the Tajikistan border in the north, out to Islamabad and beyond to the south east, a span of at least 400 miles – or 600 kilometres for Zahir. Later, 80 miles on from Jalalabad, when we had entered the confines of the Khyber Pass, and as the ionosphere lifted with the passage of the day, I knew that radio propagation would be impaired, contact would fade and that I would be cut off and isolated.

I felt it was not dissimilar in some ways to the isolation of hapless General Elphinstone of the British Army in 1842, a century and a half before me, except that, of course, he never got even half that far with his retreating army of 16,000 on 'the march of death'. Hardly before he reached the end of the Kabul Gorge, most of his men had been annihilated as they withdrew over this very terrain, with ailing Elphinstone himself taken hostage on the final night of the massacre, to die a few months later whilst still in captivity.

Briefly, the story was this. Early in 1839 the invading British 'Army of the Indus', with the broad remit from Lord Palmerston to 'take Afghanistan in hand and make it a British dependency' – which included removing the Afghan ruler Dost Mohammed Khan from his throne and installing someone more compliant – had bought their way through the Bolan Pass (which lies to the south east of Quetta), and a month or so afterwards walked into Kandahar, the defenders having fled. Advancing further north eastwards through Afghanistan the British (under the command of General Sir John Keane) fought their way into Ghazni and the way to Kabul was clear. Once there, the British placed their choice as monarch, Shah Shujah, on the now vacant throne. The date was July 1839. Not long afterwards, General Keane (soon to be elevated to Lord Keane for services rendered) and a sizeable element of his invading army returned to India.

Just two-and-a-half years later, in January 1842, the residual British garrison, humiliated by spiralling civil insurgency, attempted to leave the country by way of the Kabul Gorge. Practically the entire force was slaughtered by the Afghans in the course of five days and five nights as they withdrew from Kabul. Dr William Brydon was one of the very few to escape with his life, reaching the British fort at Jalalabad wounded and exhausted to give news of the catastrophe before collapsing from his horse.

The aberration that possessed the British force to surrender their artillery to the Afghans in return for a promise of safe conduct remains to this day inexplicable; any imagined justification went to the grave with disgraced General Elphinstone. Regardless, the ill-advised conciliation proved fatal on a grand scale. Equally, after so many years, who can say how the British Political Adviser in Kabul came to place the great Bala Hissar fortress in sole custody of the newly installed Afghan puppet monarch, Shah Shujah? Over-confidence, misjudgement, a conflation of both: the outcome was that the British invading force established their cantonments on low-lying ground that was quickly revealed to be indefensible when the subjugated Afghans turned against the occupying garrison.

As I raced along the road that day with Zahir, there was no time to dwell further on those dramatic happenings of so long ago, but I knew that undoubtedly there would be other similar journeys in furtherance of our Project – and further opportunities to explore the events of the First Afghan War. And even the Second and the Third (the Fourth being yet to come).

In Jalalabad we stopped for 15 minutes; three hours hard driving for 80 miles. There had been scarcely any accompanying traffic, apart from the occasional jam-packed bumbling minibus, swiftly overtaken and left wallowing in our wake. But we had encountered – and surmounted – miscellaneous obstacles and hindrances of a different nature: rocks, craters, would-be bandits. And the 40 roadblocks of assorted degrees of difficulty.

Now, from the semi-security of a hidden alcove on the balcony of the Jalababad *chaikhana* I could survey the busy street unobserved, drinking restorative green tea the whilst. Ahead of us, between here and the border crossing at Torkham, lay active terrorist training camps. Originally spawned by the CIA (just as, later, the USA was to support and fund the embryonic Taliban), these camps were intended to train freedom fighters – Mujahideen – during the years of the Soviet occupation of Afghanistan. And as it happened, numbered amongst the numerous foreign students was one Osama bin Laden from Saudi Arabia, Class of '84 – or thereabouts.

Tea taken, onwards we sped, trailing a billowing cloud of dust that floated dreamily behind us like a chiffon scarf of immense length. The countryside was flatter now, the chequered fields lying fallow, the colourful, hallucinatory poppies had been harvested, all was safely gathered in for another year. The land indeed was Kipling's land: 'brown and green in alternate slabs like chocolate and pistachio cakes, speckled with occasional peasants who do not utter'.

The road itself, long bereft of the benign attentions of a grader, had in places – and by some little understood geological inter-relation – worked its surface into an endless ripple of coruscations, like an estuary beach at low tide. It was a phenomenon defying ready scientific explanation (like heavy objects – miniature space craft and plastic jumbo jets and toy nuclear submarines, for example – unaccountably rising to the top in a packet of breakfast cereals, confounding logic and gravity), but the effect was pronounced and undeniable. The vibrations threatened to shake the vehicle to pieces – to Zahir's undoubted chagrin – and cause greater havoc than had been wrought by all the combined boulders and potholes of the earlier mountain road.

Rather than reducing speed, the trick was to go faster and faster still, so that the tyres hummed harmoniously and effortlessly from the top of one tiny ripple to the next. When I got it just right it set a little rhythm running in my mind, like the wheels of a steam train d-d-d-drumming over the j-j-j-joints of an old railway track – the lines laid by the admirable Victorians, mindful of their coefficients of expansion and with that thoughtful gap (now forgotten) left between the rails so that they didn't buckle on hot days. Over and over ran the rhythm in my head: *No donors no de-mining no donors no de-mining no de-mining de-mining de-mining.* Over and over. Faster and faster. Zahir closed his eyes ever more tightly.

As for the roadblocks, some we caught unawares: we were through and away even before the comatose scavengers had scuttled from their roadside shelters. As others waved us down, I slowed obligingly, shooting a sociable smile through the half-lowered window, the door firmly locked. A gracious wave of the driver's hand, '*ba omide didar* – see you soon', and accelerate away, eyes (as ever) fixed on the rear-view mirror in case of anything untoward coming our way, shoulders hunched in a futile gesture of self-preservation. No problems today. *Alhamdu'lillah* – Allah be praised. On earth as it is in heaven.

Torkham, Landi Kotal, Peshawar; thanksgiving strawberries and cream at the pink-painted Pearl-Continental Hotel; onwards down the graveyard that is the GTR – the Grand Trunk Road of ancient origin leading to the capital of youthful Pakistan. An unscheduled pause in Rawalpindi to investigate promising-sounding Flashman's Hotel – and drive on quickly, a disappointing detour.

Safely into Islamabad by mid-afternoon, in readiness for the De-mining Conference on the morrow. Time enough to visit our principal donor's offices before they closed for the day and the staff headed for hearth and home. There on the table in the outer waiting room lie erudite reports: 'The Anatomy of Poverty'; 'Humanitarian Aid – The Golden Purpose'; 'Putting Dimensions on Evolution'; 'Complementarity in Humanitarian Space'; 'Living Creatively versus Survival'.

The following morning the meeting of mine clearance representatives takes its conversant course. Throughout the day a gross bluebottle buzzes at the top right-hand pane of the conference room far window. For reasons of safety and security many of the agencies operating in Afghanistan have their offices in Peshawar. As the bluebottle turns this way and that, trying to escape, there are flashes of green and purple.

One agency specialises in the use of dogs trained to detect explosives; we learn that they are more than 90% effective. Except, we are told, they are expensive to train and have an inherent weakness: a fatal incapacity to detect trip wires linked to the lethal stick mines ... the POMZs.

Another agency focuses on the use of flail-fitted tanks to sweep hidden mines from the ground – as in Europe in World War II, as in Burma, Korea, Vietnam, and the Gulf War – detonating them in the process. You might have thought that the bluebottle would get tired after an hour or so of frantic buzzing, yet it seems to have endless stamina. The will to survive. The flail tanks, they too are assessed as being 90% efficient. It must be a strange feeling walking on ground that is 90% safely free of mines, or, more disconcertingly, land that has a 10% likelihood of erupting between your legs. Better, perhaps, to proceed behind a herd of goats or a flock of sheep, and then follow your wives, Dhofari style.

Technology notwithstanding, there was clearly still no substitute for the man on the ground: Joe Soak, using his eyes, feeling with his fingertips; Ali Bi in Pol-i-Khumri and Ali As in Jebel Seraj, armed with their extending TWFs – their trip wire feelers – and their quarter-inch diameter, pointed prodders at the prescribed angle of 30 degrees, supported by their comrades-in-arms scanning assiduously with that long-serving aid to mine clearance, the battery-operated hand-held mine detector.

Anecdotes abounded of mines on sale in local bazaars. The going price was five dollars or so; economical and handy for resolving un-neighbourly neighbourhood land disputes between farmers – they that ploughed the fields and scattered, using the latest techniques.

One Afghan de-miner related problems his group had encountered where seasonal flood waters had coursed through known minefields, shifting the danger of the PMN2s and the PMNs to new, unknown areas, even back into previously cleared safe zones.

'And they were buried by alluvium?' questioned an Australian army expert (Peshawar based), semi-rhetorically, the words twanging Antipodean style from his scarcely opened mouth (an evolutionary adaptation for fear of swallowing bluebottles) and defying orthographical representation.

The Afghan de-miner blinked several times before correcting the assumption.

'No,' he declared, politely but unequivocally. 'They were buried by Russians.'

****

Capital and conference business conducted, cosying-up to the donor concluded, time to leave Pakistan and to return home. Home to Afghanistan.

Sedately up the GTR we go, sharing the motorway – the Grand Trunk Road, highway of Alexander and the Moghul Emperors – with mentally retarded meandering bicycles, deviant buses with belching black diesel exhausts busily warming the globe mile after mile, and with those misaligned, crab-like rear axles favoured throughout the developing world; we pass unhurried, methane-emitting oxen and even the occasional camel ('with 'is silly neck a-bobbin' like a basket full o'snakes') – mandatorily supercilious, that snooty stare having everything to do with the fact that they alone amongst creatures are entrusted with knowing the hundredth name of Allah – and nothing to do with the smile on the face of the Sphinx.

For once, there is no need to force the pace; that day there was time to savour the abundance of roadside slogans, corny all: 'Save the Wildlife'; 'Pollution restricts your Life Span'; 'No Gains without Pains'; 'Knowledge is Power'; 'To Trust is to Truimph' (sic); 'Help Keep Clean Environment'.

Eventually we cross the River Indus, wondering if the disintegrating bridge will hold up for another day, or even for just another 20 minutes; thence into Peshawar we drive, taking care with two-syllable *Pesh-shar*: short – long. Colourful, turbulent Peshawar, with its matchless cottage arms industry.

Travelling in this direction our journey can not be completed in a single day; it is necessary to endure a tortuous circuit of gloomed government offices to procure a Tribal Pass (assuredly another British legacy), an essential document for transit of the mountainous road that leads us back to the border crossing at Torkham. A road that passes though the untamed, ungovernable tribal areas of the North West Frontier Province and which is flanked at intervals by the giant strongholds – manifestations of globalisation – of the international drugs barons, secluded and forbidding fortresses discreetly set back from casual view (and where eye contact is best avoided as you pass).

Accommodation in Peshawar was traditionally taken in Dean's Hotel. 'Sleep at Dean's, eat at Green's': no contest – everybody knew that. A handful of small change (the merest fraction of the proverbial *lakh* of 100,000 rupees) proffered at hotel reception would procure an echoing four-room suite in Dean's. These were suites of sweepingly grandiose proportions from a bygone era, yet simultaneously seemingly mournfully heavy with the accumulated personal woes of decade upon decade of earlier infelicitous guests and wayfarers, each inexplicably more forlorn than the last. In consequence, the only advisable way to forestall the haunting aura of foreboding was to put one article of clothing in each chest of drawers, and to hang trousers, shirts and ties (should you have them) in separate wardrobes to give an uplifting sense of homely occupancy. Appropriately, even predictably, the predominant colour throughout was brown – carpets, curtains, walls, panelling: all lugubriously brown. Even the water was brown, its impending arrival signalled from afar as, eager for freedom, it cascaded through giant ducts, titanic valves and cisterns – plumbing and pipes fit for a Maharajah, a Memsahib or a monsoon – that rumbled far, far into the subterranean distance.

The following morning the journey to the border – as with the night's repose at Dean's and breakfast at Green's – was unexceptional; nothing untoward, nothing of note. The traffic thinned as we departed the city fringes and ascended to regions more remote. Yet again, pursuing a fragment of family history, my eyes scanned the sheer rock faces of the Khyber Pass searching for the emblem of the South Lancashire Regiment, the Prince of Wales's Volunteers, assuredly painted somewhere up there sixty or seventy years ago when my father passed this way. But, disappointingly, this time my efforts again go unrewarded.

Less than an hour into our journey and we passed the turning leading to the barracks of the Khyber Rifles. There, sitting in the centre of the lawn outside the French windows of the Officers Mess, was to be found the curiosity of a rarely encountered heliochronometer. This was generally assumed to have been presented by some astronomically inclined eccentric Englishman, and was attributed to the hand of the celebrated (heliochronometrically speaking) Mr G.J. Gibbs – he who produced the design in 1906 and held the patent for 'mechanical universal equinoctial meantime sundials'. But, tantalizingly and perversely, we had no time to stop for lunch with the historic Regiment (and in any case, that day we were without an invitation).

Before ten we were at the border, our transit subject to a minimum of formalities. There is no 'Welcome' sign as the traveller moves from Pakistan to Afghanistan; equally, there is no declaration relating to the abandonment of hope. It was a matter of indifference to the Torkham authorities; they felt under no civic obligation to complicate matters with injunctions of welcome or warning. If you wanted to cross, then cross. We crossed, and onwards we went, non-stop through Jalalabad, thoughts turning to Lucky Five Street, meatballs and apple pie.

The four Mujahideen waving us down with their Kalshnikovs halfway up the Kabul Gorge that day made an unremarkable adjunct to the local scenery in those parts. I hove to, *force majeure*, doors locked, window half down, engine ticking. Never cut the ignition.

'They want a lift,' translated Zahir, his eyes perambulating preternaturally in their sockets. Could have been worse. The Muj quartet grin at me through the window enthusiastically. I give a jobsworth shake of the head, sucking in my lips like a traffic warden on duty in Battersea Park Road, keenly upholding the law.

'Tell them very sorry, but we are a humanitarian de-mining organisation and we cannot transport armed men in the Project vehicles.'

The grinning Muj nod understandingly and sympathetically in unison, tickled by my sense of humour; they had clearly been this way before. No need for Zahir's translation. Without further ado but with great agility and rapidity – plus a deft hitch of their baggy pyjamas – they help each other on to the roof of the cab, and squat there like four hairy fruit bats. *Force majeure.*

Zahir regards me anxiously.

'Sometimes silence is the best thing to say,' he suggests, softly and with infinite wisdom.

The fruit bats tapped the roof impatiently. They were ready, what was the delay?

Off we went. I felt slightly out manoeuvred, but, oh well, most things are not important in this life, and many things are not important at all. However, as a token indication of displeasure I made no concessions to our passengers on the upper deck (just lately opened) and we batted along as before, bouncing over the boulders and dodging the ruts and rivulets furrowing the track in our customary carefree style. From time to time the roof gave a complaining *bo-i-i-ing* like an old biscuit tin, and I made a mental note to write to the makers with a strengthening suggestion, knowing full well that it would be to no avail. Just like the letter I wrote about toughening the rear door fixture for the spare wheel, because it was inadequate to the stresses and strains of high speed, life and death travel over rough roads. No demand, said the company engineers. Of course not, there never is. Except from those who ask for it.

On reaching the margins of Kabul the hirsute bats thumped the roof with their rifle butts to indicate – thanks very much – that was as far as they were going, and with another grin in my direction, in quadruplicate, and a final bound, they were gone.

'*Khodaa haafez* – God be your protector!' And forgive us our trespasses.

How they had managed to stay aboard atop the lurching Land Rover was a mystery; they must have had specially suckered shoes.

Word of the unauthorised passengers later reached the ears of a senior UN official, visiting Kabul for the day. Or rather, nervously in town for a hasty pair of hours.

'You must always be prepared to manage the consequences of your actions,' he chided, darkly and obliquely meaningful, before hurrying back to his waiting aeroplane, and declining my invitation to lunch (pot luck), much to Abdul's relief.

Was he talking here about stray hitchhikers (with or without AK-47s), or international foreign policy and UN global strategies? Probably both.

As Zahir cautiously opened his eyes and eased himself down from the cab, doubting his deliverance, conscientious Karrimullah shot home the bolts of the compound gates behind us. Hajji hovered like an inquisitive ferret and Abdul clucked off to fill the kettle. Mission accomplished. Well, that small part of it.

'Boggis is here,' advised Dr Rhubar, straight-faced and awaiting my reaction, not for the first time reminding me of Mona Lisa's lesser known younger brother.

Dead on cue, Dr Boggis-Battie appeared from the wings. In fact, he looked dead on his feet. He stood there swaying in the entrance to the sitting room, the funereal hue of his ashen face highlighting the magnolia sheen of his silk pyjamas; as he swayed, the tasselled cord of his old-gold Chan Tuck dressing gown swung in sympathy and the oriental black brocade facings – beyond question the handiwork of the very same craftsman who won the contract for North Korean quilted kapok combat wear – caught the faint glow from the flame in the *bukhari* stove. B-B's feet were encased in a pair of Pluto slippers with immensely floppy ears of indescribable sadness. Spellbound we gazed at the apparition, until, after more time than it takes for a Sakar rocket to pass, its mouth moved.

'Dys-en-tery,' groaned Boggis. Then he was gone, vanishing in the direction of the bathroom. Travelling fast.

The severity of Battie's sorry state was eclipsed by its inconvenience. Why, at this rate the generator would have to be re-started to re-fill the water tank even before half the day was out, and already we were seemingly spending an inordinate amount of time on survival and housekeeping chores. There was only one thing for it. Project house style decreed maintenance of the objective at all times, and was not big on the extension of on-site counselling.

'Yes,' confirmed sharp-as-a-tin-tack Dr Rhubar, master of the good news/bad news genre, and reading my mind like the open book it is. 'There is a flight to Delhi today. But, disappointingly, the road to the airport is impassably blocked by serious *jang*.'

Blessed are the hard of hearing. Hajji re-opened the compound gates, Karimullah swung Bog-Bat's suitcase into the back of the Land Rover and Zahir found himself reluctantly re-occupying the very same passenger seat that he had so recently and thankfully vacated. I revved the engine and with a squeal of tyres we were gone.

On hearing the commotion, Abdul Ahmed scuttled from the kitchen bearing the pansy pot on his tin tray, steaming freshly with green tea and with the golden spout leading the way like an enthusiastic retriever on the Glorious Twelfth. Only to find the sitting room empty and a cloud of telltale dust settling over Lucky Five Street.

'*Bisyaar ajib*,' he breathed. 'Very strange.'

Not for nothing was the Project flag predominantly white, thought I, as we sped towards the airport – and in the direction of the general *jang* – our standard of surrender fluttering bravely from the roof rack. And how fortuitous that our Land Rovers were also white, not so much as a winter camouflage strategy, more as a result of that being the colour in which the vehicles were delivered. Doubly convenient and nicely reinforcing the message that I was trying to convey to the busy battlers on either side of the road, dashing about as they were, joyfully concentrating on the job in hand: that of trying to kill each other.

I waved graciously and metronomically to the startled warriors, giving a polished non-stop performance of a carefully perfected 'confused old codger's salutation' while simultaneously working overtime on the contents of the much-maligned flash cards.

'*Khub hasti*? Art thou well? *Bisyaar afsos.* Awfully sorry. *Sabr ku*! Have patience! *Bubakhshed*! Excuse me! *Dar dilat khosh bash*! Be happy in your heart!'

I felt like an unknowing pigeon settling innocently midwicket on the freshly rolled square on the first day of the final Test against Australia at The Oval, the bemused umpires stopping play with the most terrifying Aussie paceman of the day pawing the ground halfway through his bumper delivery. England steadfast at 128 without loss and lunch not yet taken. Imagine that! The players glare furiously at the poor unfortunate bird, the crowd boo vociferously at our feathered friend and start a counter-clockwise Mexican wave in sheer disbelief and rampant frustration.

But the reality was – we were through the *jang* unscathed, travelling fast (yes, yet again, *force majeure*) and heading for check-in.

It may already have become apparent that, for me, farewells are difficult, an un-mastered art form (with or without the intervention of flying fluorescent tubes). And yet, as I watched the socially insecure patient pass through the final barrier on his way to convalescence and a return to the comfort of familiar surroundings, I was unable to restrain a compassionate shake of the head. Boggis-Battie by name: Battie-Boggis by nature.

The retiring doctor turned at the departure gate and I had a sense of *déja vu*. Then the spell was broken as he lofted an enfeebled arm, from the end of which a hand moved weakly, to and fro. Dr B-B was waving goodbye. He gave a wan smile of gratitude – just the ghost of a sickly smile. Then he turned the corner and was lost from sight, homeward bound. Home to the Home Counties to dine out on his experiences. Good of him to have come all this way. 'Valiant of you to bring me to the airport' he had said. 'No, no. Not at all,' I had assured him. 'No trouble in the least. I think you'll feel better when you get to Delhi.' Basically, he had the shits. And we didn't do on-site counselling; no trauma or stress therapy was on hand hereabouts.

Simply a severe case of enlightened self-interest on my part. Just another Achilles' heel; like a neurotic centipede.

****

Back at the office, Dr Rhubar had already prepared his next trump card. He had an inexhaustible supply, aided and abetted by the Controller's regular exhortations from HQ London, electronic enjoinders which periodically curled and slithered their sinuous way from the jaws of the office fax machine. Messages that were more akin to speeding artillery projectiles, invariably scribed in a fiercely square hand, as though a muzzle-loading ramrod had been employed in place of a quill, liberally doused in the blackest of black inks before being generously dusted with Grade A gunpowder for greater clarity and impact, heedless of effort and expense.

'Dr Goose is coming out as replacement medical cover,' Rhubar announced casually. 'That will be good news for the Pol-i-Khumri team. Re-assuring for the de-miners to have someone on hand.' He watched to see what effect this news might have before continuing obscurely: 'Perhaps it will turn out to be "a comparison between two devils" – that's another of our sayings.'

'Dr Goose?'

'That's what the Controller said. The new quack. Anyway, very soon we will have to pack everything up and shut down. Winter is coming, closed season for mine clearance. And time for your Christmas migration homewards. Like, er … ,' Rhubar paused. 'Fat geese, winging westward. Honk! Honk!' he concluded brightly, well pleased with the absurdity of his feeble prep-school inspiration.

****

Chapter VII

INTERMEZZO

'...long afternoons, when an hour isn't an hour, but a piece of eternity dropped into your hand.'

Tennessee Williams

'Dr Goose?' said I to Dr Goose, in what I judged to be a friendly and welcoming manner, when he arrived at Kabul's blitzed airport.

'Goosens,' quacked the weary traveller stuffily, feathers ruffled. 'Dr Goosens.'

I turned sharply to Dr Rhubar, eyebrows raised. But Rhubar was sharper than that. Defying the laws of physics, my shadow was no longer at my side. Never mind, what's in a name? I migrated the affronted medic northwards to the minefields of Pol-i-Khumri, as directed by HQ.

Duty done, and hoping for a few moments alone with Lady Sale, I headed back to the terrace. No sooner were we settled in the wintry sunshine, as chill and thin as yesterday's soup, than Dr Rhubar re-appeared.

'Your fame as a sand-bagger has spread,' he announced.

Nothing more. He was at it again. I played along. Waited. And eventually elicited that the Jamhauriat Hospital, the municipal facility in the centre of town operating in arduous conditions – made more extreme by water and power problems, exacerbated by the shortage or total absence of required medicines – had asked if we might have time to visit and advise on strengthening their defences against rockets. We set out immediately to see what we could contribute.

'You can leave the tow rope,' I said to Karrimullah as we piled into the Land Rover. 'Just bring the shovel.'

We did the rounds of the crowded claustrophobic wards, anxious relatives clustered at the bedsides of the injured, shoring up the defences where necessary, bolstering doors against blast, blocking gaping windows and taping the glass to reduce the likelihood of flying shards and splinters. Sand-bagging is not an especially arcane trade: sturdy bulwarks and buttresses well-constructed – those are the basics. Bread and butter for disembarked naval brigades across the centuries, as well as for the army. Plus Karrimullah, to move the unwieldy weight of the bulging bags as though they were swansdown cushions.

The sick and wounded followed us with their vulnerable eyes as we worked. '*Har chiz khub hast*? How's it going?' we enquired. '*Shab khoob boodi*? Did you sleep well?' Except for the little girl, rigid in her bed, pocked and peppered from head to foot with shrapnel and blast marks, the children laughed and their parents smiled. It must have been the accent. '*Chansi khoob*! Good luck!' The children swung on the bed posts, giggled, and watched us out of sight.

On the very point of leaving, an Afghan surgeon, gowned and capped, hastened to detain us. Just one more thing? Please? Of course. He led, we followed. Entering the operating theatre, I hesitated. Shoes? Scrub? Robe up? The physician shook his head; not today. Sandbags were the priority of the moment. We set to, studiously ignoring the man on the table, under the knife, half his face blown away. The surgeons were tidying things up; a fleshy portion of bright red cheek splashed wetly to the floor.

Karimullah filled another bag or two, then we finished the job and tidied up. *Chansi khoob.*

****

The British Embassy in Kabul occupies a compound of some 23 acres. The fine buildings – and the magnificent towering trees – date from 1922. An era when the greatest Empire the world has ever seen was largely still intact: four years after the Armistice brought the Great War to a close, three years following the end of the Third Afghan War. In those days the strategic importance of Afghanistan as a buffer against Russian expansionist designs on British India to the south was undiminished.

Hence the grand scale of the construction, starting with the wrought iron, gilt-topped gates that were swung back by the gatehouse guard for our arrival. 'Honi Soit Qui Mal y Pense' reminded the delphic admonition encircling the splendid heraldic emblem over our shoulders as Captain Rai, officer-in-charge, did the honours (in the absence of HM Ambassador, prudently withdrawn three years previously). We signed the book. Stayed for curry lunch. All the manifestations of normality.

The steel helmets and flak jackets we had been asked to bring up from the High Commission in Islamabad were duly delivered. For wear by the guards, ex-British Army Ghurkhas. Then we walked the spacious lawns, the soothing scent of freshly cut grass in heavy contrast with life as lived beyond the walls of the compound, conjuring an image of the contented British Garrison during those relaxed summers of 1840 and 1841, incestuously absorbed with horse racing and games of cricket in their cantonment, the officers' wives elegantly visiting, up from the heat of India. While all about them were occupied in plotting their downfall.

The fountain in the formal gardens was not playing on the day of our visit, nor had the swimming pool been filled. But the trimmed symmetry of the rose beds was remarkable. Modest Captain Rai smiled appreciatively. Pruning apart, his was not an easy task. Arriving at the squash court he showed where a grenade had landed only two nights past. Then he pointed out more damage, in the forecourt to the servants' quarters.

Peering through the tall shutters into the shaded drawing room we could see the marble fireplace laid with logs, ready to warm the yet-to-be-invited guests. The sofa and the cabriole-legged gilt chairs needed but a tweak and a whisk of the covering dust sheets to bring them to readiness – ready for diplomatic intrigue. In the dining room, the imposing table was distinguishable under its green baize drape, the obscured mahogany yearning for the glissando caress of the decanters of port and madeira, brimful and richly loquacious. Confidentially, Captain Rai revealed that all the requisite silver was residing in the safe, waiting the word to be prised from its wrappings, buffed and laid. Ah, if only tables could talk.

The ballroom, echoing with evocative foxtrots, faint quicksteps and quadrilateral Scottish reels, had its grand piano; the long conservatory had its empty pots, eager to be re-united with oranges, lemons, culinary bay trees and box bush topiaries. Not that Kabul boasted an abundance of garden centres. Nor had we met any piano tuners, for that matter. Such minor impediments would surely be suavely surmounted when the day came to refurbish the legacy, to re-open the Embassy, break out the Union flag and re-occupy the adjacent substantial residences ear-marked for the Head of Chancery, the Military Advisers and other sundry attendant staff.

Ours was a routine visit, one of many, as was our custom. Except that this was to be the final contact with the guards before Kabul's bleak winter settled like a frozen shroud over Captain Rai and his men. Our intention to resume supportive liaison on our return in the Spring was left unsaid. Better the tactful voice of silence. Meantime, the gallant Ghurkhas would need all their renowned fortitude to fulfil their undertaking to hold the fort.

Thus it was that our immediate destinies were dictated by the oscillations of the universe: the movement of the planets and the consequent changing of the seasons.

From the north, hard-working Trotter and McScumble reported that their day was done, that they were dispersing the de-mining work force and returning their sensitive detectors to the store to await the thaw of the coming year. They hastened to make their way over the mountains before the Salang Highway, the Russian-built artery to the south (convenient in equal measure for invasion and retreat), was impassably blocked by snow. The radio fell silent and they were gone. No more dawn calls to Whisky Papa for the stats, nor to Oscar Zulu at Jebel Seraj for that matter: Walduck too had shut up shop for the season and was on his way to Kabul, likewise eager to evacuate and be gone.

Mid-December, thoughts turning to the coming of Christmas, even if not necessarily to the Nativity and the coming of Christ, not in Kabul.

It was a typical late-afternoon scenario in the villa. Just a touch of distant *jang* leavening the sense of finality in the affairs of the departing day, occasioning perky, end-of-term Abdul to remark: 'Now we are hearing the voices of the guns,' as he obligingly made good with the golden-spouted tea pot. 'Maybe the militias they are boring, so they are just shooting on the air,' he observed, chattily and knowledgeably.

'"When the big guns speak to the Khyber peak …"' I intoned, seeking to tease Abdul with a snatch of Kipling, and even perhaps to take advantage of his mood and to open a conversation. Instead he gives me an odd look and hurries back to his kitchen, closing the door.

Dr Rhubar had gone over to the Clinic, to see how things were, he said. To spend a few moments with his wife and with Son of Battle, *Bachai Jang*, lately internally displaced victims of the civil war. Myself, having donned my predecessor's unwanted jersey against the seasonal chill, I was up on the terrace, fast approaching the tail-end of Lady Sale. As for O'Deere, he was fiddling in the kitchen, steaming out the contents of a couple of grenades and a mine that he had chanced across in his predatory prowlings, and which he kindly intended to present to me as Xmas mementoes. Just stocking-fillers, he had explained. Excellent as pen holders and to serve as a paperweight, he thought.

Looking over the roof tops, eight points of the compass to the right of the setting sun – beyond the flat ground in the middle distance where General Elphinstone must have sited the indefensible British lines, and further still beyond where the political adviser Sir Alexander Burnes must have been living in his remotely situated house on the night of 1st November 1841 when he was murdered and his corpse mutilated by the mob – I gazed abstractedly at the familiar outline of the mountains.

One of the principal and most notable features hereabouts was the existence of a near-perfect, classically shaped saddle – *kotal* was the local word – that topographical feature beloved of geography teachers. Normally I would have given it but cursory attention (once I had established that it was still in position), but on that particular afternoon it happened to be the scene of an unlikely but compelling duel between a tank, clearly silhouetted against the sky line, and a gun emplacement, concealed somewhere down in the valley.

Out would come the tank, like a nosey crab emerging from the safety of a seashore rock, scurrying to reach the far side of the saddle. Bang! would go the guns, sending up perilous puffs of dust on the horizon, whereupon the tank would cease its advance, pirouette and crab back to safety. Minutes later, there it was again. Peep, pause, scurry. Provoking the guns to re-double their efforts – Whoompf! Whoompf! And in turn forcing the tank to scuttle for its life.

Hearing my summons, O'Deere desisted from his festive labours at the hob and joined me on the terrace. He pulled up a chair, professionally riveted by the unexpected spectacle, engrossed yet again with fields of fire, angles of elevation, the spatial thermal aspects and co-axial drift. The duel progressed and time stood still.

'What's that funny smell?' I enquired, glancing sideways at my companion.

'My God!' exclaimed O'Deere, departing with such suddenness that his chair flew from under him and toppled over backwards. It was unlike him to be so emotional.

Agitated clattering came from below. Followed by Abdul's voluble curses. That much was normal. Probably the mouse was giving trouble again.

After some while O'Deere returned to the terrace. He looked crestfallen.

'Yes,' I told him, misreading the situation. 'I'm afraid they've just finished. Sorry about that. No hits on the tank and now the artillery have given up.

Curious business but great fun, don't you think?'. Then, as an afterthought: 'Crepuscular conditions for ranging,' I added, just to test him.

'We nearly lost Abdul,' O'Deere confessed, gravely subdued, his mind elsewhere.

'Umm, nearly his home time. Or was it the mouse?'

'I forgot the grenades. And the mine.' O'Deere pursed his lips and widened his eyes. 'Your Christmas presents; they were in the oven. Gas mark max. I was only just in time. Little Abdul's pretty lightweight, he would have gone into orbit.'

'My God!' I leapt to my feet with such suddenness that my chair flew from under me and fell over backwards. Crepuscular conditions indeed – *and* we nearly lost the recipe for the meatballs.

****

One week later, de-mining done for the year, and everything was set for the westward-winging seasonal migration. I hoped the Colonel would be pleased with Project progress. Well, satisfied, anyway.

The passengers were packed into the Land Rover, no room for Zahir this time. He was happy with that. I was to drive, the stern presence of O'Deere would occupy the passenger seat. The four squashed missionaries took up their pew in the next row – veiled Isabel, be-bobbled Wilfred, bespectacled Dan and bearded Dan. Finally, feet braced on the spare wheel (which was in the back because there was no demand to strengthen its proper stowage outside on the rear door), came Dr Goosens, Walduck and the Stetson, survivors all.

Dr Goosens, safely returned from Pol-i-Khumri, had made a video of his time with the Project, and today would, he felt, provide a spectacular finale. All had been promised a copy.

I made a last check of the office, and of what had been home for the preceding long months. Lady Sale, my dear and close companion, muse – and more – for so many weeks, had retired, as graceful as ever, back to her own kind to await my return. For the moment, pending whatever the future might hold, she had been bedded down in her rightful place: top shelf, far left of the bookcase.

In the bedroom I checked the chest of drawers for inadvertently forgotten relics. I cast a fond glance over the somnolent and mute expanse of the big bed with its heavy blankets, now increased to ten, my nightly refuge. There then followed an unnecessary and superfluous excursion under the bed, to make sure I had packed my trainers (which I knew I had but I just needed to be certain), and to stow my trombone – 'not required on voyage'. And then we could be on our way.

Except that there under the bed I was more than startled to encounter a dusty pair of abandoned Pluto slippers, a vengeful legacy of poor Boggis-Battie, our one-time doctor, latterly retired hurt. The pinched faces leered from the gloom, doleful ears a-droop, surveying me like the curse of the Pharoahs (Surrey Chapter) and promising imminent retribution for past cruelties inflicted on others. My time was surely nigh.

'Anything wrong?' murmured a doom-laden voice behind me. With the inevitable effect that I jumped again, but this time in the opposite direction.

I was relieved to see it was only Dr Rhubar, who had entered the bedroom unobserved. He cocked his head quizzically. Like a nosey chicken. This he was enjoying; it was an unanticipated (if unexplained) bonus.

'No! No. Nothing. I'm fine,' I hastily assured him. I was far from confident about that but in any case, my interlocutor's mind had moved elsewhere. Unaware of the swirling spirits and negative ions that filled the room, he was gazing wistfully at the brazen bed.

Awakening simultaneously from our separate trances, Dr Rhubar accompanied me to the Land Rover, the cramped occupants impatient to be away. He spoke quietly as we walked.

'In the Spring,' he said, 'when you come back, we must build the monument. You know, the memorial.'

Rhubar was right. I hadn't forgotten the memorial. No way. It was just that all our days recently seemed to have been bought up getting things back on track. There would be more time when we returned, and we would make a good job of it. The best.

Dr Rhubar continued. 'There is a mason nearby where we can choose a suitable stone. Then he will carve the names of the three dead men, first in English and then underneath in Dari, with the date of the accident.'

'It happened about 10 miles to the north of the city, yes? The Controller mentioned it when I first went to HQ.'

'Yes, the booby trap was buried in the track leading to the village of Kariz-i-Mir, maybe 15 kilometres from here. As you probably remember, one of the men died almost immediately, the other two took longer. The tank is still there, marking the spot. You can see it from the main road. No one can move it. It's too heavy and too badly damaged. Anyway, when you come back . . .'

'Definitely. Top priority.'

We shook hands, touched eyes, old Rhubar and me.

'Happy Christmas.'

****

We were on our way. The four missionaries were silent, pondering the past, considering their future. Under his Stetson, Walduck was probably and deservedly thinking of log fires, brandy butter, carols, charades and crackers. O'Deere had gone into intense ballistic mode, his mind filled with simultaneous quadratic equations packed with kinetic energy.

Of all the passengers, Dr Goosens alone had not taken flight with his thoughts and remained of this world. In the mirror I could see him fidgeting as we sped down the photogenic Gorge, camera at the ready but defeated in his efforts to capture the scenery by the seismic lurches of the suspension. When it came, I was prepared for his request.

No, I explained as gently as I knew how, there would be no touristic diversions today, no delays could be countenanced; it was not that kind of sight-seeing situation. Remember your history, I advised, think of sad General William Elphinstone, geriatrically enmeshed in the exceptionally harsh and early winter of 1841/42, and think of the ill-fated garrison deposited in Kabul by the victorious British Army of the Indus. Think on that.

'The intention is to stop for precisely 15 minutes at the Jalalabad *chaikhana* and then again in Peshawar. Not before and nothing more.'

On receipt of which edict, Dr Goose took the news badly. In fact, he never spoke again. And the spectacular video? Another unexplained casualty of seasonal postal overload.

The jolting silence in the Land Rover gave opportunity to gather my own thoughts after the multi-coloured passage of all the changing scenery of the recent weeks in the metaphorical caravanserai of my mind. As I punctuated my reflections with rapid gear changes in response to the challenging terrain, my mind moved back to Lady Sale and her 'Journal of the Disasters in Afghanistan', published 1843. Difficult to obtain from the library – the librarian may well hesitate and ask who wrote it – but perhaps it might be found in the depths of the furthermost archives. Well-ordered citizens that they are, librarians should rule the world.

As for Lady Sale, wife of a British officer, she was taken into captivity by Mohammed Akbar Khan as hostage against the safe return of his father – Dost Mohammed Khan – to Kabul. The date was 9th January 1842 and the place was some 20 miles down the Kabul Gorge. The seizure had occurred one and a half centuries previously, on the self-same spot that we happened to be passing. Chroniclers of the time recorded that 'the snow was crimson with blood' and at night the ill-prepared camp followers of the fleeing army froze to death in their hundreds.

Following the murder of political adviser Burnes at the beginning of November 1841, unrest against the British garrison in Kabul spiralled, encouraged by the vacillation of General Elphinstone and the absence of any determined, forceful response – including a failure to move directly from the unprotected cantonments into the safety of Bala Hissar. On 23rd December 1841, Sir William Macnaghten, the Resident British political officer, fell victim of his own intrigues and died at the hands of the leading Afghan insurgent, Mohammed Akbar Khan. Dismemberment was the order of the day; Macnaghten's decapitated corpse was 'suspended from a pole in the bazaar, while his bloodstained limbs were passed round the town in triumph', his disembodied hands waving and jigging dementedly from the ends of poles. The sequence of events thereafter was ever more catastrophic.

On New Year's Day 1842, in the midst of heavy snow, Elphinstone accepted a withdrawal agreement with Akbar that supposedly guaranteed his force safe passage in return for the surrender of the bulk of his artillery. On 6th January the 16,000 strong retreating column left wintry Kabul on the start of their 80-mile march to the safety of the secondary British garrison at Jalalabad, manned by the Somerset Light Infantry (Prince Albert's); by nightfall, with the temperature plummeting, they had covered but the first five miles of their trek. It was a day in which the Afghans attacked constantly, killing hundreds, picking their targets from the exposed flanks and from amongst the stragglers. The dead and the dying were abandoned where they fell, to be mutilated and debased, decorated with the scrotum and testicles hanging from the mouth.

With much the same happening the following day, a halt was called after five more miles – the improvised overnight encampment of bivouacs being at a spot we had passed just 25 minutes after leaving the city. Thus the massacre continued: on 8th January 1842, some 3,000 of the force died whilst passing through the narrowest part of the gorge; by nightfall on 10th January the combined number of surviving troops and camp followers totalled no more that 5,000; all that remained at dusk on 12th January were some 2,500 souls, of which fewer than 200 were troops of the original 4,500-strong former British garrison in Kabul. That same evening, Elphinstone himself was taken hostage by Akbar.

As the remnants of the force attempted to flee in the darkness, the slaughter was completed – apart from a group of 65 foot-survivors who were rounded-up, surrounded and killed the following day, at a village just 30 miles from safety. A further mounted group met a similar fate a mere 15 miles from the gates of the British fort – with the exception of Dr William Brydon, the 'Messenger of Death', who, wounded and exhausted, was left to tell the tale of the disaster.

The two villages where the final killings took place all those years ago – the villages of Gandamak and Futtehabad, where the bones of the fallen may still be found – we passed that early winter's day on our way to Jalalabad, but a few weeks short of the 150th anniversary of the final bloody chapter of that signal defeat of the British Army in Afghanistan.

****

Returning (almost) to the present, it was clear that Dr Goose and his part-completed video were not the only casualties of the day.

The introspective missionaries, they too were suffering, not only from circumstances outside their control (however predictable), but also as a result of their commendable yet over-optimistic excess of proselytising zeal. Things had not panned out for them in Kabul, those difficult days for ... well, everything really. Including melodic brass duets. Abandoned in my trombone case, now under the bed with the Pluto slippers, were some excellent arrangements for Christmas Carols, rapturous harmonies. As it was, I had been forced to play them solo in the relative calm of the long, dark evenings during the preceding weeks, the unsatisfactory auditorium that was the sand-bagged living room muffling the sound and ruining the acoustics.

Hajji had tilted his beard to the sky and expressed appreciation; O'Deere had been expressively non-committal. Solo renderings leave no cover in the event of an embouchurial mishap; additionally, correct positioning of the trombone slide depends on having a good ear. Even better, two good ears.

As we pulled up outside Green's in Peshawar (breaking with custom and eschewing Dean's), the downcast group of four missionaries removed their ecclesiastical baggage from the vehicle preparatory to disappearing from our purview. As they unloaded their kit I pondered that if I lived in Sydney I might be inclined to pass any chance excess over three score and ten that came my way in watching cricket, or reading a book on the beach. Except, of course, it wasn't true. I knew exactly why Wilfred didn't sit at home; the only possible flaw was the preaching thing. Perhaps it is better when abroad not to spread the word but to receive it. In the midst of such reflections, I was suddenly interrupted by Wilfred jabbing a finger in my direction.

'The trouble with religion,' he observed, the cooking apple on his hat freezing mid-bobble with such miraculous suddenness that I did likewise, 'the trouble with religion is people.'

I was still intellectually mid-stagger, when Isabel flicked back her veil and followed up with a looping right cross.

'The fine details of your belief are not in themselves important. Have faith and be fulfilled. The important thing is to believe in something.'

Brass band music? Then they were gone, gone from our world, or at least, gone from our hemisphere. And we were the poorer for that.

After that (and everything else), anything more that happened during the remainder of the homeward migration was bound to be anti-climactical. There were however, two minor happenings of anti-climactic note, one involving a discovery, the other concerning a disappearance.

We passed one night in Green's and then – having settled our dues with manager Mr Chaudhary at the front desk – moved to the airport to take the flight from Peshawar south to Karachi, in readiness for the final downwind leg, Karachi to London. Straightforward enough, except that at the Peshawar departure barrier I encountered three armed, uniformed Pakistan security officials. Lined up accusingly across the counter in front of them (and me) were one paperweight and two pen holders of original design.

'What are these that you are having here?'

'Oh, those? Those there are just Christmas presents.' Never give more information than necessary.

'We are thinking these are not so suitable for Christmas, actually speaking.'

'Oh, you know, just stocking fillers.' Out of the corner of my eye I noticed the Stetson and O'Deere proceeding unimpeded out to the waiting aircraft.

The subsequent debate on the subject of Christian festivals and stockings and suitable presents was difficult and prolonged. The eventual compromise was that the guards kept the landmine and the passenger retained the pen holders.

O'Deere, eyebrows lifted ingenuously, looked at me questioningly as I hurriedly made an overdue entrance and belatedly fastened my seat belt (PIA – both portions present and correct).

'Christmas,' I explained. 'Always a difficult time of year.'

Thus we straggled into Karachi. Plain sailing from here, no more minefields, no Muj roadblocks; the stocking filler grenades now well bedded down in the baggage.

Unremarkably, Walduck appeared, mundanely proceeding from the direction of the Duty Free emporium, trundling his trolley, demob happy and dreaming of home. Actually, his trolley was empty. After the two marauding robberies at Jebel Seraj, his was a mere minimum of hand luggage: one humble plastic bag and nothing more, as though he had just been released back into society after serving a six-month sentence. Which was true.

'There was something I meant to mention,' he remarked earnestly as he approached.

'What?'

'Did you know that on the lawn of the Officers' Mess at the Barracks of the Khyber Rifles there is a Gibbs heliochronometer, generally considered to be the acme of sundials? He, Gibbs that is, produced perhaps as many as 1,000 between 1907 and 1914. That was the golden era of these instruments and in those days they were used to set the time on civic clocks and for running the railways and even for use in lighthouses. But, of course, the advent of the radio time signal in 1912 put an end to that and nowadays they are difficult to find, especially in the North West Frontier Province, obviously. There is one at the Royal Naval College at Dartmouth and I have heard there is supposed to be one at Windsor, and another in a village near Petersfield in Hampshire. The one that used to be down by the old Naval Hospital at Greenwich seems to have disappeared.'

I stared at Walduck intently, both astonished and taken aback by his timely interjection and apposite erudition. Interesting, too. I don't wear a watch, but I checked the time on the airport clock (quartz). 'Go on,' I said, encouragingly (our flight wasn't for another couple of hours).

'Well,' said Walduck, settling back into his professorial stride. 'I expect you know that heliochronometers are precision instruments and the main dial plates are tilted and locked at an angle exactly reflecting the latitude where you happen to be, for instance, on the Khyber Rifles' lawn. There is a sliding adjustment which makes the necessary correction for longitude, and then there is another adjuster which makes allowance for Summer Time, if necessary. It may sound complicated but, once set up, it lasts for ever. The tricky part is that the sun's apparent orbit of the earth – of course, it is really the other way round – has little known idiosyncrasies. For any given earthly point – the Officers' Mess lawn, say – it doesn't pass due South at the same time each day and can be up to 14 minutes early or late. Extraordinarily, but conveniently, the apparent discrepancy repeats itself by the same amount on the same day every year. Copernicus and Galileo called it the Equation of Time but, amazingly, it was not until Gibbs came along that anyone had harnessed these theories into a practical correction device for sundials, readable throughout the sunlit year.'

Walduck paused for breath. I paused for thought.

Unforgivably, I found that I was no longer concentrating on the fascinating sunlit operation of the wondrous Gibbs heliochronometer. There was something mystifying about Walduck's appearance that was causing me unease, quite distinct from the guilty realization that we, Rhubar and me, had never quite got around to delivering his avocado bidet. Nor the rest of the desired bathroom suite for that matter. 'Wait – Out' we had told him cheerfully, and still the poor chap was waiting. Yet – and yet – that wasn't it.

As he pontificated, Walduck looked odd, definitely odd, like W.G. Grace without his beard and without that plank of a bat of his that was twice as wide as anyone else's, but which no one ever dared mention. Or like the Pope first thing in the morning, hair tousled and without his little white cap, his perky zucchetto. Yes! That was it!

'Where's your hat?' I asked, innocently curious.

'Good grief!' cried Walduck, aghast, all thoughts of Latitude and Longitude and the Equation of Time flying from his mind.

It must be catching, I thought. Everyone's doing it; if he'd been sitting on a chair it would have gone flying backwards, somersaulting over and over as far as the Duty Free check-out.

'Good grief!' cried Walduck a second time, clearly discomfited and clutching his naked head in search of the Stetson, but to no avail, for it wasn't there. Then he spun round as though centre-stage on Olympic ice and was gone, moving fast (that was catching, too) through the crush. The judges were unanimous: a full set of 'Sixes' for artistic merit and degree of difficulty.

'Passengers are requested not to leave their trollies unattended!' I called after his departing form, self-righteously. But also to no avail; it was abundantly clear that now Walduck had lost his head as well as his hat. Ergo … Anyway, no point in being too sententious and censurious about his abandoned trolley, especially in view of my recent misunderstanding with the Yuletide carry-on paperweight.

****

Christmas Eve, late afternoon: magic in the frosty air. A hint of mist curls in the valley; on the hillside the trees are silhouetted darkly against the gold and orange of the setting sun.

The Hampshire farmhouse, warm and brightly lit, is full of festive friends and family. But out here in the winter garden, I am alone, apart, savouring the solitude and space, and indulging distant fantasies.

Collection of the fallen leaves is complete, that most relaxingly therapeutic of horticultural labours, using a besom and wooden tined rake, eschewing that infliction of the devil, the mechanical blower. Except the besom reminds me of a TWF – a trip wire feeler – and the rake pans from side to side like a super-sensitive Vallon mine detector.

Never mind; now I will plant the berries that I have plucked from the mistletoe that the children have hung on its customary nail from the big black beam that extends across the drawing room indoors. With frozen fingers I will painstakingly squash the sticky green seeds into cracks and crevices in the orchard apple trees, and then do the same along the line of poplars. It's traditional, an annual ritual. Sometimes I cut the bark and bind the seeds into the incision; on occasions I concentrate on the forks in the branches and add a little earth. I vary the direction from year to year: the north side of the tree one year, and then work round, through east, south and west; a four-year cycle. Most years the ceremony is delayed until Twelfth Night, when the mistletoe has served its purpose in the house, the berries old, drying and shrivelled. Some years I even wait until April (by which time the seeds look even more unpromising), hoping to benefit from the warmer weather. This year I have decided to plant whilst the white fruits are young, ripe and luscious. An annual ritual, but always the result is the same: no mistletoe grows in this winter garden. In small endeavours as in great, life is sustained by hope.

I gaze at a vapour trail high in the translucent sky and as I do, the low Hampshire hills surrounding the valley become the snow-capped mountains encircling Kabul. I wonder if Karrimullah managed to collect the *nan* today, unhampered by *jang*, and if Abdul made it across town on his bicycle, unhindered by snow, with Hajji ready to warm him on his squeaking arrival with the volatile *bukhari*. And what about Dr Rhubar, soft-eyed Najia, and wriggling Son of War, internally displaced refugees, now sheltering in the Clinic? No festivities for them; just enforced and cheerless hibernation in bleak Kabul, waiting for the touch of Spring.

The soft undulations of East Hampshire have become the snow-covered peaks of a distant land, and I too have been transported far away.

My reverie is shattered by the unmistakeable crackle of a Kalashnikov, the gunfire close at hand. My companion, the robin, takes flight, the blackbirds in the holly bush call with alarm as I look for cover in the gutter, diving behind the compost heap heedless of the mud.

The firing ceases as abruptly as it started, and I peer out, cautiously. My assailant lowers his weapon slowly, rooted to the spot, appalled at the havoc he has wrought. I raise an arm to indicate that I have survived the unexpected attack, and to show that all is well, dicrotic pulse notwithstanding. Whereupon the small boy of the house turns on his heel, racing back to the brightly-lit farm to inform his brother of the unprecedented success of the ambush.

Christmas went the way of countless Christmases before.

Thoughts of sand-bagged bedrooms, meatballs, mice in the kitchen and pear liqueurs – these things intruded but rarely. The handsome charger of apples in the farmhouse dining room (a giant platter of incomparable Egremont Russets, a smattering of Lord Craven's Wyken Pippins, Laxton Superbs and the house favourites, Lane's Prince Alberts, those regal cookers) that provoked recollections of Wilfred's bobble, and the flesh of the carved turkey that splashed wetly to the plate – these images were swiftly banished from the convivial scene.

January passed and faded; February took its place. The Controller made the first of two telephone calls to the farm.

'Are you available, Hornblower?' he demanded to know, using the accolade of the newly bestowed alias that he had accorded me and losing no time on pleasantries.

'Yes, Colonel,' I replied. 'Available. I was only waiting for the wind to veer to the south west so that I could put the cloches out and sow a few lines of radishes and early lettuce.'

'Captain Rai and his Embassy guards are under pressure in Kabul. Whitehall want us to get them out. It will just be the two of us.'

'Excellent. The salads can wait.' All of a sudden there was far richer fare on the menu. More than excellent. It was perfect. 'Good team player', that's what my credentials say. It's obligatory, so that's what I wrote. It's true too – so long as I am appointed team Captain, with executive powers as extensive as the situation requires. Or if the team numbers a maximum of no more than one, or at the very most, two.

When the Controller rang back, I was ready to move.

'Cancelled,' he said, his voice flat and on this rare occasion unable to disguise his disappointment. 'London got cold feet. They're going to give Rai a medal instead.' With that, the Controller hung up; it was not his way to embellish. Never explain, never complain. Just short bursts or single shots.

I too was disappointed.

It was March before I received another call.

'The snow's melting. No time to lose.' It was the Controller's voice.

'Take post?'

'Affirmative. Advance. You know the terrain.'

****

Chapter VIII

IN AND OUT

'You may muffle the drums and loosen the strings of the lyre,
But who shall command the skylark not to sing?'

Regrettably, at some time during the course of the evening, radio contact with Trotter was lost.

I kept trying until 2200 before closing down. The two Land Rovers, heavy with equipment and stores in preparation for the Spring resumption of de-mining operations, had left Kabul at 0830 that morning heading for Pol-i-Khumri. Trotter, McScumble and Zahir should have reached the security of the Project northern base by nightfall.

Having seen them on their way, I had set to work grappling with the two office generators, then turned my attention to the water pump and the temperamental *bukhari* stove – all suffering from severe gremlin infestation following the winter shut-down. We were in the final days of Ramadan, the Holy Month of dawn to dusk fasting for Moslems; nevertheless, Dr Rhubar manfully passed by Lucky Five Street. He stayed for sufficiently long to witness and admire my endeavours before observing (not altogether helpfully, I felt), 'in this country we say that you cannot hold two melons in one hand.' Then, pleading famine and fatigue, he left.

At intervals during the day the northbound travellers had come up on the radio to report their progress: slow but sure through the snows of the Hindu Kush, up and over the Salang Highway. In turn, I had re-confirmed our Kabul arrival to the Controller in his London bunker, and updated him on progress made in kick-starting our de-mining activities back to life. The operating season was short; every day counted.

The avalanche that blocked the northern exit of the Salang Tunnel (at the crest of the Salang Pass), thereby trapping the trio of Trotter, McScumble and Zahir in the black heart of the frozen mountains, also succeeded in entombing several hundred other vehicles. Throughout the 2.6 kilometre length of the rocky darkness (almost one and three quarter miles), trucks, coaches, mini-buses, vans and cars ground to a halt, jammed bumper to bumper, unable to turn and escape. As many as 1,000 vehicles used the route daily.

The tarmac within the tunnel, laid by Soviet engineers when they constructed the road in 1964 nearly thirty years previously (and subject to minimal maintenance since that time), was in the process of disintegration. The decay was accelerated by seismic movements and subsidence, so that in many places the fluctuating surface was an unstable and difficult mix of ice, mud and freezing stretches of water. The tunnel approach roads, at a height of nearly 12,000 feet (4,000 metres), were themselves subject to landslips, and to the deleterious effects of snow and rain-fed flash flooding. They were also susceptible to avalanches.

On this particular occasion, the tunnel lights (at best dim and uncertain) failed; many of the ventilation galleries became blocked by snow. In the stationary vehicles, now effectively sealed in the underground shaft through the mountains, were upwards of 2,000 travellers. Many of them were women and children; most were ill-prepared for the emergency: lightly dressed and with minimal food and water. The drivers ran the engines of their immobile conveyances to provide heating for the hypothermic passengers; the contamination within the tunnel – a cocktail of carbon monoxide and petrol and diesel fumes – increased accordingly, and the plight and suffering of the travellers worsened.

On the second day of the developing drama, I rose unsuspectingly soon after 0500. At 0620 radio contact with Trotter was re-established, thus furnishing details of the icy crisis unfolding high in the mountains of the Hindu Kush. Apparently, some vehicles had been stuck for several days; the first deaths due to exposure and asphyxiation had already occurred. I radioed Dr Nasseir (Rhubar's brother, the redundant eye specialist), already in residence at Pol-i-Khumri; in turn, Nasseir set off for the northern end of the tunnel with food and blankets, while in Kabul we attempted to mobilise aid for the victims of what appeared to have all the makings of becoming a substantial humanitarian disaster.

'Out with Dr Rhubar in heavy snow and clag,' records my diary of events, 'the deserted city a flooded, muddy morass, the remnants of the broken buildings framed and stark against a sky of dirty yellow.' The scene of devastation that confronted us was compounded by the fact that during the harsh winter nearly all the trees that formerly lined the once-fine avenues had been felled for firewood.

First to the Ministry of the Interior we went. There we saw the Deputy Minister; uncertain of the practical response to our plea for assistance, we drove on to the Presidential Palace to meet with President Rabbani's spokesman. And from there we moved to Ahmad Shah Masood's office in the Ministry of Defence, followed by (for good measure) the Ministry of Information.

Our simple request was insistent and unvarying: Help! The reaction throughout was equally constant: courteous disinterest. The unwelcome news was too difficult. These things happen, Afghanistan has many problems, one has to take one's chance.

'Snow continued all day,' records the diary. 'At the airport (to collect stores) the sheds were blasted and derelict, the frozen labourers huddled in darkened, leaking huts surrounded by squalor.' On all sides the evidence conveyed but a single message: the will and resources with which to mount a rescue attempt were non-existent.

It took Trotter and McScumble six hours to walk from the tunnel to rendezvous with Nasseir, by which time it was dusk. After a short night at Pol-i-Khumri they returned to the tunnel and on the third day, in spite of a further avalanche, Zahir was relieved as vehicle guard, having spent two nights in the contaminated darkness. '*Eid al Fitr*, the end of Ramadan. New moon sighted – but not here,' records the diary. 'Cold, grey, wet – petrol generator still refusing to start.' After passing two more nights with the Land Rovers, Trotter and McScumble were in turn relieved by Zahir, now newly accompanied by colleague driver Charwali.

On the sixth day the road was re-opened. Not exactly cleared but passable with care, and the journey to Pol-i-Khumri (140 miles/224 kilometres), normally taking well under ten hours, was completed. Ironically, prior to construction of the Salang Highway and the associated tunnel, access to the north of the country from Kabul took three days, the route looping through Herat, some 400 miles due west of the capital.

With his mission fulfilled, and his tour of duty having expired, Walduck (like so many others) was no longer with us. The Project at Jebel Seraj was temporarily in the hands of an Afghan caretaker. This vigilant watchman reported seeing buses wending their way down from the Salang Tunnel, passing the camp entrance on the main road and heading south to Kabul. He said they were full of corpses. The unofficial estimate of fatalities was 300. The official figure was eight. The press settled for 100. Who knows?

It was by no means the worst such incident to have occurred in the tunnel. In October 1982 a petrol tanker, part of a Russian convoy, burst into flames following a collision somewhere in the depths of the mountain. Fearing the threat of a guerrilla attack and the possibility of an ambush by the Mujahideen, the Soviet authorities sealed both ends of the tunnel. The death toll on that occasion was estimated to have been more than 1,000.

These things happen. Afghanistan is a country with many problems. You have to take your chance.

****

Following the Controller's directive to mobilise for the Spring re-opening of the de-mining season – the Spring offensive – the Project team of O'Deere, Trotter and McScumble had assembled in Peshawar, where two of our Land Rovers had over-wintered in the care of a neighbourly Agency. Zahir appeared magically at Green's Hotel, having found his way from Kabul (no mean undertaking), whilst I travelled to the rendezvous via Islamabad.

If my route had lain through Karachi I could have gone to the Lost Property Office there – surely a substantial concern – to enquire after the missing Stetson. As it was I passed no closer than vaguely overhead at a height of 35,000 feet and nothing further could be done about Walduck's anguished hat, carelessly mislaid on the airport shuttle the previous December in a moment of grievous inattention.

Instead, I went to the British High Commission in Islamabad, to be accorded the established arm's length greeting, extended in trepidation lest a situation might arise (horror of horrors) requiring some sort of response or action. A reluctant diplomatic *tour d'horizon* of the Afghan scene was conducted, embracing (amongst other things) failing security on the road to Jalalabad and the associated subversive training camps in the vicinity.

Yes, I confirmed, I had seen the report in *The Times* dated 3rd February: 'Bandits shoot British Aid Worker in Afghanistan Ambush'. The death count for the incident, just nine miles east of Jalalabad on the road from Peshawar, was four, with one survivor who leapt from his vehicle and hid in the roadside scrub. Yes, acknowledged the diplomatic man, the targeting of Westerners was a growing problem. Especially for travellers on the Jalalabad road. 'Probably best to play it long' was the cabbalistic advice proffered, whereupon, equally enigmatically, I nodded in accord.

Having dealt with that, the focus turned to the ex-Ghurka guards at the Embassy in Kabul, still standing sentinel over the 23 acres – including the grand piano and associated accoutrements. Yes, I said, I had also seen the other report in *The Times* dated 3rd February headed: '72 Killed in Attack on Kabul'. Over 80 wounded, the state radio claimed, as 'Rebels intensified their two-week old siege of the Afghan capital, firing more than 75 rockets'. Possibly Sakars, although it didn't say; it was just 'News in Brief'.

And yes, I had also seen the report dated 26th January headed 'Civilians Die' saying '800 people were wounded and 200 killed after hardline Islamic rebels fought government troops in the capital for the eighth day running'. And 5th February's report too: 'UN Office in Kabul Wrecked'; there was nothing about Lucky Five Street and the Moscowbitch. But it did say that 'the capital is being pulverised in a many-side contest for supremacy'. There was more: 'There is no effective government, no electricity, no running water, no police force and no telephone service'. True: just running refugees. The report was written from Islamabad. 'All or most aid organisations are expected to pull out of the city', it said. Wrong: apart from the International Red Cross, Médecins Sans Frontières (our MSF neighbours) and our own de-mining Project based in Shar-i-Naw, they had all left quite some time ago, giving their locally entered staff a few months' advance of salary and inviting them to keep things ticking. Lock the office door and hope for the best; there was no need to turn out the lights – that was already taken care of automatically by Mr Hekmatyar. Now the only sightings were of occasional day-trippers making fleeting appearances above the parapet.

After all that despondency, I went to see Mr Willow, the donor. *No donations, no de-mining.* There was a shortage of funds, said Mr Willow. He asked had I seen *The Times* report of 4th February? Yes, I had: 'Rebels fired nearly 100 rockets into the Afghan capital, killing at least 14 people and wounding 79, with at least 300 killed in the past month'. And the one in the Guardian ten days later headed 'Mojahedin [sic] batter Kabul', reporting '3,000 injured and hundreds killed in the latest fighting'. Four rockets had fallen near the Jamhauriat hospital; hopefully our new sandbags had been of some assistance. 'Government planes attacked Mr Hekmatyar's headquarters south of Kabul', concluded the report, nicely preserving the genteel formalities and courtesies of the conflict.

'We will have another De-mining Conference here in Islamabad next month. We hope you will be attending,' continued Mr Willow, presenting me with yet another opportunity to drive up and down the picturesque but dangerous Jalalabad road. 'Did you see the report headed "Afghan Truce"?' he asked. 'The one about six Afghan factions agreeing on a peace formula, with a ceasefire in the Kabul fighting and elections in less than a year?'

'Yes,' I confirmed. 'Encouraging. Except just a few weeks after that it said that 60 people were killed and at least 100 were injured by rockets ploughing into homes and into the bazaar in Kabul the day before the second round of talks.'

I moved on to Peshawar to join up with the team. There we decided that I would take my chance with the money (another swag-bag top-up for the Project coffers to meet those recurring running costs and honorariums), hitching a ride on a Red Cross flight into Kabul, while the rest of the group would take their chance with the Land Rovers and bat their way up the Kabul Gorge and see if they could race me to the delights of the waiting villa.

The boys – Trotter, McScumble, O'Deere and Zahir – left Green's at 0715. I made my leisurely way to the airport, confident of winning the day (even though the departure of my 'Beech King Air 2000' transport was delayed by the unscheduled arrival of two dozen MIG 21s – a redeployment in response to Pakistani tensions with India). When we finally got airborne, the ride over the mountains was bumpy. Stretched out below us and framed through the circle of the aircraft porthole was truly 'the loneliness of the great landscapes' – with no trace of a tell-tale plume of dust to indicate the passage of the overland band on their scenic way.

I occupied the time with my Afghan Dari flash cards – my memory rusty after the winter break and in need of refreshing: '*Ba rasti*?!? – Is that so?!?' '*Shuma makbul hastin* – You are beautiful.' '*Khar* – Donkey.' '*Who hay*! *Ho way*! – Amazing!'

When I got bored with that, I shut my eyes against the turbulent movements of the plane as it responded to the thermals rising from the arid land, and tried to see if I could remember (as a variation on Kim's Game, the memory test) details of the ten Oxfam suits that Rhubar was in the habit of wearing on appointed days of the week (seven regulars and three spare, just in case). Saturday was easy: that was the hairy milk chocolate brown tweed with turn-ups; must have been a Yorkshire farmer's market suit, 16-ounce cloth, so thick it was almost bullet proof, ideal for winter in Kabul – weather resistant and doubling as a flak jacket.

Sunday was the elegant charcoal grey, with those *outré* slanting pockets and a fancy lapel on the waistcoat, hitherto unseen in these parts; good for funerals – and even for church in general (although that was irrelevant, of course). It was single breasted ('button one, show two' the old-school Gieves cutters were fond of saying at every opportunity), with a single vent behind – 'bugger's delight' as Rhubar was inclined to say, at every inopportune moment.

Monday was the snappy hound's tooth check, ambidextrous for town and country, but again, with comfortable north-country bracers and old fashioned turn-ups.

Just at that moment we did the Stuka re-enactment thing to counter ground-to-air missiles, and the familiar scene of devastation that was Kabul airport unfolded once again beneath us. I tried to see if there were any additions to the crashed and crumpled aircraft that lay below, but everything looked more or less the same; all normal, except for the newly-spread mantle of snow. Anyway, and as I was saying, Tuesday was the dark blue pin stripe, double breasted, cheeky double vent ('bugger's dilemma' sniggered rotating Rhubar without fail every time he made his Tuesday entrance to the office).

Our brave little aircraft taxied to a halt. No missiles today; no problems with the haul of dollars I had stashed somewhere in my bags. No Immigration man either: given up, had he, probably until later in the Spring. Fingers frozen in those funny gloves, too cold to work the multiplicity of rubber stamps, the blue and red ink on the pads transformed to solid ice.

It was Wednesday and Dr Rhubar gave the game away by appearing in Arrivals in the three-piece light grey worsted. I kept telling him that black shoes would be better but he would persist with those two-tone tan brogues.

'Everything prepared, as in your fax from UK,' he affirmed smoothly and breezily, following our exuberant exchange of greetings, and after Karrimullah had surprised me by jumping out from behind the Land Rover with a slow grin of welcome, a faint bow as he touched his heart and then a bashfully extended hand.

The crispness of Rhubar's confident declaration alerted me in anticipation of the inevitable caveats and corollaries that swiftly ensued. 'Except we still couldn't catch the mouse,' he said, shaking his head regretfully to indicate the extreme effort that had been extended to that end. 'They almost unblocked the toilet, I think, and there's nobody left sleeping in your bed. Well, it's so big and with so many blankets that you can never be sure who's in there. In

Afghanistan we say that "someone else's bed can be used until midnight". I don't know what it means, actually, and I have never been sure if that's a restriction or a licence.' He gave his laugh and by a simple process of thought association sorrowfully advised that the long promised and eagerly awaited addendum to the Kama Sutra that the clerks in Banke Millie were busily evaluating was not yet available. 'They're still doing the practical research, double checking their findings. These things take time,' he explained, moistening his lip, his mind wandering.

'And our money?'

'Banke Millie are researching that as well,' replied Rhubar with a start, his line of thought abruptly interrupted. 'I had my car fixed,' he said proudly, shrewdly changing tack. '*Alhamdu'lillah.* Praise be to Allah. You remember – the Muscovitch.'

You can say that again. *Alhamdu'lillah.* Good work by Allah. In fact, resuscitation of that bombed-out heap of scrap metal was nothing short of a veritable miracle; those panel beaters must have been out of this world. Yes, I remembered the Moscowbitch, I remembered it well. Although just at that moment I was inwardly vexed because I couldn't for the life of me remember what were the Thursday and Friday suits. Well, at least dear Rhubar was just the same, and at least his hopeless old car had been restored. *Who hay! Ho way!* Amazing. Rhubar smiled and nodded happily in confirmation.

Trotter, McScumble, O'Deere and Zahir arrived in their Land Rovers about two hours later; no problems on the way, the active roadblocks of late-Autumn temporarily deserted or disinterested.

'Muddy, bumpy and boring,' said Trotter in that laconic style of his, much as he might describe a day spent in a minefield. 'What else can you say about ten hours passed scratching around in the dirt looking for explosives?' he wanted to know. As far as he was concerned, dedicated though he was, that just about summed it up.

We had lunch. Abdul served the meatballs, underarm. It was the first day of term, heralding the new de-mining season, and he was slightly harassed by all the noisy chatter and the unaccustomed demand for his catering. In self defence he clucked continuously, his tipsy *chapan* sliding this way and that on his bald head with its zero coefficient of friction like a hyperactive omelette.

Afterwards we crossed the half-frozen Kabul River with the swag-bag to trade with the money-changers, 'the watercourse lifting up its voice in the silence, talking foolishly to the rocks'. On our return we had set about sorting kit for the morrow, in readiness for the departure of the Pol-i-Khumri party. If we could get things moving smartly, then may be we could hit that target of 2,000 mines cleared before next winter.

'Kabul generally calm', reads the diary. 'Just distant explosions ("small fightings" according to Abdul). Weather clear and sunny; north wind eased but v. cold.' No banjo barometer on hand and – apart from the tell-tale mares'-tails of golden-grey cirrus cloud high in the sky that caught my mariner's eye – no hint of the coming storm. No hint of any power either, so Karrimullah and Hajji lent a hand in trying to start the lazy generators.

When we did get the diesel generator going – in a choking rich burst of black smoke, and so heavy that only O'Deere and Karrimullah could crank it – we found that the computer had died during the winter stand-down. Perhaps we needed a new stabiliser as protection against the enthusiastic surging of our home-brewed power supply as the regulator lagged in its duties and the motor hunted unchecked. Never mind, we still had the electric typewriter. Only to find that had gone the same way. Awry. So I used the old hand-driven Imperial to prepare the Controller's fax: clackety-clack, clackety-clack, long burst-short burst, long burst-short burst, just like a busy Kalashnikov. I felt empathy with the Vice President of our insurance company, sheltered from the cold in the Valley of the Archives. Ting! Thus went the little bell at the end of every line. Ting! Such that, as I flipped the carriage back against the ingenious elastic, Abdul popped up in response to the sonorous summons, waving his pansy pot.

'Shall I open for you another cup?' he enquired.

Clackety-clack, ting, fling; clackety-clack, ting, fling. 'Have re-taken the high ground', I typed, graphically yet melodiously. Signed: 'Hornblower'. Economy of words, economy of effort. The job was done in no time, a one-cup composition. I terminated with a single shot through the heart of the fax. Clack! HQ would appreciate that. Ting! went the richochet.

In the distance (over to the north-east, O'Deere said), the explosions continued to rumble round the ruins of Kabul.

Thus the Project slipped back into gear. Minimum fuss, no delay: copybook house style observance. Mine clearance work in the north got underway again, productivity resuming as though there had been no interregnum, and I garnered the stats by radio at 0630 each morning. Trotter left McScumble in charge of the re-assembled force of Afghan de-miners at Pol-i-Khumri and moved down to Jebel Seraj, mouth of the Panshir Valley, to continue and expand the mine removal programme previously initiated by Walduck.

In Kabul, Hajji and Karrimullah periodically threw back the big metal gates of the compound and Dr Rhubar led the way on our sorties through the city. Out we rolled in the short wheelbase Land Rover, or even (just occasionally, to please Rhubar) using the rehabilitated Moscowbitch. Sometimes we went in support of the well-being of shell-shocked Captain Rai and his 23 imperial acres of fresh-cut lawns and towering 70-year-old trees. On other days we drove in search of the elusive President of Banke Millie (we suspected that perhaps he was vacationing in La Paz); frequently we paid visits to the Ministry of Defence to obtain the promised minefield maps (those maps of dangerously doubtful veracity) from chimerical Colonel Sharook (ever-absent, reputed to be afflicted with gout and wintering in Herat); often we found our way to the diverting ping-pong table at the almost-empty Pakistan Embassy in search of the ghost of Mr Baksheesh, once of the Visa Section.

Meanwhile, O'Deere the demolisher ranged ever further afield in his eager search to gather industrious mounds of discarded munitions, ripe for detonation. Such was the press of Project activity that the imminent Islamabad symposium on de-mining came upon us almost without warning.

Nevertheless, on the eve of departure, time was found to organise a Grand National sweepstake, ostensibly (and after some research) to mark the sometimes forgotten visit by King Amanullah and the Queen of Afghanistan to Aintree in 1928. The 65th Anniversary of this singular (and surprising) occasion was well supported by the handful of Red Cross delegates remaining in Kabul, and by mystified members of Médecins sans Frontières. The confusion was compounded when after a false start, the 1993 running of the renowned racing spectacle-turned-debacle was abandoned.

In the absence of a precedent, instead of lamely returning the speculators' investments, the stakes were unilaterally re-cycled against successful selection of the date of the next (and inevitable) serious outbreak of sustained fighting in the capital. Serious *jang* between the warring factions battling for power – in which we would unfortunately and detrimentally be embroiled, along with all the other civilians still present in Kabul.

****

Bollard was not his real name. The correctly courteous moment for establishing his real name had long since passed. Droll Dr Rhubar jovially quipped that the alias was bestowed because he, Bollard, was stumpy, stolid and static.

Regardless of his true identity, Bollard had somehow appeared in Kabul – as off track as a swallow at the North Pole or a curate in a bordello – with the innocent administrative intent of casting his bricks-and-mortar Foreign Office eye over the real estate of the vacant, or rather, vacated, British Embassy. In turn, in a familiar moment of self-enlightened altruism (or even out of genuine compassion for his plight – reluctant though I was to own to such a weakness), I had offered him a lift in the Land Rover with Zahir and myself, imminently departing for Islamabad. Which, in the case of Bollard, meant home, and all that that implied.

Bollard himself, his prosaic work concluded (and now with the realisation that his re-assuring pre-assignment briefing had been based on flawed intelligence that bore little relation to the actualities on the ground) was – not unnaturally – keenly anxious to depart alien Afghanistan. Consequently, he lost no time in gratefully accepting the convenience of the proffered conveyance. Especially so in view of the fact that so-called 'scheduled flights' had become markedly the opposite, or as non-PC McScumble wittily observed over the radio: 'As rare as Princes Street shoppers on an Edinburgh flag day'.

On the appointed date, at the appointed hour of 0645, squat Bollard was at the gates of the office villa, punctual as a bailiff, neatly combed, expectant Gladstone travelling bag in hand. The first rays of the sun were slanting on to the terrace; a fine Spring day was in prospect. All that was lacking was driver Zahir. I fulminated; Abdul poured. In the midst of which, the radio crackled to life.

'High Commission, Islamabad,' whispered O'Deere, doing the honours with the set. 'They say that on no account is Mr Bollard to travel with you.' He pursed his lips and widened his eyes.

'Your tea is well?' enquired Abdul, solicitously but with misplaced timing.

I put down my cup and took up the microphone. 'Weather nice here,' I confirmed, obtusely. It's true: I was piqued – painfully ostracised. It was clear that overland travel via Jalalabad was not to everyone's taste; it was just a matter of differing house styles. 'Leaving now,' I continued into the mike. Well, almost now, as soon as I had finished this nice cup of tea and if only Zahir would show. 'All well in Kabul.' Historic, that.

'No! NO!' cried Islamabad. 'On no account …' Etcetera and so on.

'Fine and sunny,' I replied, persistently perverse. 'Our ETA your location mid-afternoon.' Succinct and helpfully informative.

Pleasingly, Islamabad jumped through the hoop once again.

'Confirmed,' I radioed. 'Teatime. Out.' Useful invention, 'Off' switches. I looked at Bollard; he looked dejected. There was nothing we could do. He had put his shiny little bag down on the floor, signalling defeat. He probably used that bag for his diplomatic squash kit in Islamabad, freshly laundered by his wife, or the maid. Nothing wrong with that, except that he had mistakenly wandered on to another planet. Anyway, now he and his sad little bag, disappointed both, would have to wait, un-ecstatically and stolidly – but inwardly nervously, that I didn't doubt – for an unscheduled scheduled flight.

This wasn't the way it had been planned, but there was no point in hanging about. Maintenance of the objective: that was the Project ethos. Zahir was a no-show; Bollard was a no-go. Already I was almost a quarter of an hour late. Karrimullah shot the bolts and flung back the gates, enacting the established departure routine, gaze fixed on his big toes protruding from his sandal. Abdul hid, silent and motionless in the kitchen, pre-occupied. Pensive Hajji wispily tilted his pointed grey beard through the open window of the Land Rover and looked long and deep into my eyes.

'*Khoda hafees*,' he said, solemnly. 'May God be your protector.' Fingers crossed for a second coming; nothing about the *bukhari*.

Formalities fulfilled, off I sped, the white flag of the Project close up and a-flutter at the masthead. Head down, go for it, hope to arrive – sooner rather than later. I felt I was back in the Devizes to Westminster Canoe Race, a single-minded activity of such dedicated concentration that at the finish line some of the cramped competitors have to be prised from their fragile craft and carefully straightened, re-opened like recalcitrant rusty pen-knives, long forgotten in a drawer.

Scarcely had I cleared once-upon-a-time-sedate Shar-i-Naw, when, swinging on to the wide and expansive roundabout leading to the out-of-town road I became conscious of the fact that facing each other on opposing sides of the circle were arraigned two neat ellipses of tanks. It was as unexpected as the unheralded appearance of two new moons.

There was no other traffic. None. On the surface of the road was a generous scattering of debris – the debris of *jang*. Clearly I had chanced upon the scene of some sort of disagreement, catching the players *in flagrante delicto.* Even more surprisingly, in the centre of the mess was a bent bloke with a tired brush and a rusty hand cart with wobbly wheels. That must have been his job: sweeping the circle. So he was doing just that; professional integrity, an example to all. What really caught my attention was the fag hanging from his mouth. The length of ash on that smouldering cigarette was truly prodigious. It drooped, yet it didn't fall. How did he do it? It must have been well over an inch long.

There was nothing for it other than to press on. I was committed to circumnavigating the circle. The Mujahideen seemed to be as astonished as I was. I kept my speed steady, resorted to the metronomic wave and smiled pleasantly to right and left. Nerves of steel, just like that erroneous taxi driver had said on our way to Heathrow. The white flag above my head fluttered and snappled helpfully. On the tanks, the odd gun barrel returned my greetings, waving like an elephant's giant proboscis, but in general the perplexed fighters stared fixedly at the Land Rover in dumbfounded wonderment.

'Phew!' I said to myself as I cleared the field of play, principally because there was no one else to talk to. Foot hard down with relief, I was eager to be gone. The tyres of the TDI Land Rover caught the mood and hummed like a bird. Turbo Diesel Injection, that's what made the difference. I made a mental note to write to the makers. Just then the radio spoke – actually it was O'Deere.

'Calling Juliet Lima, calling Juliet Lima.' That was me, thinly disguised, Juliet Lima. 'The BBC visitors have their film ready. Can you take it out to Islamabad?' Long pause. 'Are you there, Juliet Lima? They say they are sorry not to have delivered it as promised. … Over.'

I un-hummed the tyres and turned the Land Rover. The TDI aspect had become redundant. Perhaps I wouldn't write that letter after all.

'Do you read me, Juliet Lima?' transmitted O'Deere, knowingly giving me the Nelsonian opportunity to drive on.

'Loud and clear,' committed Juliet Lima, teeth gritted. 'Wilco. Returning. Out.'

Back at the traffic circle, nothing stirred. The sweeper had finished his mobile smoke and was taking a sedentary break. The tank men were paralysed in amazement as I fluttered through; it was like a parlour game of statues: the music had stopped just as this one was sipping his mug of green tea, that one was wiping the turret with a greasy rag, that group over there were applying a drop of lubricative 3-in-One to the roller bearings. Like a post-Vesuvius tableau, all were transfixed. I was petrified too – well, apprehensive, certainly. Then I was round the bend, gone, lost from sight. I imagined the squatting fruit bats turning to each other enquiringly. '*Marde divanaa didi*?' they would be saying.

I didn't have a flash card for it, but it must be something along those lines. 'Did you see the nut case?' Something like that. Was it real? Had that old guy really passed by again? *'Ho way*! Amazing!'

I located the house where the errant film lay, and in response to my hammering a spotty TV man stuck his head out. He had cut himself shaving; there was an unpleasant decapitated shag-spot seeping blood on his chin..

'We're just having breakfast,' he said, his mouth full. 'Can you wait?'

'I'd be quite obliged ...' I began. That's not what I said at all; in truth I phrased things diametrically differently. The Controller would have been pleased with my progress. The TV man stiffened like a trapped traveller in the Salang Tunnel. His buttered toast dropped from his fingers, landing face down in the dirt, Oxford thick cut marmalade and all, thus validating Murphy's Law in a most satisfying manner. Then he was gone; then he was back; then I was gone – with the film. The work of moments: another lifelong enemy easily acquired.

My third circumnavigation of the roundabout lay ahead. I resolved to play it by ear and (to borrow the vernacular) to go for it, even (if necessary) to 'play it long'. Which is by way of saying that I didn't have a plan. Other than to keep the circus going. I could sense the Controller frowning, but in truth, it was Hobson's choice, no options, no alternatives. Islamabad, venue for the De-mining Conference, lay on the far side of the traffic circle; my situation was akin to that of a poised, embryonic, tyro bungee jumper, verging on the distraught – there was only one way to go. At least I had the element of total surprise – no one in their right mind would traverse that explosively volatile field of play three times in the space of half an hour.

Entering the arena I immediately noticed that the sweeper was no longer in attendance. Brushing was done for the day. Ominous. No sweeper, no birds, no kites; it all pointed in the same direction: no chance. They say that when one of the senses is impaired, the remainder hone themselves to a higher degree of effectiveness by way of compensation. The hard of hearing are not only strong on non-sequiturs but also strong on telepathy, fine-tuned to the invisible. Just at that moment I could sense I was surrounded by cohorts of itchy-fingered militiamen and a veritable arsenal of twitching RPGs. Yet again I waved agreeably, while above my head the banner of surrender gestured likewise in wholehearted support, ruffling and riffling the intensity of the surrounding silence.

As I drove through no-man's land, emitting an aura of deceptive *sangfroid*, I imagined myself in the role of a streaker possessed of dismissive assets on a cold day at Twickenham, play continuing contemptuously, the crowd enraptured with the on-field action, not even a derisory snigger or chortle in my direction. One streak: nothing. Try again: no reaction. Third streak: not a sausage. In all honesty, that was fine by me, except that, deep down, I knew things were wearing thin and that I was running on 'empty' in the goodwill stakes. It wasn't on the flash cards but I could sense the muttering Muj squatting on the sidelines mouthing inwardly to themselves, with the greatest respect and fingering their RPGs with an intense desire: 'Make a fourth pass, *rafiqam*, dear friend, and we'll have you. Just one more pass … please!'

But I had no intention of returning that day: no way was I planning a re-run. And, *alhamdu'lillah*, miracle of miracles, there I was, gone. Down the players' tunnel I scampered, over the hills and far away.

The adrenalin carried me to Jalalabad in record time. Once there, I hummed right through, racing over that rippled road, the bouncing of the spare wheel in the back of the cab keeping me company on my solitary dash. No tea break that day. It was all very well to secrete myself on the clandestine balcony of the *chaikhana*, quietly observing the passers-by, but there was no means of disguising the presence of the fat TDI Land Rover parked below in the street. For the ill-intentioned it was but the work of moments to pass word of the tasty target to the nearby terrorist training camps, beckoning the subversives to step out for a touch of ambush drill.

The procedure for the assassinations of the previous month had been straightforward. Two pick-up trucks of armed men had driven up behind the defenceless UN vehicle. The first had overtaken the quarry, effecting a neat sandwich. The canvas back of the lead truck dropped down and the occupants opened fire. When everything had ground to a halt, the gunmen in the following truck stepped up to the stationary target and completed the day's work with a series of shots to the head.

All that remained was for the local authorities to hold an investigation and for the bodies of the two expatriates to be sent back to their families for the memorial services. 'They were doing what they had always wanted to do,' said the encomiums. 'Helping others.'

They always say that.

The two Afghans, who had taken their chance, were buried locally.

Foot down, all the way to the border. No one was given a chance to come up from behind, let alone to overtake me, drop their tail gate and riddle the pristine white Land Rover with bullets. The flying TDI was a match for all-comers.

Five miles beyond Torkham I came to the railway line, derelict at that time, but since renovated for a monthly tourist run, in contrast to its original strategic military purpose. It comes up from Peshawar to Landi Kotal – there are 34 tunnels and 92 bridges; I didn't have the guide book to hand but I could remember that bit. Twisting and turning through the mountains it is probably about 35 miles in length, more or less, and was built by the British in the 1920s. Same age as the trees in the grounds of the British Embassy in Kabul – it surely all tied in, even without checking the guide book: The Great Game. The Great Jigsaw of history. This was the British equivalent of that later, Russian-built, northern artery into Afghanistan, the Salang Highway. I had read the plausible claim somewhere that, at a cost (in 1920) of over two million pounds, this was 'the single most expensive development undertaken in the British Empire'; correct or otherwise, the dramatic feat of engineering underscored the value attached to the security and retention of the jewel in the crown, British India.

In Peshawar I stopped at the pink-painted Pearl-Continental Hotel for restorative strawberries. A double portion, with double cream, in recognition of a double thanksgiving; tardy Zahir would be sorry he had missed the excursion. And I was sorry not to have been more patient in recognizing the domestic difficulties that daily attended our local helpers in reporting punctually at the Project office early each morning.

Then it was onwards again, speeding down the crowded Grand Trunk Road – only to be apprehended by a duo of immaculate traffic police in their equally immaculate motor, ostentatious siren wailing.

'Overtaking is not permitted by way of the hard shoulder', they courteously caution.

I hang my head in shame; no use blaming the double portion of strawberries, no point in trying to explain the tactics of the pick-up trucks in a distant land, loaded with trainee terrorists eager to target Westerners (it being the early days of the sadly unravelling relationship). We have a contrite chat, me and the policemen at the roadside as the painted Pakistani trucks and the packed buses and the heavy horse carts and the curious camels go past; we converse animatedly on cricket, and part the best of friends.

Curiously, as I climbed back into the driver's seat I happened to notice that the Project flag had largely disappeared. Now, just a few torn shreds of tattered cloth remained adhering to the angled staff, so that it resembled the yardarm of a tea clipper emerging dramatically from the effects of a prolonged gale, a tempest of double-digit ferocity on the bicentennial-Beaufort scale.

Once in Islamabad, I immediately rang the BBC to report the arrival of the all-important film from war-torn Kabul.

'Oh, really?' they said. 'We're a bit tied up right now. Can you deliver it?'

I left the film at hotel reception. It's probably still there.

****

The De-mining Conference completed, I drove home – back to Kabul, that is.

The meeting had been much the same as last time: sniffing dogs, alluvial Australians, flailing tanks, bizarre bazaar prices for DIY minefields. No mention of impregnating mined areas with additional explosives to trigger consequential clearance detonations, nor of using airborne search radars employing ground penetrating technology mounted in helium-filled balloons to relay a revealing overview of soil density to de-mining monitors; all that was yet to come.

For the moment it was mixture as before: still no sure substitute for the de-miner on the ground – on his hands and knees – with his feeler, his prodder, his scraper, and the all-important Mk I eyeball. Except that the wearisome buzzing bluebottle had gone from the top right-hand pane of the conference room far window – and the Project donor, Mr Willow (who had never been known to smile), said he would like to fly in for lunch one day in Lucky Five Street. Welcome, I said, any time, and thought no more about it.

In Peshawar – halfway home – I settled into the haunting comfort of a suite at Dean's, put a sock in each drawer to confirm my occupancy and, lulled by the mighty winds and rushing waters in the monsoon pipes, decided not to spend the afternoon in pursuit of a Tribal Pass. This document – obtainable from officialdom in those gloomed government offices bequeathed by the British – was supposedly mandatory for my transit, solo or otherwise, of the Khyber Pass, land of the Pathans, the following morning. Somewhere, at some indeterminate moment during the passage of the previous half century, I had read the words: 'Trust a snake before a harlot, and a harlot before a Pathan'. Just another of those disgraceful calumnies, obviously, but the dictum had wedged itself in my mind with the force of a stale doughnut in a denture, periodic purges of political correctness notwithstanding.

The upshot was, instead of advertising my intended movements to the world and signalling ahead to the waiting opposition in the Tribal Areas and beyond across the border, I chose to take an early bath in the rich brown waters that cascaded from the bathroom plumbing (quite possibly the art work of the same engineers who built the arms and munitions railway to Landi Kotal) and retired to bed. As I fell asleep I was reminded that, in the unstable circumstances prevailing, it had even been fancifully mooted that a UN escort to Jalababad might be provided, on request. Disregarding this siren-call and further opportunity and invitation to shout word of my coming from the roof tops, I slept soundly – untroubled by beguiling dreams of non-existent escorts composed of squadrons of mounted dragoons in plumed helmets and shiny breastplates clinking at my side, lances at the ready. Like Hajji, I trusted that God might be my protector – plus once again, the twin supporting strategies of speed and surprise.

At dawn I am on my way, unleashing the full extent of the TDI and grateful for the unseen presence of Zahir's soft hands under the bonnet, tweaking the tappets, soothing the sprockets, greasing the gaskets and tensioning the torsion. I catch the first two military check-points flat-footed, the smartly painted barrier poles open and pointing ineffectually skywards, the sleepy sentries straining the early-morning brew through their regulation military moustaches and salaciously savouring the delights of re-living the saucy escapades of the previous night spent on the town. If they cried, 'Oi! You!' in Urdu, Pushtu or Punjabii after my fleeing form, hazy in the heat of the exhaust, then I wasn't there to hear it.

It was at the third check-point that I met what appeared to be my Waterloo. The cuckolded sentries earlier along the road had radioed ahead to their comrades to be on the alert to apprehend the dastardly runaway renegade. Not quite cricket, but there it was and there was no escape. The barrier was sternly horizontal, uncompromisingly lowered into position, the welcoming posse were assembled to accost the villain, complete with Lee-Enfield .303 bolt action rifles of World War II vintage. The newly applied oh-six-double-oh matutinal blanco was scarcely dry on their white webbing belts and gleaming gaiters, their daily-dhobied uniforms starched and pressed. Crisp as new baked *chapattis*, fresh from the *tawa* or *tandoori*, were those soldiers of the guard, my apprehenders. Not only were they as immaculately presented as my other friends, the traffic police, they were equally graciously polite.

'We are wondering where you are going?' observed the dapper Sergeant, half informatively, half questioningly. 'And, moreover, what might chance to be your good name?'

'I'm just on my way home,' I replied, eager to be seen to be giving every assistance with the official's enquiries. 'To Lucky Five Street, Kabul,' I added, helpfully.

The posse exchange knowing glances. 'Are you sure?'

I wasn't sure at all. 'Yes,' I confirmed, defying deflation.

'We are thinking you must be in a hurry?'

I had undergone the interrogation course in a previous life, 'tactical questioning' was the euphemism; I was trained in spotting tricks and traps, identifying leading questions, vaguely versed in the complexities of the Geneva Convention – name, rank and number; nothing more. The Sergeant filled the silence with another interrogative stab. The rest of the treatment – the indiscriminate cold water, the intimate electrodes – that could come later.

'You are having the Tribal Pass?'

I dug deep and tendered the Dean's account, which irrelevantly and inconveniently came to hand: One spacious suite (one solitary night – no solo supplement); breakfast included (but not taken; the dining room was closed). Total charge: just a few rupees.

'You cannot be proceeding. You must be going back for your Tribal Pass. Rules are obligations.'

I thought fondly of cock-eyed Abdul busy in the kitchen, methodically pounding and shaping the day's meatballs, perhaps even preparing one of his pies on the mouse board as a special 'welcome home' surprise. Abdul Ahmed didn't do forty-fathom figgy-duff (a sad omission in his culinary apprenticeship), but he did do the soggiest pastry this side of the Panshir Valley: forty-fathom apple pie, speciality of the house. Then I thought of Karrimullah, my self-appointed minder, and Hajji, self-appointed warden of my spiritual welfare, both loitering in the compound courtyard and feigning unconcern but taking it in turns to squint out through the peephole in the big metal gates to see if at last I was coming up Lucky Five Street in a billowing cloud of dust, dodging the stupid goats and the uncertain cyclists.

Once again I dug deep into my pocket, whereupon, on withdrawing my hand, a wad of high denomination rupee notes fell clumsily and completely inadvertently to the ground. Must have been well in excess of a *lakh*, more than 100,000 lovely plump rupees. Taking a leaf out of Hajji's book – if not

Uzbekistan
Tajikstan
China
Turkmenistan
Tashkent
Bokhara
Samarkand
Dushanbe
Termez
Wakhan Corridor
Shir Khan
Mazar-i-Sharif
Kunduz
Hindu Kush
Pol-i-Khumri
Jebel Seraj
Bagram
Toraghondi
Herat
Farah River
Bamiyan
Jalalabad
Kabul
Gandamak
Peshawar
Islamabad
Rawalpindi
Minaret of Jam
Khyber Pass
Ghazni
Gardez
Shindand
Farah
Indus
Maiwand
Kandahar
Iran
Zaranj
Quetta
Pakistan
Helmand River
Bolan Pass
0 100 200 km
0 100 200 mil
India

Afghanistan
Provinces
Mazar-i-Sharif
Jowzjan
Balkh
Kunduz
Takhar
Badakhshan
Faryab
Samangan
Baghlan
Sar-e Pol
Panjshir
Nuristan
Badghis
Bamyan
Parwan
Kapisa
Kunar
Laghman
Jalalabad
Herat
Wardak
Kabul
Nangarhar
Khyber Pass
Ghor
Logar
Peshawar
Daykundi
Islamabad
Ghazni
Paktia
Khost
Orūzgān
Farah
Paktika
Musa Qala
Zabul
Sangin
Kajaki Dam
Camp Bastion
Lashkar Gah
Kandahar
Nimruz
Helmand
Kandahar
Province

Welcome – Kabul Airport 1992

City checkpoint

Lucky Five Street – Shar-i-Naw

A city in ruins – Kabul 1992

Once a spacious tree-lined boulevard

The effects of civil war

Local commander overlooking the Kabul River

Rooftop fighters during a lull

Citizens of Kabul by the River

Author (centre) with local militia

Mines awareness course (for the remaining expatriates)

Rudimentary mine disposal – plastic explosive and fuse

Morning roll call – our Pol-i-Khumri de-miners

Wiring up the accumulated debris of war

Avalanche on the Salang Highway

A landslip impedes travellers – southern end of the Salang Tunnel

The Christian cemetery, Kabul – comprehensively desecrated (Dr. Rhubar at right)

Local fighters with T-55 tank near Mazar-i-Sharif

Village children – an uncertain future

An existence apart – colourful nomads in Afghanistan

Ageless Afghanistan – yoked oxen and wooden plough

Ruined village – post Russian occupation

A majestic land

HALO TRUST
IN MEMORY
OF
TIMOTHY GOGGS
JULIAN GREGSON
SHAH MOHAMMED
Fatally injured on this road
whilst clearing mines

In memory

his principles – I gazed searchingly into the Sergeant's eyes.

'Oh!' exclaimed the Sergeant helpfully. 'I am observing that you are dropping this.'

Whereupon he bent, recovered the inducement and returned it to its owner in one flowing motion. Just my unlucky day: men of such fine calibre are but rarely encountered these days.

One hundred *lakhs* to the *crore*: ten million rupees. I remembered that from the Christmas Quiz. A *crore*! That would surely do the trick, except that I didn't happen to have it on me. My pockets weren't that big. I was beaten and I knew it. 'All had been done that could be done, and all was done in vain.' And yet I couldn't possibly go back; it was out of the question and in any case the house staff were waiting, and I would be late for lunch.

I said as much to the Sergeant. He asked at what time was luncheon being taken. Despondently, I told him. Luncheon was always being taken on the stroke of one o'clock. Every day.

The effect was electrifying.

'Goodness gracious me!' he exclaimed, consulting the Casio on his wrist. 'At one o'clock they are serving! Why you are not saying so sooner? You must be hurrying at once on your way or you will be late, oh dear!'

So saying, he waved imperiously at his men. Rapidly was the barrier untethered and flung skywards to the full extent of its string. The entire guard sprang to attention and saluted. I saluted in return and the TDI revved with delight.

Without further ado I was gone: once more through the narrow confines of the Khyber Pass, with its towering bastions of rock (with or without the painted insignia of the South Lancashire Regiment, except I knew it was there somewhere), weaving my way into Landi Kotal, scattering the mangy dogs and the economically half-feathered chickens, onwards across the anonymously foreboding border at sombre Torkham, vanishing over the hills and far away.

As I hummed and rippled my way along the lonely road to Jalalabad, the terrorists in the adjacent training camps obligingly confined themselves to their barracks that day.

Taking the undulations in the track at seventy to eighty miles an hour, the Land Rover swayed as I sought the optimum line over the rutted surface, the plume of dust in our wake suspended in the still air of the early morning, spiralling softly before returning to earth. But the terrorists stayed put, the succulent invitation went unanswered. Perhaps they were busy with their classroom revision at the time, intently preparing for exams, or even putting up the decorations for their graduation ball. For whatever reason, I was left unmolested to reflect uninterrupted on the final months of the 1st Afghan War.

Following the disastrous annihilation of Elphinstone's army in January 1842, the British lost little time in effecting retribution. A relief force under Major General Pollock passed through the Khyber Pass on 31st March 1842, reaching Jalalabad two weeks later in mid-April. Thus, as I drove that very road early in April 1993, exactly 151 years later, I shared the journey with the ghosts of that long column of marching men, their spirits intent on exacting vengeance for their fallen comrades. The silence of the way was broken only by the creaking of the gun carriages and the clink of the harnesses on the horses of the officers. And as they advanced, the long trail of dust thrown up behind the thousands of tramping soldiers entwined with the drifting dust of my solitary passage.

At the same time, way to the south west, General Sir William Nott moved up through the Bolan Pass and similarly re-established Kandahar as a secure British garrison. Co-incidentally, Shah Shujah – the puppet ruler installed by the British in July 1839 – was killed in Kabul by his countrymen. The scene was set for the nemesis of treachery.

Safely to Jalalabad, rather than tempt fate on that day in April 1993, I kept going non-stop up the Kabul Gorge in the direction of my intended destination, oblivious to the blandishments of hesitant roadblocks and hopeful hitch-hikers, with or without weapons. For Major General Pollock, with his force largely on foot and in need of respite, things took somewhat longer. It was August 1842 before his avenging army fought their way up the Gorge. The thousands of bodies of those killed just eight months early had largely decomposed and shrivelled in the sun; nevertheless, the torn and blood-stained uniforms of the dead were still in evidence. As General Pollock's force advanced, the marching boots of the British troops and the ponderous wheels of their heavy guns scrunched across the bones of the residual skeletons littering the route, to give a reminder of the catastrophe at almost every step and turn of the way.

Safely separated and securely insulated by the long intervening years from the full impact of those terrible happenings, such occurrences have a tendency, a temptation even, to become academic. In centuries past, dying was different, surely? Merely the stuff of history books …

Kabul was re-taken by General Pollock on 15th September 1842. Not a shot was fired: as in July 1839, the enemy had again decided that discretion was the better part of valour and vanished during the night. The lessons of history … General Nott's force arrived shortly afterwards, having marched the much greater distance from Kandahar, and later the same month, Lady Sale, her diaries and the other British wives and officer hostages held by Mohammed Akbar Khan were rescued.

Early in October large areas of Kabul were trashed – pillaged and plundered – by the avenging forces. On the 11th October 1842 the British withdrew, heading back towards the Khyber Pass without incident and signalling the end of the First Afghan War. A few months later, with British connivance, Dost Mohammed Khan (Mohammed Akbar's father) returned to the throne that he had been forced (by the British) to relinquish in July 1839. Not only a lesson of history, equally a lesson in heroic futility.

****

When at last I turned into Lucky Five Street, I experienced a wave of relief. Driving the final miles on the homeward leg I had feared that my memory was failing.

For the life of me, no way could I envisage or remember the descriptive detail of the Oxfam suits that Dr Rhubar habitually wore on Thursdays and Fridays. But now I had it, total recall reassuringly restored, the colourful images brought safely forth from their temporarily inaccessible hiding places in the recesses in my mind.

Thursday was the cold mushroom soup suit, not my favourite, but there again, those were not the easiest of times in Kabul. Rhubar paired this unfortunate faded fawn cast-off with brown suede shoes – his 'brothel creepers' he said, perpetually delighted with his imagined originality. Friday's suit was a startling black confection with widely spaced Al Capone-style white pin-stripes. Quality cloth, but mercifully (as it was Friday), it spent most of its time in the wardrobe, as did the three spares (also thankfully) – the bookmaker's suit, the caterpillar cabbage-green mad-scientist's two-piece, complete with belted jacket, and the standard issue lightweight tropical beige (for which there was limited use hereabouts, never mind Yorkshire).

Dr Rhubar (Tuesday: dark blue double breasted pinstripe – bugger's dilemma) was blandly awaiting my return in the sitting room. I composed myself, prepared for his eclectic mix of inswingers, outswingers and googlies. That, come to think of it, was surely where the occupying British went wrong – they kept to themselves overmuch, failed to teach the Afghans the rules of cricket and thereby eschewed the opportunity to alter the course of history.

'No news,' declared Rhubar nonchalantly, wearing his metaphorical resident-manager's hat on the back of his head. 'None. Nothing happened whilst you were gone. Well, except the de-mining, of course. That's going fine.'

I sensed a trap. Best to attack.

'The Project donor's coming to lunch,' I announced. 'Mr Willow.'

Abdul pricked up his ears apprehensively under his '*kolah*', the collapsed pancake that hid the little-known secret of his shiny nut-brown head – the traditional Afghan *chapan*, invested in his case with jaunty, lopsided bravado.

'Of course, he's not really the donor, just the donor's representative,' said I, hastily trying to play down the forthcoming event. 'But these people are all the same, labouring under the same illusion. They think that theirs is the blessed hand that personally bears the largesse, so we need to put on a good show for Mr Willow.'

'My frying pan she is not so fine these days,' interjected Abdul, immediately hopping nervously from one foot to the other at the thought of impending culinary pressures.

'"God sends meat, the devil sends cooks",' unhelpfully interceded Rhubar, who had clearly picked up rather more than just the ten crumpled Oxfam suits when he was studying in England. 'The lunch will be even more important than you think,' he added solemnly, having unsympathetically torpedoed the cook. 'This donor, Mr Willow, is the one the Controller pinned forcibly against the wall of his office.' He paused for effect, successfully.

'Go on.'

'Apparently there was some sort of misunderstanding. Just a rumour, of course. Entertaining hearsay, so everyone repeats it until it becomes fact. Which reminds me …'

I looked at Rhubar, now well into the swing of his knowledge-is-power mode, waiting for the inevitable.

'The Controller made contact whilst you were away. I almost forgot.' Rhubar tapped the side of his head. 'He wants you to investigate possible escape routes in the north. Through Tajikistan, that sort of thing, in case of, you know, emergency evacuation, possible enforced temporary suspension of the Project because of the situation, even though obviously we hope that won't be necessary.'

Pause; silence. Wait.

'And another thing: Walduck's relief is on the way, except that I can't remember his name. Bones, something like that.'

Abdul made his escape and went off to put the kettle on, fretting about the future.

'Oh yes!' Rhubar was enjoying himself. 'There's one other point that nearly slipped my mind. You recall I mentioned President Najibullah, our neighbour? Near-neighbour, I should say. Well, when the Russians pulled out – retreated, that is, like all our other visitors over the centuries – his position became increasingly difficult. The Soviets went in 1989 as you know, and by early 1992 – the beginning of last year it was, *Bachai Jang* was about six months old – he, Najibullah, was forced to take refuge in the UN compound just down the road. That's when the Mujahideen entered Kabul, in April and May. He's an ex-President now, of course, but still alive, and he's asked if we can possibly help him out. I'll tell you more when you've settled after your journey.'

'Hang on. Help him out of what?'

'No more news,' asserted Dr Rhubar confidently, meaning that would be all for now, until he happened to remember something else. 'None. Nothing at all.'

****

Chapter IX

IN SICKNESS AND IN HEALTH

'For the pillars of the temple stand apart,
And the oak tree and the cypress grow not in each other's shade'
Kahlil Gibran (The Prophet)

There is something about a freshly blown-off leg.

When we got to the Jamhauriat Hospital there were no beds available; no trolleys, no stretchers either. So we laid Said Abdul Salem on the stone-tiled floor in the entrance foyer and stood round in a circle while arrangements were made.

The accident had occurred south of Jebel Seraj. The Médecins sans Frontières doctors had provided field casualty treatment at their Charikar clinic, staunching the pulsing flow of blood, tidying things up the way they do on these occasions; debriding: cutting away some of the non-viable mangle of muscle and dead and injured tissue that dangled loosely from where the leg used to be, the white bone splinters contrasting against the blackening morass.

Things didn't look good, in spite of the tidying up. No trace at all of the foot and calf, the rest was a mess – beyond the reach of any modern miracle of reconstructive micro-surgery, not here in Kabul, not anywhere. The point of amputation would have to be somewhere around the upper thigh. Always better if the knee joint could be preserved; but not this time – it wasn't there any more.

This wasn't the way the Victorian chroniclers would have us believe it. In their accounts, limbs flew off neatly with minimal trauma.

'Egad!' the afflicted hero would exclaim, as the severed limb soared high over the battlements. 'That's my leg they've taken clean away!'

'Zounds, Sir!' the nearest subaltern would confirm. 'How confounded right you are!'

This was different. There was nothing clean or neat about it. No one spoke. Someone found a strip of sheet and draped it over Said Abdul Salem's good leg and then, involuntarily and out of habit, over where the other leg, the bad leg, had been. The hollowed contour of the sheet accentuated the victim's altered silhouette, his changed profile. That was the thing about a freshly blown-off leg. It left a void.

As we waited, and in spite of the pressure of the field dressing, the blood seeped through the sheet.

Of course, the mine – probably a PMN or a PMN2 – hadn't been designed to kill. That would have been too simple. Anti-personnel mines are intended to incapacitate, to maim, as a general rule. Casualties with one leg blown off – screaming in fear and agony, covered in blood – are bad for morale. Not only that, it takes two more combatants to carry the wounded man to relative safety. Once in hospital, the broken cripple is a further drain on the enemy's resources. Incapacitated for life: high maintenance. Killed in action: low maintenance.

Lying there on the floor, Said Abdul Salem fastened his eyes on me. It was not the moment for the flash cards, it was not the time for anything. He was going into shock. It was not the time for saying: 'You're going to be fine. You're going to start a new life'. In any case, he didn't ask; Said Abdul Salem was an Afghan. He just gripped me with his eyes.

Once upon a time, fifty long years ago in Kentish woodland – another place, another time – I had chanced across a rabbit trapped in a poacher's snare. The wire wound tight around the rabbit's neck had yet to complete its work. As I approached, the animal fastened me with its eyes. Unblinking. Just like Said Abdul Salem. Club me to death if you must, or set me free. It's up to you. I am in your hands.

The accident had occurred before Christmas. The morning's de-mining work had been progressing routinely. Except that nothing is routine in Afghanistan – or in the centre of a minefield. As always, the swept channels – those safe lanes across the land, those parts of the suspect zone that had been checked and cleared of lurking mines – were plainly marked with white tapes. Eye-catching tapes that fluttered and gyrated in the breeze. That was the drill, the SOP, the standard operating procedure.

After two hours or so of sweeping and scrutinising, probing and advancing, little by little, step by step, the time came for the mid-morning break. It was demanding work. Work that called for care and concentration, a job that Trotter had described as 'grindingly boring, but dangerous'. It was in the boredom that lay some of the danger.

Said Abdul Salem straightened from his labours, stretched and relaxed.

He was in need of a pee before he had his cigarette. He ducked under the eye-catching, re-assuring white tape to relieve himself. The pressure of his foot activated the buried mine, and his leg blew off. Untidily.

Those were the days before protective clothing. No body armour for the de-miners; no Kevlar plates, no reinforced low hanging apron. No non-flammable natural fibre overalls to preclude the tendency for synthetic materials to melt and fuse with the skin; no shielding visor for the eyes and no safety helmet. No huge inflatable moon boots either, for treading softly, as favoured by the French, regardless of the difficulty of reaching down to the ground and the propensity for punctures. Not even specially strengthened safety boots, subsequently modified after it was found that the metal insert running through the soles caused additional repercussive detrimental damage to the victims (the designers were reputed – erroneously, no doubt – to have purchased amputated limbs from the previous owners for testing purposes).

The Project mine clearance teams were trained professionals; yet it took but a single moment of untrained, human aberration to produce a one-legged professional.

The incident involving Said – the most recent accident in the minefields – took the Project overall casualty toll for the de-mining programme in Afghanistan into double figures.

When we got back to Kabul in the Spring, Said Abdul Salem was still hospitalised, but had been moved from the civic hospital to the military establishment at the edgy end of Shar-i-Naw. There he could share the company of other youthful amputees.

The process of recovery was proving lengthy and he remained bed-ridden; however, the deep wounds suffered by his 'good' leg were healing, while on the other side, the lurid stump – all that remained of his 'bad' leg – was settling slowly. When it had stabilised – when the bulgy skin had shrunk and strengthened – then we would see about getting a prosthesis fitted, perhaps in the comparative northern calm of Mazar-i-Sharif, possibly across the border in Pakistan, in Peshawar. In both places were specialist clinics, well experienced in the task. Meantime, we attended to the insurance claim in the office.

Most days I visited Said, usually in the late afternoon when the business of the day had been knocked on the head. Or in the early evenings as the days lengthened, pedalling to the hospital on Abdul's rusty old bicycle. It was less formal than the Land Rover. A lot less. The guards at the hospital entrance would start laughing when I was still a hundred yards away, opening the gate in readiness for my squeaking arrival and waving me in with their Kalashnikovs.

'Why are you using the poor cook's bicycle, *rafiqam*?' they liked to enquire, their grinning welcome a profusion of black whiskers and yellowed teeth.

'So I can be sure nobody will steal it,' I would tell them opaquely.

Then, as they nodded in agreement at the unarguable wisdom of this, I would ask them to look after it for me and go off to find Said, top floor of the second block, end room, the ward with seven other one-legged young men, the iron beds squashed in so tight that there was hardly any space between them, certainly no room for fresh air. The invasive smell was the usual sick-room pot-pourri: yesterday's stew, stale sweat, fresh urine, old bandages. The blankets on the beds were grey, to match the sheets.

Said was in better heart now; he was adjusting. That's what you have to do in such circumstances. He helped with my Arabic script. If, when writing my name, the all-important dots above and below the letters ended carelessly in the wrong places, or worse still, were absent-mindedly omitted, then we could end up with 'June Loon' by mistake, or an assortment of similar variations.

The other occupants of the ward remained impassive to my visits, impervious to all overtures. They were resolutely indifferent, or silent with tangible, smouldering antagonism. I didn't know why and I never found out. I was left to wonder: race or religion? Certainly it was an increasingly unravelling relationship, although not a new phenomenon, and patently not just about me. Nothing personal. Was it a question of unbridgeable faith? Or was it because I was one of the *firengee gowrah* – one of the 'red-faced foreigners' – an unwelcome reminder, a historical throwback? Or was it simply because, having two legs, I was the odd man out? Probably all three. But principally, I told myself, never be deluded: not too deep down, most people don't like foreigners. Especially a plague of them.

There were no other visitors to that stuffy, eight-bed, eight-legged ward. If Said had any family, I never met them. A familiar story. As they say, we were all in it alone together – the loneliness of trying to live the life that lay in front of us. Especially in Afghanistan.

Pedalling round Kabul on Abdul Ahmed's bike became a daily habit, a break from life as a lower case head of mission, a change from de-mining stats and all the attendant administrative trappings. It struck me that if we had two bikes we could have gone on rides together, although perhaps Abdul might not have seen it that quite that way. Whatever, diligent oil was regularly applied to the moving parts of his rusty steed, but to no effect. The squeaking was as much a part of that bicycle as were the cracked-chrome handlebars. It must have been built that way, a specific design feature and its USP – unique selling point. Certainly – and this was helpful – it gave advance notice of my coming and no one was startled or taken unawares. Heads would poke out from fortified positions along the route, invitations for a cup of tea were forthcoming. On the cook's bicycle I was at street level, accessible, non-threatening, in touch. Especially if I wafted along one-handed or, better still, no-handed. Who would want to waste an RPG on a dusty chap on a rusty bike going his whistling way down the street? In the white Land Rovers, well-known though they were, we were in an ivory tower, out of reach, out of touch. Yet not out of range.

Bicycling was good 'hearts and minds', though it would never have done to suggest as much to the Controller. He would have shot a stare of heavy calibre astonishment in the direction of the speaker. 'Hearts and minds?' – went one of his cherished expostulations – 'Never mind the hearts and minds! Just grab 'em by the balls and the rest will follow!' (the primordial seizing of the assets expression on loan from Field Marshal Sir Gerald Templer and taking me back to the Malayan Emergency).

With the Spring weather gradually improving, the late-afternoon cycling outings became more and more established. First to Said; do what I could, practise the Arabic script. Then down to what was left of rocketed Chicken Street, sometimes to chat with old-world reliqual Mr Samir (the master cutter left behind from the peaceful days of the monarchy), the tailor with the *ting-a-ling* doorbell, racks of finely crafted clothes and no customers; at other times to visit closely adjacent Flower Street, running parallel and whimsically named, in the vacant hope that there might be something new, although I was not sure what and there never was.

Abstractedly I bought some 'elephant's foot' Afghan rugs, supposedly old; in an act of faith they were parcelled up and addressed to the farmhouse in Hampshire. And months later, they arrived. It was before the invention of retail therapy, but I did it nonetheless and with that purchase I was a true pioneer.

On occasions a visit was paid to the Jamhauriat Hospital. There to see how the sandbags were holding up, and to pass the time of day with my flash cards and the wide-eyed patients, those incidental, haphazard casualties of war, advancing with the Afghan Dari and making the children giggle as they swung on their mothers' skirts and peered at the *firengee gowrah*, funny man that he was.

My beard grew longer, partly out of convenience in response to the chill darkness of six-o'clock mornings without electricity or water, partly as a gesture of blending solidarity with my fellow citizens of Kabul. Every two weeks I pedalled my squeaky way to the barber's. Dismounting, and leaning the bike on the chipped and tilting kerb outside, I would take a seat within to await my turn: the only one in the patient row of long-haired customers without a Kalashnikov propped between his knees, listening to the tick of the 1930's mahogany mounted clock that marked the quarter hours with Westminster chimes and wondering how it came to be there.

The barber had one style and one style only: medium-short back and sides, give or take, with a few peaks, clefts and furrows if his attention wandered. Like when he was distracted by gunfire and other ordnance. The customers habitually took their pre-warmed place in the plastic covered chair in sombre silence, and work got under way without further ado, chit-chat or delay. Yet, exceptionally in my case, he always received me in that chair with interrogatively raised eyebrows to ascertain my desires of the day. 'Rococo like a coco,' I would respond, with appropriate gravitas; whereupon – the minuet completed – he would incline his head deferentially, click his scissors a few times to limber up, take the much-used comb from his top pocket with a professional flourish and a quick flick to dislodge any foreign bodies and livestock, and off we would set on another hairy adventure.

On holiday Fridays I roamed further afield. Once, before they went home (retired hurt), I rode across town to have lunch with the disappointed, deluded missionaries. The invitation, curiously, was to attend at the empty Russian Embassy: there were just nine of us present that day – refugees of our own making – Isabel and Wilfred from Australia; two Finnish financiers without names – 'there's good money in poverty'; two American hydrologists scratching their heads over what to do about the millions of acres of previously fertile land in southern Afghanistan now rendered saline by World Bank irrigation schemes; a Canadian journalist; a German paediatric nurse; and a man on a bike from Hampshire. There are some things in this world that are difficult to explain. Perhaps the invitation card should have decreed fancy dress; theme: 'Flotsam and Jetsam'.

Another day I biked to the great fortress of Bala Hissar, to circle the towering ramparts, to greet the ghosts of murdering Mohammed Akbar Khan and his father, Dost Mohammed Khan. Shah Shujah, the puppet ruler, he was there too – and all the ghosts of the 200 men of the British Empire who were entrapped and killed by insurgents in the narrow streets that starlit night of 1st November 1841 when they marched out vainly to try and save Sir Alexander Burnes, besieged by the mob in his burning residence. Too many tortured spirits were sheltering in the dark shadows thrown by those high walls on the day that I passed; there were no living beings in the vicinity for company, no birds flew overhead, no coloured kites tugged at their strings and danced in the empty silence of the clear blue sky. It was not a place for lingering; I pedalled homewards, late for tea, keen for the company of Karimullah, Hajji if he was at home, and cock-eyed Abdul. I hurried along as the sun set and the shadows lengthened and the busy world was hushed, whistling on my way, no-hands.

When night fell on our villa in Lucky Five Street, up went the metaphorical shutters. Curfew-breaking sorties after dark (aside from the improbability of compelling social commitments) were not to be countenanced. Dusk was the time when Abdul reclaimed his bicycle and with a *shab bakhair*, would bid us good night. '*Ihtiat ko*!' we would tell him. 'Be careful!' At which he would give a determined tug on his *kolah*, crank the perverse pedals and head off into the gathering gloom. Shuffling Hajji would slipper silently in to the living room to turn up the *bukhari*, and Karrimullah would swing on the recalcitrant generator, the reluctant contraption no match for his determination. The lights would glow and the throb of the running machinery would conveniently exclude any sounds of distant *jang*.

So snug – if not impregnable – was our stronghold that the night we forgot we had invited our friends from Médecins sans Frontières to watch our only video, their hammering on the compound gates went unheeded. Eventually they had to climb over the wall of the villa to gain admittance, only to find that irremediable technical shortcomings, either in our projection equipment or in the variable quality of our home-brewed electricity reduced the murky underwater scenes in 'The Hunt for Red October' to total invisibility, detracting markedly from the highlight event – quite aside from the translation aspects.

Nocturnal visitors to the house were the exception; the tranquil scene of de-mining Project after-hours domestic bliss went generally undisturbed. Supper dispensed with, the pear liqueur would come forth from its not-so-secret stowage to be poured by the self-appointed sommelier of the day into two generous tumblers (in the advantageous absence of dedicated liqueur glasses, those mean-spirited, lamentable thimbles). Then we settled with our books in the armchairs on either side of the spluttering *bukhari*, O'Deere's weighty 'War and Peace' versus 'Flashman' (unlikely successor to Lady Sale, but similarly produced by BBC Suzi).

When the pressing need for a set of dumb bells was declared – a bar and weights for use on rainy evenings unsuited to bicycling – it was Suzi again who met the requirement. Using reportage contacts she produced an assortment of re-cycled cogwheels taken from the gear box of a Russian tank – a T55 or a T62 that had long since been immobilised by the Mujahideen. The wheels had been welded on to iron bars in varying ratios and sizes, a modern version of swords into ploughshares. It was explained that they once belonged to Wingood, but (whoever he was and whatever he did) he'd gone now. Wingood? Gone? Yes – he wouldn't be needing them anymore. It was that euphemism again. For Wingood, he who had clearly 'obeyed the voice of the Great Summoner and been gathered to his fathers', time must have merged itself into eternity, thought I, plagiaristically. Thereafter his heavy legacy alternated nightly with the trombone: one evening passed in the company of the slush pump, the next pumping iron.

On the portable music stand, the December carol sheets were replaced by '101 Hits for Buskers, Volume I'. Hajji was spellbound, Karrimullah too; O'Deere less so. A difficult man to please. He asked whether, by any chance, there happened to be anything else in the repertoire. Whereupon I switched seamlessly to '101 Hits for Buskers, Volume II'. Out with the beguiling 'Windmills of Your Mind', and 'Ob La Di Ob La Da' dealing with Desmond's barrow in the market place; in with 'Burlington Bertie', 'Jeannie with the Light Brown Hair' and 'Happy Days Are Here Again'. Varied audience reaction is the lot of all the world's great artists. Here the facts spoke for themselves – not once did we receive an unsolicited RPG through the windows of the villa.

There was but one thing that disturbed the calm of those culture-crowded and cerebrally elevated evenings. And that was the monumental upheaval and commotion caused by the nightly appearance of the resident mouse. Hardly had we turned the first few pages of our respective books, great and small, when, unfailingly, that self-same mouse would make a reconnaissance run across the worn carpet, skittering for cover so fast that we were left wondering if it had been an illusion. The mighty nightly mouse knew the form. Giving us a minute or two to recover our composure, it would follow up with a second high-speed pass. This time there could be no doubt about it.

'Mouse! Mouse! *Mosh didi*? Did you see the mouse?' we would cry, leaping to our feet and grabbing the broom and the mop, handily placed in preparation. It was enough to bring Karrimullah running from the kitchen, knife at the ready, ever eager for diversion. From the other direction in would hasten Hajji, devotions or ablutions temporarily abandoned. Under the sofa we would rattle with the long-handled broom, heedlessly shaking the blameless curtains, banging the resounding sideboard with the mop so that the innocent candlesticks rattled and the candles slumped sideways in protest.

Without warning the fearless offender would break cover for another quick circuit of the room, jumping for joy. Whang! Bang! The broom and the mop would thud heavily in pursuit, O'Deere busily assessing target velocity, movement right to left, crossing speed left to right, aiming off for projectile time of flight. I relied on instinct, hand and eye co-ordination. Thump! Thud! Reload! The effect was the same. The head would fly off the broom, the whirling mop would up-turn the tumblers of pear liqueur, Hajji and Karrimullah would dance about in their *pirahan tonban,* baggy pyjamas flapping, sandals slapping and clapping. Left with bare poles we would fight on, equally ineffectually.

Wheeee-eee! Thwack! Clomp! Nothing. Wait! Shsssh! Down on hands and knees. Quiet! Wheeee-eee! Too late again … We never, ever, came near to catching that mouse. Quicker than lightning was he, faster than a speeding Sakar. By the morrow, another nibbling attack would have been effected on our stock of favourite Afghan biscuits, fresh from the bakery at the far end of the road. And equally fresh droppings would adorn the bread board, causing Abdul to cluck and curse, not-so-sotto voce.

Cease firing! In dispirited silence we would return our cudgels to the corner, ready for the following night, puffing after our exertions. '*Sabr ku. Dafai digar…*' Hajji and Karrimullah would console as they withdrew, heads shaking. 'Have patience. Next time…' '*Ahysta, ahysta* – softly, softly.' It was the signal for O'Deere to shut down the generator and to light the two hurricane lamps, one for each side of the *bukhari,* to accompany the two refilled tumblers. Reading would resume, the flickering of the lamps throwing long shadows across the sitting room. Domestic equilibrium restored, just the rustle of the turning page. All that was needed was to replace the two horse hair slumpers with a couple of rocking chairs either side of the matrimonial hearth, and to add the somnolent tick of a large kitchen clock.

'Ah, well,' O'Deere would sigh, finishing yet another fulfilling chapter and carefully inserting his book mark. 'Good, better, best,' said the marker. 'May you never rest, 'Til your good is better, And your better best.' It was leather, from Tunbridge Wells.

'Oh, well,' I would sigh, placing my marker with equal care (Royal Horticultural Society, red and blue anemones, inscription: 'Tomorrow is another day').

O'Deere would go to the glass house under the stars, I would go to the big boudoir under the stairs, barricaded behind the bulging bags of sand. It was one of those marriages of inconvenience with separate beds in separate rooms, reasons not discussed, never divulged, patently obvious to all.

O'Deere brooded about that mouse, concerned that his calculations never resulted in a hit. I brooded about the biscuits – the delicious but forever-nibbled *kolcha* – assuring O'Deere that there was probably nothing wrong with his mathematics or with his assessment of the related spatial gradients. It was just that the mouse had an in-built radar that sensed danger. Hadn't he seen how high it leapt when the mop was descending, right on target and all seemed lost? Dr Rhubar added his extensive knowledge, overseas training and experience to the debate.

'It's like fox hunting,' he explained. 'And fishing. The mouse enjoys the chase. Fear is not a factor, there is no question of suffering. Haven't you noticed how it turns and charges from time to time, just to put you off?'

I thought hard about the charging mouse. Truly, Rhubar had indeed acquired far more than a mere ten suits when he was studying in England.

****

'No ping pong today,' I declared, satisfactorily catching Dr Rhubar totally off-guard with a successful pre-emptive strike hardly before he was halfway through the office door (Thursday: mushroom soup suit with fungal creepers). 'We're far too busy. I'll go to the market with Karimullah and see if we can pick up some drums of fuel for the vehicles and a cylinder of gas for the kitchen. You see if you can help O'Deere in the Ministry of Defence. Colonel Sharook might be back and then you can get those minefield maps they promised us. Trotter and McScumble are impatient for them, and I agree; we've waited long enough. Meet up back here at 1230 sharp for the donor's lunch.'

Before setting out I needed to brief Abdul. I could hear him clattering around in the kitchen. 'What about some apple pie and meatballs for Mr Willow?' I suggested helpfully (ignoring the fact that he didn't seem too pleased to see me), before adding knowledgeably: 'You can stick a tomato on top to give it plate appeal.'

It's little known and not generally appreciated that I studied Catering in the Royal Navy. Just the Short Course.

Abdul looked doubtful.

'Well, do what you like,' I said impatiently. 'Or rather, *koshish ko*, do your best. By the way, I've had a brainwave about that low table we use in the sitting room. It's a coffee table really. Mr Willow, our guest, is very tall, at least two metres high. So if you could put some bricks from the garden under it, that will save his back a bit, make it more comfortable for him.'

For me, too. Simple. Much easier than trying to excavate the proper dining table, seeing as it had almost disappeared from sight under the computer, the pounding Imperial, the erratic electric typewriter, the printer, the HF radio and the un-filed office filing system. Abdul looked even more doubtful – positively alarmed in fact – so I left him to it. It was not a day for tolerating temperamental artists.

When we returned at 1230 (sharp), Karrimullah and Hajji grappled with the load of diesel and gas that we had acquired while I went straight into the house to ensure that all was prepared, everything spot-on for receiving Mr Willow. He was unlikely to make a habit of visiting us in Kabul: this was the moment to impress him with our attention to detail and simultaneous grasp of the big picture in the context of humanitarian de-mining.

'*Nan tayar ast*?' I remembered that – 'Is the food ready?' There was no sign of Dr Rhubar and O'Deere. No sign of Abdul either. '*Abdul kuja ast*? – Where is Abdul?'

In the sitting room, the coffee table we had improvised for eating off was tilting, unusually, to one side. It was listing heavily, in fact, like a shipwrecked freighter after a storm, left hanging on the rocks as the tide receded. I proceeded to the galley; the kitchen door was shut, possibly locked.

'Abdul?' said I, man to man through the keyhole, recognising that this minor and sabotaging contretemps was capable of simple and ready resolution via the application of elementary human resource management procedures. Failing that, of course, I could always resort to more traditional methods to quell the mutiny and have Abdul shot at dawn. Or sooner.

'*Bali*? Yes?' countered Abdul from within, radiating wholly justified suspicion through the closed door.

'*Nemaz*? Prayers?'

'I have finished my prayers.'

It dawned on me that he must have done the resistance to interrogation course.

'Then what are you doing, Abdul?' I enquired gently, maintaining my fraudulent stance as the prisoner's friend. '*Abdul khow hast*? Is Abdul sleeping?' Next move was to offer him a cigarette – except that he didn't smoke – and to ask about his wife. '*Famili shuma chitor ast*?' That was the nearest I could get with the flash cards. I stooped lower and squinted into the lock. 'How is your family?'

'I am mending my sock.'

Further dialogue and cajolery was interrupted by the arrival of five-foot Hajji, escorting seven-foot Mr Willow. Not only was the donor immensely tall, he had a tiny head, as though the maker had run out of materials by the time he had got that far and it was early closing in the hardware store. Mr Willow resembled a Victorian hat-pin. Maybe it was this faintly ridiculous *trompe-d'oeil* that had so provoked the Controller to launch the alleged attack that supposedly left Mr Willow crumpled and tearful in the corner of his office. Reasonable enough.

Then I remembered why he was there, or here, so I agreeably led the way back to the sitting room – where we sat. If Mr Willow spotted the unusually angled table then he didn't say so. He was a Buddhist. I knew that in advance. Inscrutable.

Anyway, we sat and we conversed for an hour or so. It was a good opportunity to brief our visitor on Project progress. I had all the trappings prepared: whiteboard, de-mining statistics, charts. No Powerpoint though; no power.

No sound came from the kitchen. The hole in Abdul's sock must have been enormous. I wondered how his wife was. I took the opportunity to run through my presentation again – 'just to make sure everything has been covered', as I said to Mr Willow at the time. Working lunch, I explained. Mr Willow was courtesy personified.

Then I took the donor out to the lawn and explained the way we conducted the Mine Awareness Indoctrination Courses, which were particularly important for the returning refugees when they went back to their farms. Especially the riveting bit about how we buried a PMN mine in the grass just where the audience were standing, for realism, and that the activating mechanism could be responsive to pressure, tension release, pushing or pulling, or remote command using electronics. And that you could use a round of ammunition as a percussion cap.

Taciturn hat-pin that he was, Mr Willow listened without commenting. An articulate silence indeed. I found myself siding with the Controller. And still there was no sign of Rhubar and O'Deere.

Without breaching the fragile boundaries of political correctness I contemplated how Mr Willow had chanced to become a Buddhist; it must have been an act of discernment – checking through the proclaimed and apparent virtues of all the manifold religions on offer and then choosing what was best. Rather like selecting an internet service provider. Speedy and secure access to the information highway, ditto for the after-life. Thinly veiled Isabel, the missionary lady, would have approved of that: the main thing is to believe in *something*, the details are just that – *details*.

I was interrupted (as was the cathedratic silence) by a scraping noise from the direction of the kitchen. I presumed it to be the mouse, finishing my biscuits. As it happened, it was Abdul, turning the key in the lock and emerging defiantly. He obviously hadn't prepared any lunch; instead, he had prepared a speech.

'The linings on the table and the cookeries are not important,' he declared boldy, smoothing the front of his off-white apron with his knuckles and then hurrying on as though in fear of contradiction. 'We in Afghanistan have very deep hearts.'

From on high Mr Willow's loosely attached little head nodded supportively, like a brainless bobbin in a cotton mill. Thus needlessly encouraged, Abdul continued, avoiding my glare. The next part of his oration was less well prepared.

'This is very, very problem,' he explained. 'I am revolutionary cooker, except when the feet in my kitchen are sometimes too many.'

I took the point, but I did wish Mr Willow would stop his needless nodding; definitely this must have been the source of his past friction and misunderstandings with the Controller (alleged). Wholly predictably, Abdul was further encouraged and finished with a defiant flourish, albeit sacrificing a touch of fluency in the excitement.

'I make him this cooking diesel fine for Karrimullah. He don't know for this one!'

Whereupon Abdul left, exiting stage right. Moments later I heard his bicycle – our bicycle – clunking down the back passage.

'Well ...' sighed sagacious Mr Willow. 'Time to be moving.'

'Yes …' sighed I, but rather more heavily. Adding automatically, without thinking and borne of habit: 'Tomorrow is another day.'

Just then O'Deere strolled in.

'Sorry,' he said, less than explicitly. 'Spot of bother.'

'Where's Dr Rhubar?'

'He said he wasn't hungry.'

Curious, but not the moment to pursue. Mr Willow stood up, practically festooning himself with our cheap chandelier hanging from the centre of the ceiling, his miniscule head taking its place amidst the cluster of 40 watt lamps so that it almost disappeared from view, like the top of Everest when the weather breaks.

Karrimullah chose this memorable moment in which to make a triumphant entrance with the steaming pansy pot, in a noble effort to redeem what was fast becoming a tricky and rather disappointing occasion. Ever willing and eager, he placed the well-filled pot ('with extra sugar to give happiness to the tea') on the rocky table, which promptly listed heavily and violently from port to starboard, with the inevitable consequences.

If Mr Willow noticed anything (his field of vision being somewhat impaired at the time by the chandelier on his head), then he didn't say so. What Karrimullah said as the piping-hot tea ran into his sandals was definitely not on the flash cards; for my part, I made a mental note to add the invaluably graphic oath to my lexicon at the very earliest opportunity.

I watched from the terrace as the UN flight bearing our donor's representative (the telescopic Mr Willow) droned overhead, turning to the security of that south easterly heading.

'So,' said O'Deere, coming up behind me and looking over my shoulder. 'That went off all right then?' He gave me the high beam and the wide eyes.

'Truly a momentous and memorable event,' I confirmed. 'Possibly life-changing.'

'He's a Buddhist, you know,' continued O'Deere, in chatty mode. 'I'm going to have to re-work my thesis slightly.'

I wondered where this was leading, feeling somewhat less than chatty and affable myself.

'Which thesis is that?' I enquired, reluctantly and distantly.

'You mean you've forgotten?' The lips pursed, the eyes crossed. 'You know, my proposal for a revised Geneva Convention. I've been developing this idea that it should become contrary to international law – illegal, that is – for any soldier of any country to be less than sixty-five years of age. Persons under that age will have to work off their testosterone and that sort of thing via other activities – playing football, you know, partaking in compulsory sport generally, long walks, cold baths, bromide in the tea and so on. The effect will not only be an immediate saving in the loss of young lives, but warfare will be revolutionised. Well, eradicated, actually.

'Just think of it. Night warfare would become a thing of the past; old people can't see in the dark and anyway they don't go out at night. Too dangerous. Similarly with the pre-dawn stand-to, historically always a perilous time. That would disappear because the veterans would still be paddling around in their pyjamas, you know, putting the cat out, checking for the postman and watering the houseplants, busy, busy, before going back to bed to listen to their wireless and the weather forecast with a nice cup of tea. Then, when they smelt bacon frying on the enemy side they would put their own eggs in the pan and pass word across the lines in the hope of some company and a bit of a chat.

'As for the latest advanced equipment, well they would spend all their time checking the manual and being confused by the battlefield real-time computerisation, trying to work out gobbledygook conundrums like Network Enabled Capability and Effects Based Programming versus old-fashioned commonsense. It would be totally innovative, casualty-free combat. I don't anticipate any mishaps, but in the unlikely event of an accident, well, it wouldn't be such a big deal for pensioners, would it?

'I should think that in the afternoons these new battalions, or rather, old battalions, would settle to a snooze after lunch, so that, generally speaking, action and active service would become misnomers of the past. Anachronisms, that's what they would be. If there was any activity at all, I think rather than digging foxholes and trenches, the old chaps would probably dig their allotments, do a spot of weeding and hoeing, tickling up their beans and the onions. You know, adjusting their brassicas.'

'And pruning the roses,' I added, keying in and helping out.

'Absolutely,' enthused O'Deere, seeing that I was getting the hang of it. 'Of course, it would result in massive stalemate at the frontline, all that inactive service, so all the Generals back at HQ would have to be a minimum of 75 years old. That way they wouldn't notice what was happening – or rather, not happening – and they could pass the war in peace, writing their memoirs and sticking their snapshots in their albums, and not bother about the duplicity of the politicians, because their futures would be all behind them and they would have no hope of promotion and in any case the economies in munitions expenditure would be astronomical. I just need to work in the Buddhist dimension. I noticed that Mr Willow was possessed of an inner tranquillity, which of course, is highly relevant.'

'Quite so. Brilliant. So what happened to Dr Rhubar?'

O'Deere widened his eyes. 'Ah,' he said. 'There was a spot of bother.'

I narrowed my eyes. Repetition. 'Exactly?'

'Well, Colonel Sharook wasn't in his office, of course, nor were the maps of the minefields, so we went to the bazaar to get a few things before hurrying back. Regrettably we got caught up in a bit of *jang*. Well, it was a domestic, actually, but it came to the same thing and you know what Kalshnikovs are like in a confined space. Noisy. It was all around us and Rhubar took fright, went wobbly, you know, windy, and dived to the bottom of the car, so I decided to drive round the block again, slowly, back through the centre of the turmoil, until he pulled himself together.'

O'Deere further widened his gaze and looked me in the eye. My move.

'Dr Rhubar's had a hard time in recent years. Very difficult indeed. You know what they say about the nuts and bolts of life? Most of us manage to handle that side of things; it's the pieces of broken heart and shattered hopes that are harder to gather up. Something like that. These things tend to be cumulative.'

'Is there any apple pie left?' asked O'Deere politely.

'You can check, but I don't think so. As things turned out, Mr Willow was very hungry today.'

****

Early the following morning we were in receipt of a fresh fax from Mr Willow. He must have composed it the moment he got back to his office after touching down in Islamabad.

I read it – the ink still shining as it slipped from the machine – with some trepidation.

He said thank you for the noteworthy working lunch (*he could say that again*), for the innovatively structured agenda for his visit (*hmmm … damming with faint praise*), and particularly for the comprehensive de-mining briefings (*unnecessarily punctilious use of the plural, I thought*) which were most informative.

And then, in the second paragraph, he was pleased to confirm that a further tranche of funding would be made available immediately to support continuance of the excellent humanitarian mine clearance work being pursued by the Project in trying and testing circumstances.

Alhamdu'lillah indeed!

I skipped through to the kitchen – hop, step and a jump – and gave astonished Abdul a hug, and another one for luck. Rendered more than apprehensive by this unexpected *volte face* he decided the safest course of diversionary action was to make a cup of tea, and he busied himself filling the pansy pot at best speed, warily glancing over his shoulder in my direction, his *kolah* hat knocked comically skew-whiff by my warm embrace.

For myself, I vowed there and then to look deeper into this Buddha business, although what with one thing and another I haven't had time yet. As for Abdul Ahmed, in that intuitive way of his he divined that something abnormal had come to pass. So he belatedly made an extra large apple tart for lunch, with extra sugar for happiness.

****

'You forgot to ask me about ex-President Najibullah,' accused Dr Rhubar, even before he was through the office door, catching me off guard to his entire satisfaction with a successful reactive strike.

'As I mentioned to you before, he wants to know if we can help him out,' Rhubar continued, hardly giving me chance to swivel in my chair and organise my defences.

'Don't forget that this morning we have to collect the new man for the Pol-i-Khumri team from the airport,' I countered, trying to regain the initiative.

'Bones,' replied Rhubar helpfully. 'You remember that Najibullah replaced President Barbrak Karmal under the Russians and that since April of last year, 1992, he has been hiding in the UN compound?'

'Does he want us to get him out?'

'Not yet. Perhaps later. He happens to be a bit short on supplies, that's all. I don't think I've ever told you this, but you've just reminded me that when we had the mining accident involving the tank at the end of last summer and had to repatriate the two survivors, the authorities here thought it was an attempt to smuggle Najibullah out of the country. Because of their burns, the two casualties were completely bandaged, from head to toe. Like those mummified remains in Egypt. The guards at the airport insisted on sending them back and then unwound them to make sure it wasn't a trick. The evacuation flight was delayed. Not that it made any difference, of course. The severe burns were not just external; they were internal as well, as a result of inhaling burning fuel. Untreatable.'

'How can we help?'

'Butter. He's run out.'

'Salted or unsalted? Do you think he's got any videos to swap?'

Just a latter-day variant on 'guns for butter'; there was no harm in enquiring. If he wanted, he could have 'The Hunt for Red October'.

'I can ask,' nodded Rhubar absently as we prepared to set off to meet the incoming Delhi flight (expected but not entirely certain).

Of course, at that time no one could have foreseen that in September 1996, after four-and-a-half years in confinement, ex-President Najibullah was to be dragged from his refuge by the Taliban, stripped, and hung naked from a gantry in front of the Kabul mob, for their general amusement and entertainment.

At the airport, the new de-mining recruit stuck out a friendly hand.

'Pendleberry,' he said brightly. 'Pendleberry.'

The brimming optimism of unsullied youth, thought I. Then I looked at Dr Rhubar.

'That doesn't even rhyme with "Bones",' I protested.

'No,' agreed Rhubar, complacently unruffled. 'Strange.'

I looked again at the eager, non-rhyming newcomer. Pendleberry was under thirty. He was ex-military. Single. That rang a bell. I thought back to the Controller's recruiting criteria.

'Are you an orphan?' I asked.

The new boy was uneasy now. 'Where's Hornblower?' he enquired, looking round anxiously.

We drove back to Lucky Five Street without incident, the silence broken only by Rhubar, humming softly and tunelessly. If Pendleberry had any other questions in mind, then he refrained from enunciating them, so we never knew. On the morrow I would personally drive him up the Salang Highway, through the infamous tunnel and on to our base at Pol-i-Khumri. I needed to go that way to investigate the feasibility of northern escape routes. Just for contingencies. As suggested by the Controller, in case.

****

Chapter X

IN THE NORTH

'I will lift up mine eyes unto the hills, from whence cometh my help?'

Book of Psalms

The new man, Pendleberry, alias Bones, had to be delivered to Pol-i-Khumri. At the behest of the Controller I needed to conduct a reconnaissance in the north of the country. Abdul, previously in disgrace but now on the path to redemption, needed nevertheless to re-confirm his cordon bleu credentials as a matter of urgency. And Zahir, also on probation after his woeful absence from his place on duty on my previous long-distance journey, needed to recover his position of mechanical indispensability (assured incomes, such as those paid to our Project local staff, being as veritable gold dust in Kabul).

In such a manner – a convoluted matter of supply and demand – everything fell neatly into place.

Abdul clucked around on the terrace with the early-morning eggs, Zahir loaded the necessary snow chains into the back of the Land Rover and Pendleberry stepped excitedly from the pristine pages of the '*Boys' Own Paper*' to take his enthusiastic place in the passenger's seat. I seated myself behind the steering wheel and all that was needed was for Karrimullah and Hajji to conduct the ceremonial send-off. Which they did, throwing open the clanging compound gates and wishing us well.

'*Ba aman-e Khodaa!* Go in the safety of God!' came through the offside window.

'*Khodaa haafez!* God be your protector!' was the nearside injunction. May he cast His care upon us. And may we cast our cares upon Him.

All we lacked was 'God speed!' and a bottle of Champagne lapping over the bows of our vehicle and all who sailed in her. Instead, Karrimullah flapped up belatedly alongside my door. 'I put the shovel in,' he confirmed. 'And the tow rope.'

Out through the muddy suburbs of Kabul we drove, the glistening tarmac of the road merging with the dun-coloured dirt at the roadside, the lean stream of humanity at the margins of our route wending its unceasing way to somewhere, hither and thither. The low dwellings, drab, bleak and uninviting, thinned as we cleared the outskirts of the city, leaving behind the litter of broken vehicles, rusty cranes, deceased diggers, dumpers and earthmovers, trailer parks and container farms – all the debris of industrialisation, if not the detritus of happier times.

Twenty minutes out of town and we came to the trail leading off to the left, little more than a narrow path pointing the way to the village of Kariz-i-Mir. Slumped astride that path was the dead tank – the Project tank – blown up by the booby trap the previous summer, the massive explosive charge detonating directly underneath so that the fuel tanks were ruptured and the interior became an inferno, the ball of fire gushing upwards through the turret hatch – to the fatal detriment of the three men caught inside. That flail-fitted de-mining tank was immobile now. It sat like a fat toad, squatting ominously across the track that gave inviting access to the picturesque village lying beyond.

Ahead of us rose the mountains of the Hindu Kush, soaring to 21,000 feet and higher still, the second highest mountain range in the world, topped by 24,557-foot Nowshak (7,485 metres), the snowy peaks appearing to be so closely packed that they gave the sensation of permitting the traveller to step from one dramatic summit to the next. However, that was yet to come, and at this point in our journey the land surrounding us was mainly flat, extensively planted with tumbled grapevines, now abandoned. Under the vines wild tulips bloomed, Persian tulips – pink, mauve and purple; *la la*, that's what the villagers called them. It was only the presence of the anti-personnel mines that were undoubtedly skulking in the undergrowth that dissuaded us from leaping down and gathering an armful or two of the decorative flowers to gladden the gloom of the office back in Shar-i-Naw.

As though any reminder were needed, there was a point along the road where a stick mine, a Russian POMZ, was clearly visible, neatly wired so that it would be triggered by any wayward wayfarer – or inattentive de-miner, such as poor one-legged Said Abdul Salem lying in his hospital bed back in the city. And in turn, that prominent stake mine was in all probability itself protected by a couple of hidden PMNs – buried anti-personnel mines – so that its removal and neutralisation would be anything but straightforward. Just for good measure. That was the way.

Pendleberry took note. Not only of the mine, or mines, but also of all the other relics and rusting legacies of the Russian convoys that had daily fought their Herculean battles along this road during the long years of the occupation, 1979 to 1989 – an invasion (as Dr Rhubar had reminded me) that cost the lives of 14,000 of their men, and the lives of an estimated one million Afghans. This was the route to and from the Salang Pass, to and from the former USSR that lay beyond – a highway that was daily ambushed by the waiting Mujahideen. It was the road where young Russian conscripts died in their hundreds. Pendleberry took note of the debris of war that lay along the way: the twisted chassis of the broken transporters, the detached and upturned driving cabs, the demolished tanks, the frequently encountered Soviet T55s and T62s, busted and abandoned. The debris of death. In the land where no one wins.

On we went past our Médecins sans Frontières doctor friends at their Charikar clinic, handy for tidying things up after accidents. A brief stop for *chai, kino* and *kolcha* – tea, tangerines and biscuits – at the Project mine clearance base at Jebel Seraj; an opportunity to get the news first hand and to renew acquaintance with the ever-expanding work-in-progress. With a pang of conscience I pledged to deliver that pending bathroom suite at the earliest opportunity – if not before – writing the whilst to lately departed Walduck to give him the glad tidings.

Then we started the serpentine climb up the mountains to reach the top of the Salang Pass, and the tunnel, at 12,000 feet. Ahead of us the long line of heavy vehicles, brightly painted Central Asian juggernauts and a bevy of buses breathing black fumes, grinding their snaking way upwards to the clouds, were clearly visible as the road twisted and turned. As always, the TDI made short work of the slow-moving opposition, a deft downward change, accelerate and move up another notch towards the head of the column. Pity they ever introduced syncro-mesh; double de-clutching through the gears, heel and toe, would have been more of a challenge. If I got time, I might write a letter about it.

As the height of the snow banks either side of the road increased, Zahir itched to demonstrate his expertise at setting the tangled snow chains over the Land Rover wheels, but it was not yet the moment. Pendleberry donned a pair of sunglasses against the glare – shades, that's what he called them – and gazed astern, back the way we had come, across the vast expanse of Afghanistan that was open to our view. A quarter of a million square miles: bigger than all of France, but not as big as Burma. I remembered that. A quarter of a million square miles of civil unrest; a country one and a half times the size of Iraq.

We entered the Salang tunnel without incident – the highest road tunnel in the world, it was said – the benign influence of the advent of the Spring sunshine had partially transformed the frozen, wintry nightmare that had so delayed the Pol-i-Khumri expedition led by Trotter only a few weeks previously. But not entirely: the towering drifts of snow from the deadly storm were still substantial and on the upper reaches of the approach road we had moved on a single track cut through walls of ice over 10 feet high in places. Now that we were in the tunnel itself, the giant icicles picked out in the Land Rover's headlights ran with water, filling the flooded potholes in the broken tarmac under our wheels, the blue haze of fumes in the semi-darkness merely threatening mental atrophy rather than imminent asphyxiation.

When we burst into the sunlight at the far end of the tunnel to commence our descent, the highway snow plough was parked lazily against the mud-bespattered banks of snow at the roadside, idle for want of blizzards – and for want of fuel, the allotted quota for the month having long been expended. No matter, for the day was fine.

Down we went, well on our way now, making good time. Half-hidden by ageless, twisted walnut trees and occasional pink blossomed almonds and apricots were tiny farmsteads, visible through the white trunks of slender silver birch, where flashing brooks ran alongside the handkerchief-sized pockets of cultivation. Close to idyllic was the pastoral scene, except for the scattered bequest of buried mines, designed to shred, maim and blow apart the families of the innocent, unsuspecting returning refugees. And to discourage further influx.

In the villages were the gaunt remains of deserted dwellings, each house shelled or blasted to uninhabitable ruination by helicopter gunships in Russian retribution for the Mujahideen ambushes – and to deny refuge and safe haven to the attackers. The Soviet helicopters would circle unopposed, completing their leisurely business of revenge and denial. Leisurely, that was, until the Mujahideen obtained supplies of the shoulder-mounted, heat-seeking Stinger ground-to-air missiles from the United States of America. After that, the attacking pilots were more circumspect, more hurried and less conscientious in their work.

I slowed to negotiate an interesting-looking roadblock that lay ahead and glanced at Pendleberry. He was enjoying the outing, lots to write home about. As we drove along he had been tucking into a bag of oranges that I had thoughtfully provided for his lunch and general youthful sustenance on the long journey. He ate as he lived, cheerfully but tidily, working his way through the oranges segment by segment. In between turning busily this way and that, so that not a single detail of the new and unfamiliar sights should escape his notice, he was dreamily squirting the fruit pips out of the open window, squeezing them between his thumb and forefinger to see how far they would go in an unconscious demonstration of a scholastic skill acquired in his formative years.

Yes, carefree Pendleberry was enjoying the novelty of the experience, untroubled by premonition and oblivious to the foreboding lurking in the barrier now confronting us.

There was no reasonable prospect of bouncing our way over this particular blockage, the unravelled tank track laid out across our path effectively put paid to any such ideas. Not only that, the four, armed ruffians manning the impediment to our progress, AK-47s at the ready, had a particularly menacing air about them, scrofulous robbers that they were. However, and despite their shouts, I did manage the precaution of bumping our way to the far side of the obstacle before coming to a halt, whereupon one bandit loitered ahead of us, one went to the back of the vehicle to molest uneasy Zahir, while the other two aggressors proceeded to either side of the cab and tried the doors.

Mine was locked, window scarcely open; Pendleberry's door flew open and the next moment he was half gone himself, wrestling desperately to stay put and only restrained by his seat belt. I nodded pleasantly at the assailant on my side, who was rattling the locked door with increasing ferocity, and by some inner thought process I came to the conclusion that it was time to go. We had a busy schedule and I was hungry.

'Hold tight!' said I superfluously to Pendleberry, who by this time was already clinging on for dear life, although I noticed that he was losing his battle to remain in contact and was fast disappearing from view. I was still in gear, engine ticking. Up with the revs so high that I could feel Zahir wincing at the whine and then, bang! Foot off the clutch and the good old TDI leapt from the blocks like a startled stag on a thistle, and the poxy man at our radiator leapt for his life. I shot a glance at Pendleberry as I moved up into second, just to check if he was planning to continue the trip to Pol-i-Khumri with us. Astonishingly – and fortunately – he chose that very moment to make a re-entry to the vehicle, springing back upright into his seat like a bewitched bungee jumper suffering a sudden change of heart. Good man, he was still with us – just – door flapping in the slipstream, but well on the way to recovering his composure. Yes indeed, lots to write home about.

As for the bandits, my man fell back in surprise, mouth agape; the irritant behind us growled with rage and started to un-sling his rifle, while Pendelberry's mugger (displaying lightning reactions as we made to depart and speed away) somehow managed to reach on to the dashboard and grab the brown paper bag that had been nestling there. A small price to pay, thought I, concentrating on putting some distance between ourselves and our new acquaintances, and moving smoothly up into third. I felt the familiar instinctive hunching of my shoulders as I looked into the rear-view mirror. Perhaps if I wrote a well-composed letter to the vehicle makers then they might consider armour plating the back of the driver's seat. Well, and the passenger's too, for that matter. Speaking of which, it was Pendleberry who spoke first.

'Got my shades back!' he gasped, happy and victorious.

For want of anything better to do I looked again in the rear mirror for a final appraisal of the situation before we rounded the up-coming curve in the road and went safely on our way. Bizarrely, I saw that the bandit with the brown paper bag was dancing with rage in the centre of the thoroughfare, hurling the contents high into the air. His three compatriots were jigging around him, convulsed with merriment, all thought of firing at our fast-fleeing form driven from their minds.

I asked Pendleberry, 'What was in that bag?'

He looked at me in surprise. 'Rubbish,' he said. 'Peel. My orange peel.'

I decided there was no need to mention the unlocked door: Pendleberry was unlikely to forget a second time.

We made such good progress along the road that five miles short of Pol-i-Khumri we stumbled across McScumble still active with a dozen or so of the Project de-miners working on arable land adjacent to the highway.

'Keep back!' warned McScumble, hard at it and by way of greeting. 'We'll just detonate this fallen stick mine which they've located and that will be it for the day. Usual drill,' he added, looking towards Pendleberry. 'We've placed a small charge of plastic explosive alongside the offending POMZ, inserted one detonator and attached a length of fuze. Basic, nothing complicated. Just add in the box of matches – safety, of course.'

McScumble paused, deadpan, and looked in my direction before running on.

'There we go – whoosh! Doesn't look much from here but it's surprising how things fly around, so it's best to keep well clear – 50 metres, that's what I always allow. At least that, just to be on the safe side.'

As the smoke drifts lazily and the dust slowly subsides, McScumble waits before continuing. 'What we really need' (and here he looks at me again) 'for this type of work are a few flame-throwers to burn off the scrub to give us easier access to the land, rather than cutting by hand which is very slow and can be dangerous. It's bad enough without that. And of course, all this vegetation makes it harder to spot trip wires, even though we use the TWF – the thingummy-jig – the extending feelers.

'As you know, any contacts we see or feel, or detect with the Vallons are normally probed and investigated using a bayonet or knife. But here's something of interest. The de-miners are taught to go in from the side, carefully, obviously, to avoid activating the top of the mine, if that's what the contact is. That's the theory. Earlier today we came across a mine that had been deliberately laid on its side with the intention of obstructing the clearance operation and fooling the de-miner. Well, blowing him up, actually. As it happened, we were fortunate on this occasion, but it's one more thing to worry about.

'The secret is not to accept anything we find at face value. Goes for a lot of things, I suppose. There are many kinds of combinations, tricks and traps. You can put a primed grenade under a mine, stick one anti-tank mine on top of another, ATM on ATM, that is. Or APM, anti-personnel mine, over ATM; or APM on APM if you like. All designed and intended to catch the other side on the hop, keep them guessing. So we don't try and lift mines, as a rule. Just blow them where we find them. It makes for a quieter life. Fortunately most of the mines we encounter here are a bit dated. What will happen when the new crushable fuzes become commonplace is anyone's guess. They activate via a chemical reaction rather than with a metal firing pin. Put that in a plastic case, and our detectors won't be much help. That'll be my time to retire.

'Anyway, we've finished here now. One more happy farmer. Or rather, another fortunate family. They're the ones who suffer most. There's a recent case quoted about one returning family where by nightfall of their first day home the mother had lost a leg and of the children, who went down to the river to get water, one was dead and two had lost hands. And my guess is that's probably not unique. So we need to keep going. We've done pretty well so far this season, and tomorrow we'll try and start at a new area, beyond

Baghlan. It's sort of on your way to Mazar-i-Sharif, so you can come along in the morning, if you want.'

****

Supper was served early at the Project base; the de-miners had worked a long day.

No Scrabble or Monopoly after the food. Just the folkloric re-enactment – for the especial benefit and enjoyment of the visitors (particularly eager Pendleberry, the new recruit) – of the hilarious day the Project staff in Kabul nearly got themselves blown up by a Sakar rocket, and the Head of Mission showed that he could run faster by far than any of his colleagues. Except, that was, for O'Deere the demolisher.

Fleet of foot O'Deere had become renowned for having filled his rucksack with handy keep-fit rocks, donning his jogging shorts and embarking on a cross-country training run on his first visit to Pol-i-Khumri. Only to be playfully sniped at by gunmen unknown when he was halfway across the mountains. After the fifth or sixth warning shot he accepted that he might do best to abandon his plans and return home.

Which he did, wide-eyed, lips pursed, shaking his head in perplexity at the injustices of life.

****

At 0630 the following morning we were ready to move, braving the 'tearful glimmer of the languid dawn'. But McScumble was pre-occupied; no poetic connotations for him. There were rumours of fighting up ahead.

Sure enough, five miles out of town we came across a tank parked beneath the trees at the roadside, half hidden under the dozen or so Mujahideen decorating its upper-works. The black-bearded combatants looked at us with curiosity. Their interest was not unfriendly, merely more inclined to indifference and not sufficient to cause any movement in the ranks, hirsute and lugubrious. Each to his own, was the general concensus; if we wanted to fiddle around clearing old mines, well that was odd but it was OK by them. So long as we didn't interfere with the ones they were using. That wasn't on, no way.

Halfway through the conversation between the leader of our mine clearance group and the tank commander, a shell seared across the sky above us. It was a memorable noise, like the tearing of cartridge paper except that, in the circumstances, it had that extra edge and something of a snap to it.

Less than a year later that sound came back to me, albeit on a reduced scale. At the time I was standing on the Maslenica Bridge enjoying a cup of tea en route to Dubrovnik when a gunman, Serbian or Croat, it mattered not, decided it was time we moved along. My colleague of the day, Krumpir by name, fell to the tarmac as though poleaxed. I thought he'd gone for good, only to realize that being an ex-Royal Marine, he'd been quicker on the uptake and his concern was for the safety of his silver thermos of sweet Darjeeling. Two further shots followed, cracking close behind; gathering up the thermos, scarper we did. On occasions it helps to be able to identify the origin and source of such sounds; and, more importantly, the implications.

As it was, and as another shell passed by on its rasping way to some distant destination, it was clear that we should go no further. I would take an alternative road with Zahir to complete our northern reconnaissance, and McScumble would transfer his attention to other pastures. There was no shortage of those. The tranquil fruit bats perched on the tank casing watched dispassionately and unconcernedly as we turned the vehicles and made to reverse our tracks. They were almost motionless, placid even, only the occasional shift of an RPG from one shoulder to the other betraying an aching joint, or the change of hands holding a Kalashnikov indicating an easing of the onset of pins and needles. In the serenity of that moment it occurred to me that for those whom fighting is a way of life, there is no urgency about such things, no imperative to rush into combat. That way lies the way of death.

Just as we were pulling away I wound down the window on impulse and leaned out. '*Zenda bashi*!' I called to the soldiers with a wave. 'May you live! Good luck, chaps! Bye, bye!'

There was a moment of hesitation before the bats stirred. A ripple ran round the assembled AK-47s, a frisson passed through the clustered Mujahideen. Teeth flashed smilingly, and the warriors waved as one.

'*Manda nabashi*!' they called in reply. 'May you not be tired! Biyee, biyee!'

I looked at Zahir.

'Bingo!' I breathed.

'Bingo?'

His eyes rolled as he let in the clutch.

****

Northern escape routes, investigation thereof: that was the task in hand.

Not too difficult, really, providing that the escapees could get away from Kabul and over the intervening mountains. If General Dostum (warlord in these parts) was amenable, then a flight to safety from Mazar-i-Sharif was the most expeditious way to go, if not the most exciting. More interesting by far would be to equip oneself with a fistful of visas and (ignoring the twice-weekly Aeroflot service to London) to press on through the forsaken towns of Hairaton and Termez on the banks of the River Oxus, the boundary with Uzbekistan. From there the way was open northwards to the legendary splendours of Samarkand and thence westward to the ancient citadel of Bokhara, heavy with history and intrigue. Or we could head north north-eastwards to the walled city of Tashkent, and from there point due east to investigate the delights of Osh before traversing Kyrgyzstan to skate on the world's finest ice at Almaty (the "Father of Apples"), in Kazakhstan, "Motherland of Tulips".

The possibilities – both escapist and touristic – were many, although the civil war in Tajikistan made Dushanbe, a mere 200 kilometres to the north east, a more dubious proposition and, judging by the extensive refugee camps in northern Afghanistan, the general flow of humanity lay perversely in the opposite direction. In fact, from a population of five million, it was assessed that one million had become refugees as a result of the fighting. Theoretically, the end of the civil war coincided with the timing of our reconnaissance – April 1993. Yet, said a contemporary report: 'Fighting goes on in the mountains. To quell this tendency, all opposition parties have been declared illegal.'

That's the way – simple.

There was no cause for excessive conjecture or micro-planning – it would be sufficient to formulate a broad contingency plan for evacuation, changing it as necessary on the day. The Controller would approve of that.

Duty done, we returned to Mazar for long enough to liaise with the panoply of humanitarian agencies conglomerated in the city, including the Red Cross prosthesis centre, planning ahead on behalf of newly one-legged Said Abdul Salem. In one instance, as a result of a navigational misunderstanding, we were 25 minutes late for our scheduled appointment. Whereupon, on our tardy arrival and while apologising profusely to the Country Director of the organisation (a suave official of long experience), we were disarmingly referred to the clock on the office wall. There, with the utmost courtesy and sub-continental consideration (and by deft sleight of hand), the timepiece declared that our arrival was punctual to the very minute.

The conversational carousel completed, we finished by prudently determining the whereabouts of various visa-awarding Consulates, possibly to come in handy at a later date, as yet unspecified.

As a reward for these taxing endeavours on behalf of the Project, our final act before leaving Mazar-i-Sharif was to visit the city's magnificent mosque, topped with shining domes of gold and blue, a shrine to the warrior son-in-law of the Prophet. After being mortally wounded in battle (or murdered, depending on source) in the year 661 in distant Kufa (once the capital of the Muslim world) on the western bank of the Euphrates (south of Baghdad and close to Najaf), the remains of Caliph Ali were recovered and transported far away from ancient Mesopotamia, to be buried in a secret grave, hidden from the knowledge of his ill-intentioned enemies. There are those who believe that Mazar-i-Sharif ('the tomb of the exalted') was the final chosen burial site, hence the origin of the grandeur of the Caliph Ali Shrine and Mosque.

Before sunrise the following day we were gone, Zahir and me homeward bound in the faithful Land Rover, antlike, hurtling heedlessly across the billowing plains that lay in our path, always with the seemingly inevitable Afghan backdrop of snow-covered mountains. Timeless, observing, mockingly indifferent.

No traffic imperilled our progress; this was a land of Biblical, or rather, Koranic antiquity, untainted and untroubled by so-called progress and civilisation, those two-edged swords. The diary of the day records that we 'encountered donkeys laden with vast burdens of brushwood, flocks of sheep and herds of goats tended by shepherd boys, straggling lines of colourfully clothed nomads, *kootchihah,* their camels weighted down with cumbersome loads, projecting tent poles and possessions'.

Our rolling road intersected fields of vivid green stretching out to velvet hills beyond, cut through with the dramatic silver threads of stream-filled gorges. Young leaves were sprouting on the trees, white and purple with spring blossom. This was the Afghanistan of thirty, forty, fifty years before, the Kingdom of Afghanistan, untouched by civil war, blessed with 'the great immutable rural peace' with 'green todays flowing into green tomorrows'.

Homeward we flew, swooping across the fields and the hills, the valleys and the plains, our wheels humming busily along the road, not pausing in Pol-i-Khumri on account of the uncertainties and delays that might lie ahead.

As it was, the roadblock that had almost occasioned the loss of Pendleberry's treasured shades was unmanned, the aggressors having dispersed with their loot after a few days of earnest plundering. This time it was the turn of the Salang Pass to impede our passage.

Again, the diary tells the tale: 'Clear run almost to the tunnel, weather fair. Conditions worsened progressively as we climbed, finally meeting with driving snow.' Zahir leapt to the fore with the wheel chains, fingers frozen, braving the vicious wind – Kipling's wind, that biting wind 'as thin as a whip-lash what carries away to the plains'. 'Road conditions rough,' say the dairy, 'but no major delays until the downward descent through the galleries was nearly completed.'

On emerging into the daylight we saw that a major fresh avalanche had occurred, sweeping at least three or four container trucks several hundred feet down the mountainside. A single 'dozer battled to clear the way, powered by a thimbleful of fuel preserved for just such an emergency as this.

It took three and a half hours to create the beginnings of a single track through the morass. Incongruously, I read Silas Marner (on loan from O'Deere), resumed the travelling diet of oranges and biscuits, the *malta* and the *kolcha*, and slept intermittently. Zahir checked our chains, blew incessantly into his hands, and prowled around and conversed with his countrymen.

The first bus to attempt the newly dug passage to freedom skidded violently this way and that, and then got wedged solid, to be towed out backwards, ignominiously humiliated. By common consent it was our turn and I took the wheel, selecting the lowest of low 4WD. We followed the grader through and were gone, like a cork out a bottle. Descending from the mountains, the snow turned to heavy rain, the road muddy and flooded.

The roadblocks were many and tedious that evening, the way was grey and wet. It was dusk when we entered the city, the cloak of darkness descending heavily and literally over the deserted streets and thoroughfares – a metropolis devoid of lighting, without electricity, bereft of fuel. A darkened city of uncertainty, where its very soul was under siege. The rain had set in for the night; Kabul in the rain has little to offer.

On arrival at the villa I discovered that during the day, in spite of the weather, Hajji had passed his time by taking the bus out to the neighbouring vineyards, where he had gathered a bunch of 'Persian tulips'. On his return he had carefully arranged the flowers – the pastel-shaded *la la* – in one of the liqueur tumblers and placed them in the centre of the sitting room, where, delicately coloured, fragile and graceful, they greeted me.

Dr Rhubar had also been active. He had left a note under the flowers. 'Butter delivered, half a pound (unsalted). No luck with ex-presidential videos.'

****

'If you want,' suggested O'Deere from the unfathomable depths of his armchair on the far side of the *bukhari*, 'I can go with you to Jebel Seraj tomorrow and you can deliver that bathroom stuff Walduck wanted. The other day I noticed a stack of old rockets left at the roadside just past Charikar. I can dispose of them on the way, if no one's using them.'

And as the hurricane lamp flickered he widened his eyes at the prospect, forever eager, itching to wire up and light the fuze.

Fly-tipping, I thought gloomily, a universal social malaise. Still, there was nothing I could do about it just at that moment, so the following morning Karrimullah trotted the avocado bidet, the matching basin and the rest of the bathroom suite round to the back of the Land Rover. Zahir was summoned from his tinkerings with the ill-tempered generator and reluctantly climbed in to the passenger's seat. Hajji did the honours with the big bolts, clang, clang. Abdul wisely lay low and kept out of sight after his recent reprieve from summary execution. I drove and off we went.

It was just a routine sortie, we would be back in good time for the meatballs. Unlikely to be any apple pie on the lunchtime menu, I reflected, but perhaps some *firni* might make an appearance on the tilting table, a conciliatory scoop of Afghan milk pudding.

Past the blown-up tank we went yet again; as we looked at it in silence I resolved that without fail I would go with Dr Rhubar that very afternoon to select a handsome headstone for the memorial. The best.

On past the neglected vineyards we drove, taking in the carpet of tulips flowering under the straggling tendrils, and the protruding POMZ mine with its hidden trip wire; and I pondered anew how Hajji had gathered armfuls of those pastel blooms and survived to tell the tale.

It was just a routine sortie.

****

Chapter XI

IN EXTREMIS

'When God calls, no man is indispensable.'

Anon.

As I drew up at the roadblock, O'Deere was dozing behind me. I don't know where Zahir's mind was but suddenly he stiffened, like a rabbit sensing danger.

Sure enough, standing there at the barrier was Walduck's woolly wildman, the *marde divanaa*, scourge of the Stetson. The madman's two cronies lounged amiably at the roadside with their rifles, disinterested spectators awaiting developments.

The pistol that whipped through my half-open window caught me unawares. Yet there it was, the barrel pressing hard and cold against my temple, so that, involuntarily and lopsidedly, my head tipped towards the passenger's side. There was no gainsaying that our fortunes had taken a precipitate and significant downward turn. And mine in particular.

At my elbow, Zahir was plainly unhappy with events; behind me, O'Deere was no longer dozing. In fact, his mathematical, methodical mind had moved into overdrive and he was busily engaged on calculating the executioner's arcs of fire, working out how many nano-seconds he might have at his disposal after the firing of the first shot in which to wrest the weapon from the grasp of the assassin, and to break his arm and smash his face at the same time.

For myself, I was troubled by just one minor technical difficulty in connection with my memorial service, or rather, the thanksgiving service, as it would euphemistically be termed. Not, of course, that I would wish for anyone to be saddened or inconvenienced by the occasion. The music was fine, I'd got that nicely organised already. It was all listed under the blotter on my desk in the Hampshire farmhouse: Elgar's 'Nimrod' and 'Land of Hope and Glory', naturally; 'Jerusalem', clearly a sine qua non; a touch of trumpeting, elevating brass, Jeremiah Clarke or Purcell, soaring to the rafters; beefy hymns

– 'Thine be the Glory', 'Eternal Father Strong to Save', hymn 540, I knew that off pat; that scintillating trio, 'Trombones to the Fore'; at least two or three Captain Ricketts (alias Kenneth J. Alford) military marches – 'The Standard of St George', 'The Gladiator', 'Army of the Nile' – all that sort of thing. Same again and more by rhythmical Mr J.P. So of the US of A: 'Liberty Bell'; 'El Capitan'; 'The Thunderer'; 'King Cotton'.

That should pack them in and set the feet tapping, no difficulties there, none whatsoever. If you want to fill the church, be sure to die tragically early. That, or very late, so the mourners may imbibe your longevity. No half measures. Oh yes, and reverting to the musical menu, why not 'The Voice of the Guns' to polish things off? Abdul might go for that – assuming he pitched up. But leaving room, naturally, for the resounding Toccata from the familiar Symphony No.5 to be played as a sort of voluntary extroit with all the stops out. And, come to think of it, why not a slice of Gounod's Judex whilst we were at it? No point in having all those talented musicians hanging around doing nothing. I would leave it to the organisers to fit that in.

Of course, the process of assembling a brass band of appropriate size and qualifications, plus the additional accommodation of an entire formally attired concert orchestra and attendant soloists in the chosen chapel might make for one or two logistical and administrative problems, but then again, it was the unwritten duty of the deceased to tease the bounden executors with the odd challenge from the after-life.

It was the eulogy that gave the real cause for concern (not that the musical programme would leave much time for oratory, which was a blessing, undisguised). They would say (as they usually did): 'He died doing what he always wanted to do: helping others'. Except it wouldn't be true. Not at all. In fact, the plain truth was that at this particular moment I was simply absent-mindedly delivering an avocado bidet, five months after Walduck had asked for it (and three months after he had left). And not even the nostalgia of a melodious rendering of Ketelby's 'Bells Across the Meadows' as the recessional would be sufficient to rectify the grave misrepresentation. Indubitably – and this was the problem – this ignominious incident would surely become known as 'the sad case of the late avocado bidet' …

I looked again at the two indifferent Mujahideen sprawled untidily at the wayside. My thoughts went back to the global problems of litter and fly-tipping. The *marde divanaa* gave the barrel against my temple an encouraging jerk to attract my attention.

'What's the form here?' I asked O'Deere, catching his eye in the rear-view mirror, he being the expert in such matters.

He returned my gaze. 'Well,' he advised solemnly, 'that pistol is cocked, the safety catch is off, there's one up the spout, so to speak, and unless I am very much mistaken, there's about to be one down the drain.'

I knew I could have enquired the make of the weapon and the size of the bullets if I felt in need of further information. But I didn't.

'It's hard to say precisely what kind of pistol it is,' pondered O'Deere, squinting hard as he concentrated and now taking a close professional interest in proceedings, 'and I'm afraid I can't be quite sure of the exact calibre.'

As it happened and as I just said, it was not important, as those were the last things going through my mind. I noticed that the madman was following the conversation like a Centre Court fanatic, growing increasingly restless and agitated the longer the rally continued. O'Deere had picked up on this, too.

'Anyway,' he continued, a warning note entering his voice, 'I suggest you jump out sharpish. Otherwise, that bullet will be next thing – and the last thing – that goes through your mind.'

'Tell our friend,' I said to Zahir as I clambered out, 'that he can shoot me if he wants as I am quite old, but I'm sorry he can't have the vehicle because it is almost brand new. It's our best one.'

Zahir leapt down from the Land Rover saying no such thing, and I knew he had wisely decided it was better if on this occasion we spoke 'with the voice of silence'.

'*Chai tayar ast*?' I asked the two roadside drifters as the madman drove down the road in our best vehicle, complete with bidet, basin and the rest of the precious avocado bathroom suite clinking and chinking in the back. 'Is there any tea? Is the tea ready?'

The utter shame of it – losing one's transport. Before Christmas a Red Cross expatriate worker had arrived in Kabul and achieved the distinction of losing two Toyota pick-ups in a single week. Then she went back home in a state of shock for the festivities. The first time the hijackers dropped her off at a minibus stop; the second time around (showing commendable foresight and conscientious to a fault), she got a receipt for the cab. Donors always appreciate that kind of thing.

'*Hawa khub ast*,' I remarked to our new acquaintances, maintaining the feigned nonchalance as they passed round the steaming mugs. 'Nice weather we're having.' It was quite incorrect: it looked like rain again, even a storm brewing. Sometimes my Afghan Dari vocabulary had its limitations. Accordingly, in spite of a personal sense of disappointment, I got the Mujahideen to help me with the flash cards, writing my name with the dots in the wrong places so that, heads bent as one over the exercise book, June Loon and Co. could enjoy the fun of trying again and getting it right.

After half an hour of driving up and down in the Land Rover, screeching the brakes to attract our attention, Walduck's woolly wildman got fed up with being ignored. Disgruntled, he parked – clunk! on with the handbrake – strutted about a bit, undecided, and then came over to join us for a cup of tea and to help with the spelling of June Khoon as it had become, and the dodgy dots. Erratic mood swings, attention deficit disorder, passing whims (such as a desire to blow someone's brains out) – occupational stress – that was my layman's diagnosis.

And in no time at all, it was time to go. How time flies! Zahir needed no prompting, no second bidding as I mouthed the injunction in his direction. I could see he was well up on this episodic psychotic pendulum syndrome. We swallowed our tea whilst the going was good, shook hands effusively as though there was no tomorrow, and – as one – the Muj warmly wished us all the best.

'*Boro bakhair*' they said. 'Go well!'

We would; we did. We drove up to Jebel Seraj and left the stuff for the plumber (miraculously it hadn't cracked) and then we went home.

So in the end everything passed off pleasantly enough, although O'Deere thought it was strange the way things had turned out, as he had been convinced I was a write-off. Anyway, he said, not to worry, as he could deal with those old rockets another time.

When we got back to Lucky Five Street, we found that Abdul had made a milk pudding. Perfect validation of the Project house style. 'Rejoice with they that rejoice!' Although when Hajji learnt of the happening he gave an admonitory, finger-wagging shake of his head, oblivious to Karrimullah standing behind him, alternately grinning from ear to ear and chuckling cheerfully. Near miss, no harm done. Enjoy! 'Weep not with those who weep.'

****

That afternoon, after lunch, I went with Dr Rhubar to the stonemason's yard. It was quite close to where we lived, no more procrastination.

There we found a really solid piece of stone, a fine memorial tablet, in everlasting granite. Then we gave the monumental mason the piece of paper on which Rhubar had written the date of the accident – that day last summer when the tank blew up – and the names of the three men who had been inside. Rhubar's piece of paper was in Arabic, and I had written the same in English underneath, in block capitals so there would be no mistakes.

The mason said he would set to with his chisel that same afternoon to cut the inscription, which was good. Then we said goodbye and went home for tea.

When we arrived back at the villa, of Hajji and Abdul there was no trace. Instead, we discovered O'Deere and Karrimullah active on the lawn.

Much more of this kind of thing, I frowned to myself, and that turf will be permanently damaged. Especially after the recent rain. Heedless to the horticultural aspects, O'Deere looked up and beamed contentedly. He gestured at the large metal canister placed in the centre of the grass and which Karimullah was attacking feverishly with a hacksaw. It looked like a bomb.

'The Big One,' smiled O'Deere happily, as though the scene was totally normal and self-explanatory.

'Right,' I said, playing my allotted role. 'So I see.'

'My friend will be pleased with this.'

'Right,' I said, repeating myself. Just a verbal tic. 'I should think so too.'

'We could hardly get it into the back of the Land Rover. It's huge.'

Karrimullah paused from his work to glance in my direction and nod in confirmation. Huge. Heavy, too.

'Yes, I can see that,' I said.

'That's why we're cutting it in two; it'll be more manageable. Fortunately it fell in soft sand. So it's unexploded.'

'Yes, I can see that,' I said. Tic. 'Or rather, I assumed that might be the case.'

At least, it hadn't gone off yet, that much was reasonably clear.

'Er, um ...' I offered. 'Do you need a hand?'

'No, thanks. Everything seems to be bang on track. You're familiar with the principle, I imagine?' O'Deere couldn't wait to enlighten me. 'Fuel/air bomb, that's the trade term. Technically advanced, state of the art. Explosion, implosion – Wham! Bam!' O'Deere clapped his hands as an improvised audio-visual aid. 'Double value, the size of a football pitch blown away. Totally obliterated.'

Tautology. I would have to speak to O'Deere about that.

Karrimullah again nodded enthusiastically, this time without ceasing with his irresponsible saw. I considered going off for a spin on Abdul's bicycle, probably to check things out on the far side of town. RHIP – Rank hath its privileges. Conversely, IAHIO – It also has its obligations.

'Right,' said I. Tic, tic. 'In that case, I had better attend to some urgent paperwork.'

So saying, I went to the top shelf, far right of the book case, and taking long neglected Lady Sale in hand, went to the terrace where we settled comfortably into my favourite chair.

I looked down on the busy scene of work in progress and then sized up the strip of endangered lawn, complete with the bordering lavender. All told, far from being the size of a football pitch, I would say it was about a quarter of the size of the penalty box. At most.

Whilst reflecting on this I was reminded that I still hadn't pruned the roses. On the other hand, it seemed possible that Karrimullah and O'Deere were on the point of saving me the trouble.

****

Chapter XII

IN THE LINE OF DUTY

'Life is a voyage
The winds of life blow strong from every point
But each will speed thy way along
If thou with steady hand while tempests blow
Will set thy course aright and never once let go.'

Anon.

I was busy oiling the Imperial typewriter and adjusting the tension of the elastic on the carriage return mechanism (always a fiddly business) when O'Deere came into the office.

'Doing anything special today?' he enquired, clearly with something alternative to offer.

Without looking up from my delicate task, I nodded in affirmation, suspecting a booby trap, like a PMN mine laid sideways or one of those inverted MS3s, activated when the pressure is released.

'Ping pong,' I explained. 'It's the final of the inaugural International Series. Me and Rhubar, Great Britain versus Afghanistan. Want to come along? I could probably get you a ticket.'

'I was hoping we could contact my contact ...'

Obediently, I carefully replaced the little red top on the plastic spout of the 3-In-One oil tin, gave the carriage elastic a perfunctory final friendly tweak out of habit and off we went to a place possessed of the necessary technology to make a call to O'Deere's friend.

'We're very interested,' said the distant voice over the secure line. 'We can fly a C130 Hercules transporter up, if you like. Or a helicopter, perhaps?'

'No,' said O'Deere, flatly. 'Perhaps you don't quite appreciate how things are here. *We* will have to make the delivery.'

O'Deere passed the microphone to me. 'Best if you speak to him,' he murmured behind his hand.

'Obviously your friend doesn't understand the terrain,' I whispered. 'Anyway, what's his name?' I asked, long years of naval indoctrination making me averse to conducting an anonymous conversation.

O'Deere put a name to the vibrating voice, now murmuring so sotto, sotto voce that I could scarcely hear.

'Hello, Pillock,' I said loudly and affably, switching the mike back to transmit.

Silence. I turned the other ear to the receiver and tried again.

'Are you there, Mr Pillock? Hornblower calling. I'll be passing your way next Saturday, so if you like, I could drop in then. It will be a sort of out-of-hours, extra-mural activity, but I will do it. Over.'

'That's uncommonly kind,' O'Deere's friend replied after an uncommonly long pause.

'Not at all,' was my genial response. 'We need to buy a couple of new bicycles, as it happens. One for me and one for Abdul, the cook. He works in our Project office. De-mining.'

'That's awfully decent of you,' I heard Pillock say. 'Are you quite sure?'

'Oh, yes, certain,' said I. 'He can be a touch temperamental, and his repertoire is a bit limited, but he's not a bad chap, really. But you should *see* his bike! It's absolutely knackered, so I decided it was the least I could do, and then I thought whilst I was at it, why not get two? We'll ditch the old one.'

'Right,' responded Pillock, rather impatiently, I sensed. 'So, how much do you want?'

'Oh, nothing at all. As I said, you need to see it first, it's just scrap iron really.'

'No, forget the bikes. How much do you want for the delivery?'

I hadn't thought of that. COD – cash on delivery – wasn't part of the plan. I was just helping out, in a manner of speaking, as I happened to be passing by anyway. I looked at O'Deere quizzically. He pursed his lips, widened his eyes and shrugged. He was technical; finance was supposed to be my side. Demarcation. I gazed absently at the microphone in my hand, mouth opened wide. Whereupon the curiously cross-connected relays of my mind produced an image of my dentist, albeit hazy (as I hadn't been able to afford him for so long).

'Ten thousand pounds,' I quipped glibly. 'Over.'

The receiver gave an electronic gulp. 'How do you work that out?' it demanded to know.

'Easy,' I replied, ready for that and light on my toes. 'That will serve as a down payment for the annual check – tap, tap, tap, here a bit, there a bit – followed by three dental implants, with X-rays, a few random extractions, some equally casual cosmetic fillings, the usual whitening rip-off, a soupçon of root canal chat, and a couple of serious sessions scraping away with the hearty hygienist. Or put it another way, five audiences with the Consultant Endocrinologist, private rates, punctuated by alternating, eye-watering Colonoscopys and Sigmoidoscopys, without follow-up histiology. Or even – if there's any loose change – an audiogram to establish the degree of conductive and sensorineural hearing loss suffered as the result of a ruptured eardrum on account of being in the wrong place at the prime time of an explosion.'

There was a long pause, just the spooky crackling hiss of the uninhabited ether.

'Are you still there, Pillock?' I enquired, thinking perhaps he might be a bit deaf.

'We don't have that kind of money,' declared O'Deere's friend.

'Oh yes you do,' I countered, already feeling the readies slipping through my fingers.

'Oh no we … NO!' said the other end, putting a halt to the pantomime.

'OK, Pillock,' I soothed, signing-off genially and without rancour. 'Right-ho. Well, I'll drop by on Saturday anyway.' I bid him bye, bye and flicked the switch.

O'Deere gazed at me thoughtfully. I shrugged resignedly and returned his gaze. What else could one do?

'I'm sorry if you misheard …' he began, as though not sure how to continue. 'His name is Philduck.'

****

The necessary preparations for the journey were made.

This would be my sixth transit of the Khyber Pass in as many months. Not to mention the equally historic Kabul Gorge, passing through Sarobi and all the other checkpoint hot-spots, thence to the road beyond Jalalabad and onwards to the border crossing at Torkham, fraught with uncertainty. And if I chanced to come back, then that would be the seventh such safari. I felt as though I was beginning to live in the TDI. Soon I would be eating all my meals in the cramped Land Rover, and we all knew what had happened to Walduck.

At the last moment, a locally based expatriate journalist (Hooper – he said he was a stringer, but I didn't want to get into that) asked for a lift. Seeing my momentary hesitation, he offered to travel on the roof. Curious, that.

'No, no,' I assured him, 'that won't be necessary, even for a stringer. Unless you have a Kalashnikov and special shoes, and anyway, it's not very strong.'

'What's with the big box?' Hooper asked, professionally inquisitive. 'Looks like groceries!'

I was trying to forget the big box. Next he would be asking me if I had packed it myself. Could anyone else have slipped in anything untoward? Yes, definitely – the whole caboodle was untoward, and quite a lot seemed to have been slipped in there. How did I know what O'Deere had put in the monster carton?

'Oh, you know,' I said. 'Just bits and bobs.'

Just one letter short of complete accuracy. After that Hooper the stringer subsided and we had a quiet run to the border. Except for the big box, which bounced around a bit as I hurtled down the road. It struck me that if anything, well, untoward occurred, it wouldn't just be a case of the back door being blown off. No letters of complaint to the makers in that eventuality; 'vaporised' was the word that came to mind. And if the trainees emerged from the terror camps for a spot of RPG practice, they would surely get the most devastatingly enormous surprise of their lives (and serve them jolly well right, too – express delivery of four-and-twenty virgins notwithstanding).

But as it was, the journey was a placid affair and we bombed along without incident.

I had been reading up about the Second Afghan War: remarkably and even depressingly similar in several aspects to the First. On the other hand, there were some equally notable differences, without exception occasioned by the redoubtable and robust approach of the outstanding British commander, the remarkable Major-General Frederick Roberts (already holder of the VC, won in 1857 during the Indian Mutiny, and whose son was also to win the same decoration posthumously in 1899 during the Nile Expedition).

The prelude to the conflict, which started in November 1878 (just 36 years after the conclusion of the First Afghan War), was the formulation of a grand strategy for a combined Russian and Afghan force to invade – and conquer – British India. The intention was to take advantage of diversionary events in Eastern Europe, where the Russians were on the point of capturing Constantinople, thereby provoking war with Great Britain. In the event, the European crisis was resolved and the Russian adventure through the Khyber Pass was hastily abandoned.

However, evidence of the intent to attack was more than sufficient cue for a British force to march on Kabul. The campaign objectives were uncomplicated: to put the Afghans in their place and to serve as an unequivocal territorial marker to the meddlesome Russians. Initially, events proceeded along familiar lines. A three-pronged invasion was initiated: Lieutenant-General Stewart moved through the Bolan Pass to Quetta, and thence onwards to consolidate Kandahar; Lieutenant-General Browne's troops marched from Peshawar to take first the Khyber Pass and then Jalalabad; Major-General Roberts advanced up the Kurram Valley, thereby giving access to central Afghanistan. Whereupon, winter set in.

In February 1879 Sher Ali, the offending Emir of Afghanistan, died (he having lost the will to live when faced with the realisation of the overwhelming superiority of the invading force, 'thrown off the dress of existence and relinquished the robe of life'). Thereafter his son, Yakub Khan, lost no time in acknowledging the inevitability of defeat and swiftly accepted a peace treaty. It so happened that this was signed at the village of Gandamak, site of the slaughter of the surviving remnants of General Elphinstone's army 37 years previously. Amongst the terms of the Treaty of Gandamak of 26th May 1879 – which included ceding control of the Khyber Pass to the British – was the re-establishment of a British Residency in Kabul.

Accordingly, in July 1879, Sir Louis Cavagnari, following in the footsteps of Sir Alexander Burnes (murdered in November 1841) and Sir William Macnaghten (murdered in December 1841) proceeded to take post as British Envoy. He was accompanied by a minimal escort of 50 infantry and 25 cavalry. On the 2nd September 1879, from the confines of Bala Hissar, the newly installed British Resident reported from Kabul: 'All well'.

On 5th September the small British contingent was butchered and the head of Sir Louis Cavagnari was paraded through the city.

The punitive force despatched by the Viceroy of India moved exceptionally quickly, in spite of the fact that the three British occupying columns were either in process or on the point of withdrawing from Afghanistan. General Roberts (newly elevated to Lieutenant-General Sir Frederick Roberts and stationed in Simla at the time) rejoined his men in the Kurram and arrived in Kabul in early October. Shortly afterwards, and with equal expedition, 100 of the Afghan mutineers hung dangling from gallows that had been erected 'facing the scene of their infamy'.

As surely as winter succeeds autumn and night follows day, the upshot of this drastic retribution was equally violent and predictable.

My historical recollections were interrupted by our arrival at the Torkham border crossing. We took our place in the short line of vehicles edging forward towards the waiting officials and armed guards. I was uneasy about the grocery box.

'Can you tell them I am ill?' groaned Hooper the stringer unexpectedly, rolling over on the back seat unconvincingly. 'I haven't got a passport. I forgot to tell you.'

I forgot my manners. 'Why not get out, Hooper, and tell them yourself,' I ordered, heedless to the probability of getting a bad press. My erstwhile guest the stringer got out. Followed by Zahir.

'I just need to change some Afs for rupees,' he explained, and disappeared on his untimely errand before I could protest. I disentangled the vehicle from the queue and parked myself invisibly at the side of the bustling bazaar. The border guards and police strolled past in pairs at intervals, looking in at me and the groceries with idle curiosity.

Eventually Zahir the zephyr returned.

'Just a little bit of shoppings for the family,' he told me, smiling disarmingly and rustling the plastic bag of trifles and knick-knacks in his hand bashfully.

We were on our way even before he had closed his door, and Zahir will never know how close he came to forfeiting for a second time his strawberries and cream at the pink-painted Pearl-Continental Hotel.

****

I made the delivery to the man in Islamabad, O'Deere's friend. He took the box, bade me good day and showed me out.

Hardly was I back at the hotel when the telephone rang. It was the man.

'About the groceries …' he began.

'Well, not quite a Fortnum & Mason hamper,' I responded. 'Did you know they were established in 1707? That's 132 years before the First Afghan War.'

'No, seriously, we really are most awfully …' and he paused, rummaging for an apposite expression. 'Grateful!'

'Oh, think nothing … of it,' I assured him. 'Of course, with a Fortnum's basket you would get Royal Blend Tea and the usual tin of Sandringham Coffee. There's no jar of piccalilli either, I expect you noticed that.'

'I need to come and see you.'

Bull's eye.

'Of course. If you're passing, do drop in.'

'Give me five minutes; I'm on my way.'

The man arrived in four minutes.

'Er, do you know the contents?' he queried, seamlessly continuing the conversation directly from where we had left off.

'Naturally,' I confirmed. 'Normally they include Traditional English Mustard, Traditional Pickled Walnuts and the Butter Biscuit Selection, of course. Usually with Icy Mints, you know, with the bitter chocolate. I don't know about you, but they're my favourites.'

'No, no – do you know what's in the other grocery box? Our box?'

I hadn't the foggiest notion what O'Deere had put in there. Well, hardly. He was hands-on, I was hands-off. Demarcation.

'Our box? Certainly I do,' I declared stoutly. I put my tongue in the side of my cheek, narrowed my eyes and tapped my nose. The significance of the gesture was lost on me, but I related it to similar clandestine circumstances in thrillers when the hoods meet up at the Pig and Whistle hostelry to deliver the bullion and diamonds in a supermarket carrier bag in the outside unhygienic Gents behind the pub.

'What?' asked the man, seeking to put me on the spot.

But I was equal to the occasion.

'Goodies,' murmured I, giving a faintly perceptible lift of the head.

'Exactly,' murmured he, replicating my movement.

The man put his tongue in the side of his cheek, narrowed his eyes and tapped his nose.

Bingo!

'We'll be in touch,' he promised.

****

On the way home, whilst passing back through Peshawar I bought two bicycles for the Project office. Phoenix, they were called, made in China. They had little brushes on the wheels to remove the sand as you sped along and gaily coloured woollen bangles on the hubs for no particular reason other than for just being a decorative appurtenance.

Zahir looked at the shiny bicycles as we stuffed them into the rear of the Land Rover and he thought enviously of Abdul, although I could see he didn't want to say anything divisive. So I told him that when we got home to Kabul we could all share the new bikes.

The road to Jalalabad and back up the Gorge beyond was quiet for our return journey. For one thing, no other agencies were using the route since the assassinations of the UN people. There was no sign of the student terrorists; perhaps the training schools were on half-term.

As for the Second Afghan War, hostile reaction to the Bala Hissar hangings of the 100 ringleaders held responsible for the earlier murder of the British Political Agent (Sir Louis Cavagnari) culminated in a force of some 60,000 rebellious Afghan tribesmen advancing on the small British garrison in Kabul in late December 1879.

Once again the British, numbering a mere 6,500, were quartered outside the fortress of Bala Hissar – this time in the Sherpur cantonments ('the Aldershot of Kabul', the site of which was identifiable from the terrace of the Project villa) constructed not long previously by Sher Ali (who had since obeyed the 'call of the Great Summoner').

The impending confrontation was menacingly similar to that which faced the British invaders in December 1841. Except that, unlike General Elphinstone, the admirable General Roberts (himself the son of a General and later to become Field Marshal The Earl Roberts of Kandahar, Chief of the Imperial General Staff) had the measure of the situation. To the extent that when the hordes of tribesmen attacked in the small hours of 23rd December 1879 the British not only held them off, but by midday when the battle ended they had killed more than 3,000 Afghans for the loss of just five of their own men.

However, although the immediate threat had been more than satisfactorily dispersed, with the throne vacant (Yakub Khan having judiciously abdicated as Emir and moved to India) the British had reluctantly become de facto rulers of Afghanistan. Withdrawal was impossible without plunging the country further into anarchy – leaving the way clear once again for the renewal of Russian influence. This situation prevailed until mid-1880, when Abdur Rahman, the grandson of Dost Mohammed Khan and the nephew of Sher Ali returned from exile to fill the vacuum. Abdur Rahman was declared Emir on 22nd July, whereupon the British thankfully handed over control and prepared to leave.

But, needless to say, this being Afghanistan, the anticipated withdrawal did not run as smoothly as might have been hoped. Almost coincidental with the proclamation of Abdur Rahman as the new Emir, word came in from Kandahar of 'one of the worst defeats ever suffered by the British in Asia'. The then ruler of Herat, Ayub Khan (cousin of Abdur Rahman) had determined to evict the British from the country and to take the throne of Afghanistan for himself. Accordingly he had advanced on the British garrison at Kandahar with a force that grew to some 20,000 strong.

The local British commander, Brigadier-General George Burrows mistakenly set out to meet the attackers with 2,500 troops (having under-estimated the capability of the enemy) and early in July 1880, at the village of Maiwand, he suffered 'total defeat and dispersion', leaving 1,000 of his force dead on the field of battle. The British survivors retreated under cover of darkness and straggled back to Kandahar, 40 miles to the east. Having inflicted this shattering defeat on the British garrison (even though at the cost of 5,000 of his own men), Ayub Khan then laid siege to Kandahar as a prelude to completing the destruction of the isolated outpost.

It was at this juncture that formidable Lieutenant-General Roberts in Kabul was apprised of events. With a field force of 10,000 he covered the intervening distance of 280 miles to Kandahar in 20 days. On the day of his arrival at the scene of action, he immediately conducted a reconnaissance of the Afghan positions and the following day he attacked. By dusk the Afghans had lost 1,200 men and fled; British casualties were 40.

Thus the Second Afghan War drew to a close. With Abdur Rahman secure on the throne and the objectives of the campaign having been achieved, the way was clear for General Roberts to complete his withdrawal back to India in an orderly and prestigious manner. Nevertheless, it was not until 4th May 1881 that the last British troops were finally extricated from Afghanistan and the war officially over.

****

'Ah!' exclaimed O'Deere on my return to Lucky Five Street. 'There you are!'

Evidently surprised by my re-appearance, he pursed his lips and widened his eyes to authenticate the existence of the apparition before him.

'Yes,' I confirmed blandly. 'Here we are. All done. We got the new bicycles. Everything OK this end? All turning and burning in Jebel Seraj and in the north? I had another meeting with Mr Willow in Islamabad and was able to thank him personally for the funding.'

'You realise that if anything had gone wrong, you would have vanished? Never seen again.'

I stared at O'Deere in disbelief. He was not normally given to exaggeration. 'The Land Rover as well?'

'Yes, that too. Disappeared.'

'Gosh! I wish you had mentioned that earlier,' I admonished. 'I used the new TDI, the Turbo Diesel Injection. Our best vehicle. The Project has picked up well, but there are so many things still to be done.'

****

Chapter XIII

IN MEMORIAM

'For him in vain the envious seasons roll
Who bears eternal summer in his soul.'
Oliver Wendell Holmes

When we arrived, the memorial stone – the everlasting granite slab – was standing at the front of the yard awaiting collection, the stony face of the tablet freshly inscribed as instructed.

The names of the three dead men were recorded, followed by the date of the accident, first in English and then repeated in Afghan Dari with the Arabic script.

'Fatally injured on this road whilst clearing mines, 19th July 1992.'

That's what the inscription said. Nothing more.

The monumental mason, hammer and chisel in hand, hovered anxiously as we checked for errors. There were none, and Dr Rhubar gave him a reassuring smile of appreciation before making payment, handing over a bundle of notes.

I wondered if we shouldn't have been more ambitious with the inscription. Perhaps we should have added a simple text.

For example: *'Cause of Death – Helping Others'*.

Or perhaps we might have gone for a longer epitaph, something like those words that read:

'To try is to risk failure
To believe is to risk despair
But risks must be taken
The greatest hazard in life is to risk nothing
For those who risk nothing
Do nothing, have nothing, are nothing
Only those who risk are free
To live is to risk dying'

Our dead colleagues would have identified with that. Before his death one of them had written: 'I have always advocated a bit of a gamble. One can't argue if the gamble is lost.'

But Rhubar said no: the more we wrote on the memorial, the greater the chance of it being desecrated, used for target practice and demolished. As it was, we would have to get permission from the Mullah in the adjacent village before we erected the stone. The selfsame Mullah who had been implicated in laying the booby trap in the first place.

Karrimullah picked up our chosen piece of stone and heaved it into the back of the Land Rover. The suspension sagged ominously and the rear axle creaked complainingly. Nevertheless, I decided against writing another letter; there was no demand for transporting this kind of load in suburbia.

The conscientious mason, dusty leather apron flapping against his legs, made his way back to the little house at the far end of the yard. He stood there in the doorway to watch us out of sight, accompanied by his two bright-eyed, bright-cheeked, tousled-haired children, holding hands, one on each side.

In a day or two we would take a bag of cement and a couple of shovels and all drive out to the village of Kariz-i-Mir. There, under the baleful gaze of the blown-up tank, we would gather sufficient rocks and build the monument to the dead de-miners, our erstwhile companions and predecessors.

One of the undertakings that had obliquely befallen the Project office was to determine the condition of the Christian cemetery in Kabul, and to initiate a programme of renovation, as necessary. To be followed, sanguinely, by establishment of a care and maintenance routine.

On investigation, we encountered a site of some two acres, protected by a perimeter wall two metres in height, entered by gates set in a gothic arch. Within, the grass was fresh and green, inter-laced with spring flowers.

Not a single tombstone or grave remained intact. Without exception they had been toppled and shattered. The shading trees had been cut and removed in the harsh winter months for firewood – cooking and heating; survival. A local resident, curious as to the purpose of our inspection, stated that the cemetery had been used as a command post during recent fighting in the city. Now it was used as the neighbourhood latrine. The diary entry for the day remembers that the cemetery was 'a sad and forlorn place'.

Most of the tombstone texts had been defaced and rendered illegible. But not all. Two in particular caught the eye. The first commemorated an English family of four, the parents aged 30 and 28 years; their little boy was aged four, the little girl was three years old. The inscription read simply: '*Motor accident on the Salang Pass, 30th June 1969*'.

The second stone commemorated the short lives of two Sheffield University students. One came from Lincolnshire, one from Worcestershire, the so-English names of their home counties sounding far, far distant in that Kabul graveyard.

'*Shot near Shajui*', said the cold stone, almost poetically. Just the three words to summarise the execution. He was 21 and she was 19. It had happened on 4th August 1971, hardly more than 20 years before, but it could have been the epitaph on any one of ten thousand unmarked British graves in Afghanistan over the previous 200 years: 'Shot in the Kabul Gorge', 'Murdered near Jalalabad'; 'Killed at Maiwand'; 'Butchered and beheaded in Kabul'; 'Blown-up at Kariz-i-Mir'.

As the first phase in our renovation work, it seemed that our new friend, the mason, might be able to assist with the repair of some of the headstones in the cemetery. But a few days later, when we went back to see him, his busy yard was a scene of desolation, his family house was a pile of rubble.

Shit.

'Sakar-ed,' observed Rhubar, staring unblinking at the devastation. 'Blown away,' he added quietly, by way of embroidering the epitaph.

Blown away, like his little laugh. Folly to get involved, naturally, but who will bury the undertaker? And who would do the honours for the monumental mason? And his wife? And the two raggedy-anne little girls that so, so recently had stood in the doorway and held his hands?

On the Thursday we went out to build the monument. Dr Rhubar, O'Deere, Zahir, Karrimullah, Hajji and me. Then Abdul said he wanted to come and squeezed himself in at the back and sat on top of the granite stone in his off-white cooking apron, alongside the shovels and the cement and the old bucket for the water. In the end we decided it would be easier to take two vehicles. We drove in silence. It was a fine spring day. There were tulips out amongst the mines in the vineyards.

At Kariz-i-Mir some of the farmers were working in the fields, their single-furrow wooden ploughs yoked between pairs of oxen. They posed stiffly for a photograph. Then the brightly dressed children came and stood to attention in an awkward row for their picture to be taken, hands loosely at their sides, uncertain whether or not to smile or be serious and ending up doubtfully in between. One of the older boys had a long musket that reached up to his shoulder.

We made a good job of building that monument. Everyone helped, collecting the rocks, bringing water from the stream, finding sand for the cement. Rhubar was in his Thursday suit and tie for the occasion, the cement dust blending with the mushroom colour of the cloth as he took his turn with the shovel. I don't know why, but I wore the grey sweater and the comfy camouflage green socks that had been left behind in the wardrobe in the villa. The old jumper and socks that wouldn't be needed anymore.

In the near distance sat the wrecked tank. The booby trap in the road had been laid so that the mine clearance flails mounted on the front had activated a small anti-personnel mine. In turn, that was wired back to detonate the huge explosive charge buried deep in the road and set directly under the tank, igniting the fuel reserves in a ball of fire and producing a glowing inferno. The three occupants had struggled out through the hatch to emerge from the smoke and flames, staggering several hundred yards down the track before collapsing at the main road. The will to survive.

The monument that we made that day was not so high as to invite unwanted attention; just sufficiently substantial to endure. Certainly bullet proof against casual pot-shots and even RPG resistant.

By the time it was finished to our satisfaction, it had gone midday. It was agreed that I would continue up the road to drop Karrimullah off at his village for the weekend (which, he said, was not so very far away, and I said that it was no trouble at all, thinking that at last I could see where he lived and even meet his family), whilst the others returned to the villa to pursue the business of the day. A formal act of remembrance for the departed, and dedication of our forenoon's work would await a date in the future, yet to be determined, when Trotter, McScumble and Pendleberry could also attend.

Karrimullah's village proved to be further than anticipated. The countryside was generally deserted and silent, omens of unease. Rumour had it that serious fighting would erupt in Kabul any day now. Talks were being held in Jalalabad. Mr Hekmatyar's Hezb-i-Islami fighters were already blockading roads to the East, West and South of the capital in confident anticipation of the breakdown of negotiations.

As for the two shots that were fired at the Land Rover as I drove Karrimullah to spend the holy day with his family, it was difficult to say precisely where they came from, or indeed how close the bullets had passed. Following the echoing crack of the unmistakeable reports, Karrimullah turned to me, expressionless, and I pressed on to fulfil my undertaking. In the event, just as the low roofs of his hamlet were coming into sight and as we rocked slowly along the approach track, he jumped down from the car, gave a shy little wave of thanks and farewell, turned, and was gone.

Oh well, perhaps next time.

Driving back alone, I gave the TDI full rein along the empty highway, the slipstream whistling and the cab swaying gently in the lullaby. When the gunman leapt into the centre of the road some one hundred yards ahead of me, I didn't even think of the brakes. I pressed the accelerator hard to the floor to give yet more power. As my assailant fired, my right hand maintained control of the steering wheel, my left hand moved up to my forehead, hand cupped outward to catch or deflect the bullet which assuredly was aimed to drill me neatly between the eyes. It was an involuntary gesture, as futile as the two-word oath that escaped my lips. It had no rhyme or reason to it, but that's what I did.

As it happened, the gunman aimed high. It is a known phenomenon, often observed during night encounters but also when the aimer is distracted, for example by a charging elephant, or by a Land Rover approaching at close on a hundred miles an hour. The man leapt for his life, just as I had jumped for mine. I looked into the rear-view mirror; he failed to re-appear, the road remained deserted. Rejoice.

On regaining the newly built monument, I stopped to admire our handiwork anew. The farmers were still ploughing, one furrow at a time. They wore a picturesque uniform of baggy white pyjamas with drab-brown loose fitting waistcoats. It was a peaceful scene.

'*In death there is life*'. Or was it: '*In life there is death*'?

Some distance behind the new memorial was the broken tank, inert and obstinate, going nowhere. It would take an eternity to rust to oblivion. Now I saw it as an integral element in the story, an unavoidable part of the backdrop.

At one side of our obelisk was a thin sapling, a young almond tree. The pink of the spring blossom was in gentle contrast with the white of the snow on the distant mountains as they reached upwards into the vivid blue of the sky. It was an idyllic spot. The soft wind from the hills flattened the grass in the fields and there was the sound of larks high overhead.

Idyllic, except that in the midst of life there is death. An idyllic spot in which to die.

'Fatally injured on this road, clearing mines'. Short of writing a book, we had placed the right words on the granite tablet in succinct tribute to those three brave men.

One of the dead had declared: 'Taking death too seriously is a mistake'. In turn, we could have said:

'Weep not for those whom the veil of the tomb,
In life's early morning, hath hid from our eyes.'

Or we could have had the mason score deep into the granite:

'Ask not how did they die?
But how did they live?
Not what did they gain?
But what did they give?'

Better to leave it as it was and to let the onlooker, the observer, the curious passer-by compose their own epitaph in memory of the three who had been fatally injured on this road, clearing mines.

****

Chapter XIV

IN THE END

'May the road rise to meet you
May the wind be always at your back
May the sun shine warm upon your face
The rains fall softly upon your fields
And until we meet again
May God hold you in the hollow of his hand.'

A Celtic Blessing

Letter from Afghanistan, May 1993: *'As I write this from the balcony overlooking the garden, Kabul is enjoying yet another balmy, early summer's evening. A light breeze sighs in the fir trees next door, where a pair of nesting doves bill and coo, to join the sound of bird song that fills the air, just as the gardens are soon to be filled with roses. Honeysuckle is out on the trellis arch and the profligate new growth on the grape vine is a vivid green. The fruits of the mulberry and this year's apricots are already setting. In the near distance rise the battlements of Sherpur Fort – or Shir-poor – 'Lion-son' Fort, silhouetted against the snow-covered mountains of the Hindu Kush and practically unchanged since it was last used by the British in 1879 during the Second Afghan War.*

Soon the bats will emerge in the warm twilight, the signal for Karrimullah to start the generator. For Kabul is without power. The hydro-electric station in the Kabul Gorge lies in Hezb-i-Islami territory and Gulbuddin Hekmatyar is blockading the city again. No electricity, no water; no food or fuel coming up through Jalalabad. The civil war has re-started after eight short weeks of phoney truce following the Islamabad Accord. On the first day of the fighting, the death toll was estimated to have been around 100, with 600 wounded. Those who get caught by high explosive and disintegrate, or those who get buried in the rubble, they don't even leave this world as a statistic. Uncounted in life, uncounted in death. We are now on the sixth day, so the toll will be at least 600 dead, with well over 3,000 injured.

Sometimes the conflict starts before dawn, around 0445. On other days the Wahdat, the Ittehad, Jamiat, Hezbi and Dostum's Uzbek fighters re-group, re-arm and wait until nine or ten, especially if they've had a late night of street fighting. The tanks and armoured personnel carriers – APCs – they race through Kabul at any moment. Keep well clear. The Jamiat tanks and artillery of Ahmad Shah Masood have taken up position in the Shar-i-Naw residential area (the familiar human shield principle) with the result that now we too get our quota of Hezbi rockets. Outgoing fire is marked by the firing detonation, then the searing sound of the shell as it tears away, followed by a distant boom or crump. Incomers are marked by a warning whistling which precedes the traumatic impact of the jarring explosion. They say that if the whistling gets louder and louder, don't be proud – hit the deck. And if there is no whistle and you fall down, that means things are getting really warm. The rocketing is random, no warning. They come in threes, fours or sixes – listen for the distant 'whoosh' of the launchers.

If you are driving and everyone is fleeing the other way, or if the street is deserted with just a few late scuttlers running hell bent doubled for cover, consider if your journey is really necessary. Or put your foot down. The street fighting is a problem. Strange too: an all-out battle in one quarter, people in the bazaar shopping in the sunshine just a mile or so away. On occasions it erupts all around you, the crackle of small-arms and RPGs whizzing past. Keep cool, drive steadily, hope for the best. At night you can sometimes hear outbreaks close by, heavy machine gun fire and the crack of the AK-47s. Trust in Allah and the sandbags; turn over and go back to sleep.

For the last few evenings the artillery have been bombarding the opposition on the mountain ridge to the west of us. If we have time and inclination, we pull up chairs and watch. Surreal. You can see the tanks on the skyline firing back, with huge clouds of dust when we score a good shot. While next door, through it all, our neighbour keeps mowing his lawn.

Today we were down at the hospital, re-positioning the sandbag fortifications and putting yet more tape on the windows against the bombs, shells and rockets. The Government are using jets to attack the Hezbi positions, but accuracy is not their strong suit. Consequently, it's the civilians who bear the brunt of the fighting as they huddle terrified in their little mud-brick houses. No ambulance service here; if you need to go to hospital then take a taxi. The bright yellow cabs pull up every few minutes, unloading screaming casualties, women and children covered in blood. Just inside the hospital entrance the injured lie on makeshift beds, stained red with the blood of the last occupant. A shrieking mother cradles a dead two-

year-old boy, waxen-faced, cut almost in two by shrapnel. Children with distorted limbs lie on the floor, wide-eyed, faces empty of expression, shocked. We visit the operating theatre to check the sandbag bulwarks that we have built. It's just a makeshift field station really; it's too dangerous to use the proper theatre two floors up. On the table is a patient with his torso torn open. The surgeons are doing their best but this time the shrapnel, the jagged lumps of flying metal, will probably win.

Out in the street there is a pathetic trail of homeless families going past. Internally displaced refugees, that's the official terminology, the euphemism for broken lives. As always, the man pushes the barrow load of bedding, the bundles and the pots; the woman carries the baby while three or four little children straggle behind, holding hands. Going nowhere, anywhere. The forgotten war.

As for the Project, after the winter snows we are now re-established in Afghanistan. We do what we can – clearing mines and unexploded ordnance, running health clinics with limited resources and ferrying the injured to hospital. But this beautiful and majestic country – the land where no one wins – seems set on self-destruction.'

As things turned out, by the time the letter landed on the doormat of her house in England, my mother had died.

****

The swallows had returned to Kabul for the summer, swooping heralds of the fine sunny days that lay ahead. There was apple blossom in the garden, the pink petals falling and scattering on the lawn like butterfly mines tossed from a Russian helicopter. The first roses were in bud, swelling by the day and glistening in the showers.

'Blossom out all over the city, the racemes floating like white laburnum,' says the diary, adding: 'Smartened up the house, sharpened up the staff'. The Anniversary of the founding of the Islamic State of Afghanistan was imminent: a parade was scheduled and the centre of the city was to be illuminated with coloured lights.

Captain Rai, commander of the diplomatic guard, passed by the Project villa with a bunch of asparagus, fresh-cut from the fertile grounds of the empty British Embassy, plus the earnest request for us to ask if HQ London might send out a flea collar for his dog, suffering Sultana who scratched from dawn to dusk, and through the night as well, hind legs scrabbling at the bites. That and other minor irritations aside, Captain Rai reported that everything was fine. 'All well at the Residency'.

By the same token, regular radio contact with callsign 'Whisky Papa' McScumble and with 'Oscar Zulu' Trotter confirmed that our de-mining operations centred on Pol-i-Khumri and Jebel Seraj were progressing apace, more or less safely distanced from the immediate conflict. We were well on track to surpass the season's goal of clearing 2,000 mines – and more.

Taking advantage of the fair weather, a UN representative flew in from Islamabad for the day. But he was not hopeful about the outcome of the Jalalabad talks, forecasting an early breakdown in negotiations, to be followed by yet more serious fighting. There was an upsurge of investment in the 'Great Kabul Jang Sweepstake'. The National Day parade was cancelled and the coloured lights were blacked out by Mr Hekmatyar, ostensibly the Prime Minister, petty vengeance substituting for statesmanship.

'Hot and sunny,' says the diary for 7th May. 'Thunderstorm and cloudy mid-afternoon onwards. Intermittent fighting all day. Power off. Topped up water tank from the well using generator. Rumours of kidnappings and car thefts. Bicycled to Red Cross to enquire about stretcher stocks. An evening of *jang*. Played the trombone.'

Sunday, 9th May: 'Cloudy and cool. PM brisk *jang*'. The following day: 'Moderate *jang* in western city'. Tuesday 11th May: 'Visited Said Abdul Salem in Wazir Akbar Khan hospital – on the mend but a bit quiet. Wards full of major gunshot, mine and rocket casualties – shattered legs, quadriplegics, both legs gone – civilians, ages 15 to 25.'

Wednesday, 12th May: '*Jang* started 0445. Typed up-date fax for HQ London. Heavy fighting in Kabul and general rocketing around the city. Out with Karimullah in Moscowbitch; four rockets fell near Ministry of Defence during de-mining liaison meeting with Colonel Sharook. PM attacks continued, moving through Shar-i-Naw in direction of Wazir Akbar Khan. Wrote submission to obtain wheelchair for Said Abdul Salem. Read "Kipling's Selected Stories" on the balcony; one or two close rockets. To British Embassy with O'Deere after tea to cheer Captain Rai and his guards, much rocket debris and wreckage en route, plus casualty at the roadside. Round to see Suzi, busy with her BBC World News reports. Paid out on *Jang* Sweepstake; Claude, the erstwhile architect, now occupied with Médecins sans Frontières logistics, takes the jackpot.'

Thursday, 13th May: '*Jang* wound up slowly. Heavy rocketing in Shar-i-Naw by mid-morning, some near misses and one straddle. Direct hit on near-neighbour Kareem's house, window frames all blown out, tended casualties at Clinic. Fighting, widespread, continued. House behind us received three hits. Read in garden after lunch, sound of the lawnmower from next door, children busy playing volleyball. Exercised with gearbox "weights" at dusk before supper, watching the flashes of heavy fighting from the balcony in the twilight.'

Friday, third day of serious fighting. 'Moderate background *jang*. The Islamic day of rest. Out on the new company bicycle to check the scene. Flower Street closed, no shopping. Managed half a haircut at Faisal's before he decided to close as well. In the barber's shop the remarkable, ornately carved walnut wall clock, complete with those dulcet Westminster chimes, continues sounding softly every quarter of an hour. Very heavy gunfire, then fierce street fighting in the direction of the British Embassy late afternoon.'

Saturday 15th May. 'Quiet start to the day, followed by sporadic shelling and rockets. Routine administration. Crossed river to change money, lodged list of Project personnel with Ministry of Repatriation. City generally shut down and deserted; exodus of refugees northwards. Weather: Cold front PM, cloud and rain.'

Sunday, 16th May: 'Fifth day of concentrated *jang*. Government (Jamiat) air strikes on Hezb-i-Islami positions in western Kabul. Jamiat artillery directed to south western hills. Occasional incoming rocket. Small arms and heavy machine gun fire. Fair weather. Passed the afternoon reading on the balcony, studying the Third Afghan War – an inconclusive, untidy and limited campaign in the Landi Kotal region, 3rd May to 8th August 1919, 38 years after the Second Afghan War. Fighting was provoked by Afghan interference with the fresh water supply. Independence for India came 26 years later – this was the last of the three Afghan Wars fought by the British "in defence of the Empire".'

Monday, sixth day of fighting. 'Down to Jamhuriat hospital to re-check sand-bagging defences against rockets. New arrivals: one dead child and many badly wounded. On to airport. No flights today. The shuttle service to Jeddah for the Hajjis – the Haj pilgrims proceeding to Mecca – was sent to Delhi empty overnight. Read on balcony again. Captain Rai called with some sticks of early rhubarb which he had forced in the garden under an old ammunition box. All well. Nice sunny day. Steady firing.' Tuesday, 18th May: 'Early start to rocketing and artillery – 0530. To Jamhuriat hospital again. Gave blood with

Rhubar. Steady stream of casualties. One man with femur exposed arrived in a wheelbarrow. PM rocketing continued. Red Cross figures for recent spate of fighting: 1,000 dead; 5,000 injured.'

Wednesday, eighth day of fighting. 'Early morning bombardment. Collected two sacks of rice – standard payment for our blood donations. Passed the food on to Hajji, Abdul and Karrimullah for their families. Rocketing – large fire towards British Embassy, got caught up in shelling investigating. Returned to villa; O'Deere back from Pol-i-Khumri demolitions in time for lunch. Debriefed PM then read on balcony in sun. Nice breeze.'

Thursday, 20th May: '*Jang*, day 9. Up 0515, routine radio calls and checks. Out with Dr Rhubar to see the President (Afghan National Insurance Company) to confirm Third Party cover. Heavy rocketing. Arrival at Jamhuriat coincided with casualties: family house hit by missile – little girl with one leg, small boy with punctured head and arms, mother and baby injured, nine dead. Discovered that the hospital lift operator was charging wounded patients and relatives a fee each time they moved between floors. Heavy conflict and shelling continued throughout afternoon. South western half of city abandoned by residents. Pall of smoke over the fighting, continuous air strikes.'

Inconveniently, unexpectedly, personal condolences arrived from the Controller, from HQ London. Another death, another place. Another bereavement. The funeral was in hand. No service of thanksgiving. Only a burial. Just the one freshly dug grave. Just the one coffin to be embraced by the 'deep peace of the quiet earth', to rest under the wide and timeless tranquillity of the shining stars. A simple funeral; a family affair. My family.

I might have left immediately, hurrying down the Kabul Gorge yet again, to take green tea, *chai sap*, on the hidden balcony of the Jalalabad *chaikana*, before pushing rapidly onwards for strawberries and cream at the pink-painted Pearl-Continental Hotel in Peshawar. And thence across the Indus on the rickety bridge, bound for the peaceful depths of Hampshire that lay beyond.

As it was, I lingered in Kabul. Unnecessarily, I suppose, but that's what I did. Packing everything back into the big suitcase – the one with all the world-wide labels, reminders of past excursions and assignments – turned into something of a psychological hurdle, a task of immense complexity that never got finished – or even started.

The Controller's remit had been met, the object of the exercise had been achieved: the Project was back on track, back on an even keel. But I was in no hurry: Kabul was where I was, and where I was, was home. Moreover, before I could depart I had noticed some outstanding administrative points requiring attention, some loose ends to be tended and squared away – there was always an abundance of those hereabouts. There was a little seamanlike tidying to be done and it wouldn't do to rush off in an overhasty manner. In any case, the airport was closed. In the absence of flights I was bound to miss the family funeral service, the interment – wherever it was. I never got there, and so I never found out.

I pedalled round to see Said Abdul Salem using one of the new bikes. I asked Abdul Ahmed if he would like to come along for the ride but he was unaccountably busy with his cooker and his English was not so fine. I told Said Abdul Salem that his wheelchair was coming, the insurance was in hand and the marker was down for the prosthesis.

I went to say goodbye to Captain Rai and to tell him that the special collar for Sultana the dog and the summer fleas was on its way. It took a whole day to tell him that, because we had to have another curry lunch with the Embassy guards – the gallant Ghurkhas from Nepal – and stroll on the rose-bordered lawn afterwards in the shade of those imperial trees, hands behinds our backs like two intriguing ambassadors.

Reverting to the collar, the request had gone to the Controller, marked 'for action by Purchasing Branch'. The latter was a figment of the imagination (we were safely separated and removed from the Colonel's huffing indignation) yet those phantom procurers never failed to deliver. So we had no hesitation in adding a post script to the message: 'Plus two small boxes of Oust Kettle De-scaler (Champions 95p) for Dr Rhubar's wife, by express request, on her Second Wedding Anniversary', secure in the knowledge that there would be no disappointment. Merely, possibly, a slight rise in blood pressure in the London bunker.

Then came the realisation that there were no more attainable loose ends to be tethered, there was no more tidying I could do, and that, try as I might, no more excuses could be found to justify delaying my departure. Our Project mine clearance work in the north at Pol-i-Khumri, and closer to hand at Jebel Seraj in the mouth of the Panshir Valley was moving ahead satisfactorily, thanks to McScumble, thanks to Bones alias Pendleberry, thanks to Trotter, thanks to O'Deere the demolisher running on six cylinders and happy at his work, and thanks to lately departed Walduck. And much appreciation also to telescopic Mr Willow for his vote of confidence. Yes, we were definitely going to hit that target of 2,000 mines swept in the season.

But here in Kabul, well, the manifold loose ends that still remained were largely far beyond the scope of the Project.

A contemporary report in *The Times* summed up the situation: 'Any pretence that there is a government in Afghanistan has been shattered by the latest tank and rocket barrage. The signs are that inter-Muslim fighting will intensify. Gulbuddin Hekmatyar, nominally the country's prime minister, continues to batter the city with rockets and artillery from his base south of the capital. He wants to dislodge the government, which is dominated by Tajiks and Uzbeks, and return Kabul to Pashtun control. A mosaic of conflicts makes peace a remote prospect, complicated by tribal, ethnic, linguistic and personal rivalries.'

A few days later the story was continued, more of the same: 'Dozens of casualties swamped Kabul's already crowded hospitals as government troops and their guerrilla foes fought to break a stalemate in the Afghan capital. Government jets made at least eight bombing runs on positions of Gulbuddin Hekmatyar, the hardline rebel leader in southern Kabul as his rockets pounded the city. Fierce rocket and artillery fire was concentrated around a strategic road junction near the centre of the battered capital where troops loyal to the Islamic coalition government were fighting off a new offensive.'

Word came in of a lull in the fighting, the possibility of a flight out, to Delhi or perhaps to Peshawar. That's when we discovered that my visa had expired. But the Indian Embassy had long been closed and now Mr Bhaksheesh of the Pakistan Embassy had similarly shut up shop. All was locked and barred. No table tennis, no consular service. Everything had expired, or so it seemed.

I sat with Dr Rhubar on the terrace and while we studied the roses in the garden and enjoyed the sunshine, Abdul brought sustenance in the faithful pansy pot. Whereupon we idly discovered that all that was necessary to extend the visa was to moisten our thumbs with the contents of the golden-spouted magic lamp and, after a little while and a little rubbing, we found that the recuperative green tea possessed hitherto unimagined restorative powers, such that, miraculously, six months became 12 months and thereby the out-of-date visa became in-date once again. Which, coincidentally, saved Mr Baksheesh the trouble of going to his office, which wasn't his intention anyway. As for ping pong, there was no time for that.

I carefully folded my predecessor's grey jersey and the two pairs of comfy green socks and put them back in the dark recesses of the wardrobe where I had found them, together with the Pluto slippers. They might come in handy for my successor.

'You won't be needing those any more,' said Dr Rhubar, re-discovering his little laugh, unable to resist a sideways glance at the big bed. 'And by the way,' he continued, 'there's one other thing I've been meaning to say to you.'

I waited, poised, my mind leaping to thoughts of the resident mouse and then moving on to the plumbing.

'When the Banke Millie people finish that addendum to the Kama Sutra, then I'll send you a copy,' Rhubar promised generously.

Abdul stuck his head round the door to see if he might cook for us another cup of tea. Was that an unbidden tear shining in the corner of his eye? No? Then it must have been in mine. Especially when from behind his back he produced the pansy pot with a flourish like a conjuror, and then watched and supervised as Rhubar helped me stuff it into a corner of the big suitcase, the one with the labels that had been so difficult to pack. I still have that teapot, even though, sadly, the secret recipe of how to make Terrace Green Tea with extra sugar for happiness did not come with it.

Glancing my gratitude to Abdul, the flash card Afghan Dari momentarily abandoning me, I saw that he looked quite cheerful and relieved at the thought of my imminent departure – positively chirpy, in fact. I couldn't blame him.

'Don't forget I'm coming back next month with Mr Willow for another lunch,' I said to Dr Rhubar. 'So please make sure everything is ready, four course luncheon and so on.'

And Abdul was gone, faster than a speeding Sakar. Ha! All square.

Karrimullah and Hajji were ready by the big gates of the compound. Abdul looked out silently from the gloom of his galley where he had taken refuge, peering into the sunlight, our shiny new bicycle propped proudly against the wall.

'*Ba aman-e Khodaa*,' said Karrimullah on the right. 'Go in the safety of God.' Easy come, easy go.

On the other side Hajji gave a tilt of the wispy beard and gazed into my face, still working on the Western puzzle, and trying to fathom what made these red-faced foreigners tick.

'*Khodaa haafez*,' he intoned. 'May God be your protector.' And may you always be in the right place.

Zahir rolled his eyes, softly slipped into gear and gently eased out the clutch. And with that, my nine lives expended, I was gone from Kabul.

****

Chapter XV

CODA

'Life has been a great experience, a grand adventure. What matters if it is also a stupendous mystery?'

Admiral Sir Reginald Bacon

Back in London, I was summoned to a de-briefing rendezvous with the Controller.

After lunch at the Club, co-incidentally the former home of Lord Palmerston (instigator of the 1st Afghan War with the directive to 'take Afghanistan in hand and make it a British dependency' – *plus ça change*) we sat in the summer shade of the immense plane-tree that eavesdrops and whispers in the corner of the courtyard at 94 Piccadilly.

There, under the rustling leaves of the self-same tree that surely similarly shaded the British Prime Minister a century and a half previously, the Controller – distinguished and dashing warrior, one-time politician, latter-day knight in shining armour – spoke of his dreams to pursue mine clearance projects all over the world, wherever the need arose.

Together over coffee that June afternoon we read the latest report on the situation in Kabul. 'Forgotten war for a city in ruins' declared *The Daily Telegraph*. 'The prime minister dare not enter his capital; the president is afraid to drive out of it; and most of the cabinet have taken refuge beyond the border ... [President] Rabbani, head of the Jamiat-i-Islami faction, reached Jalalabad [for talks] via a flight to Pakistan because he could not risk travelling the lawless roads outside his capital. Cars are checked every few miles by guerrillas of Hekmatyar's Hezb-i-Islami at bunkers bristling with weapons ... The Red Cross says that more than 1,000 people were killed [in the May fighting] ... "everyone wants to rule in Kabul but no one is strong enough to do it on his own. They will just keep fighting and whoever is left will be King of the Ruins".'

I met the Controller but once more: by chance, somewhere in the mountains between the Black Sea and the Caspian where we happened to be variously engaged on pursuing our projects of the day. After that, I never saw him again. And I was sad for that. Well, I went to his memorial service, but that didn't count and it wasn't the same.

On the day, St Columba's Church in Pont Street was full. No one there could doubt that the redoubtable Colonel had gone now – moved on – and there were those amongst us with regrets for not having been able to pass more time with him, for not having tapped his fund of brisk, no-nonsense wisdom more assiduously.

The younger members of the congregation fidgeted, no doubt wondering how it could be that you could live for so long that you grew old. The more senior participants looked around and wondered who was next. The aware had astutely dedicated their lives to writing their obituaries, but had they done enough? Live in *Who's Who*, die in *The Times*.

****

At the farmhouse in Hampshire I pressed ahead with putting the dahlias into their freshly dug, richly composted trench. I was later than usual, unavoidably delayed. On the other hand, it didn't do to be too early. The valley bottom was a notorious frost pocket, the cold night air sliding down the hillsides as surely as an avalanche on the Salang. Either way, the late-summer show was invariably as spectacular as a Jalalabad poppy plantation. The secret lay in the compost.

Planting completed, I wandered round the orchard to see if, just by chance, any of the Christmas mistletoe had germinated. Nothing. Perhaps next year. Or was there going to be a next year? I had been back a month, and strangely, my thoughts were still of Kabul – the almond blossom, the wasps at the grapes, the monumental mason and his family, the backdrop of majestic mountains iced with snow.

Stranger still, I missed rock-like Karrimullah spinning the heavy generator like a toy so we could fill the water tank for the day, and wispy phantom-like Hajji, appearing as a genie from a bottle, tending the explosive *bukhari* stove, and then vanishing again. I worried about perky Abdul crossing the city every day, and I hoped that no one would steal his new bicycle – or rather, our new bicycle. Comic, cock-eyed Abdul, *kolah* askew on his shiny head, chasing the mice with the carving knife, fending for his unseen family, and ever on hand with the pansy pot.

I wondered if Said Abdul Salem had got his new leg yet and if the wheelchair we had ordered had arrived. As for Dr Rhubar, perhaps he would personally deliver the updated, expanded version of the Kama Sutra – the one the clerks in Banke Millie were validating. He would bring ten copies probably, one for every day of the week, and three spare, just in case. Then he could stay for a few days, or better still, for a few weeks, and I could catch up on all the news and his dirty jokes and he could give me the de-mining stats for the donors and surprise me with a drip-feed of red-herrings and plausible misinformation.

It was then that the telephone rang. Or perhaps I imagined it.

Mr Cherry, Richard Cherry, it said. From Whitehall. He wanted to come and talk to me.

'About, you know, the delivery … we said we'd be in touch.'

'Oh, the groceries. Yes, of course. Come whenever you like.'

So Mr Cherry came to the farm in Hampshire and invited me to lunch. Another 'thank you' lunch. At the Bat and Ball, on Broadhalfpenny Down close by.

It was clear that Mr Cherry's real name was probably Mr Plum, Gordon Plum. Or even Greengage. Charles Greengage. He never even mentioned the groceries. And he certainly didn't have £10,000 in his pocket. I knew he wouldn't. Faithful O'Deere had already told me that I had been cut out of the deal.

No need to worry about him, said the Friends, referring to me, in the back of whose Land Rover the interesting extra-mural bomb had bounced all the way down the Kabul Gorge along the route of General Elphinstone's march of death and onwards to Islamabad through the Khyber Pass. Don't worry about him. No honour amongst thieves.

'What will you have?' asked Mr Cherry. 'And do please call me Dick.'

I wanted to, I really did. But I couldn't.

'Oh, I'll try the meatballs, please. And a fresh fruity tart. With cream.'

Mr Cherry said to the girl serving: 'Same for me. Dear.'

'And a pint of pear liqueur,' I added. Dick.

Word of the required victuals was passed through the serving hatch, which slammed shut at the effrontery of the order; only to slide open reluctantly some time later, when the desired selections were passed out. By a disembodied hand. Like a chicken's claw on the butcher's rack. Or a glove on the railings in the park.

After Mr Cherry had finished toying with his tart to his entire satisfaction he said, well, if that was the time then he had better be pushing along as tomorrow was another day.

'Toodle-loo,' I said, testing him to ensure he had access to the need-to-know coded response.

'Bye, bye,' he said, riposting in turn with what I took to be an arcane double-double bluff.

Bingo!

Which left me free to return to the farmhouse in the valley to continue my work in the long herbaceous border, tidying up generally and clearing the debris of winter from the soft march of nature before mowing the lawn with the hand machine, the one with the back roller that did the stripes. The soothing balm of the soil.

The south westerly breeze was freshening, sighing softly in the tops of the cedars, and looming over the surrounding hills there was a hint of rain, foretold by the curls of cirrus high in the sky and the advance of the more lowly shreds of cumulus.

And I knew then that I too must be moving along. Unencumbered by baggage, forever curious to see what lay in the next valley. And then the one beyond. It was time to move on.

****

THE END

EPILOGUE

'... today I met a traveller from an ancient land who said ...'

The internecine struggles of the Mujahideen (principally the forces of President Rabbani versus Gulbuddin Hekmatyar versus General Dostum) continued in Afghanistan throughout 1994.

That same year the extremist theocratic Taliban militia emerged and rapidly made substantial advances against the Rabbani government. With further gains in 1995, the Taliban took Kabul from Rabbani and seized power in September 1996 (whereupon they executed ex-President Najibullah, dragged from the UN compound where he had sought refuge). The Taliban enforced and consolidated their restrictive and repressive regime during 1997, completing their territorial control of most of the country in August 1998 with the capture of Mazar-i-Sharif in northern Afghanistan.

Immediately following the Twin Towers terrorist attacks on 11th September 2001 (which in turn occurred two days after the assassination by an al-Qaeda suicide bomber of Afghan Defence Minister Ahmad Shah Masood), the US-led bombing of Afghanistan coupled with Allied in-country military support enabled the Afghan Northern Alliance to re-enter Kabul. This they did on 13th November 2001, thus taking control and effectively removing the Taliban regime from power. Importantly, however, the bulk of the Taliban supporters were dissipated rather than eliminated, rapidly assuming a cloak of invisibility by merging with the civilian population in time-honoured fashion.

An Afghan Interim Authority was established at the end of 2001, with Mr Hamed Karzai inaugurated as Chairman on 22nd December that same year. A nationwide Loya Jirga (Grand Assembly) was held in June 2002, followed immediately by the formation of the Transitional Islamic State of Afghanistan with Karzai as President.

The Transitional Authority convened a Constitutional Loya Jirga which sat from 14th December 2003 to 4th January 2004. The resultant new constitution for Afghanistan was signed on 16th January 2004 with the intention to hold nationwide elections in June 2004. Meanwhile, reconstruction of the country was placed under the aegis of the NATO International Security Assistance Force (ISAF).

In the event, the fragile internal security situation dominated by heavily armed local warlords and bands of Taliban guerrillas – particularly in the south east of

Afghanistan – led to the subsequent postponement of the planned Presidential elections to 9th October 2004. Eventually, and as a result of that poll, Mr Hamed Karzai was inaugurated as President of Afghanistan on 7th December 2004.

Successful regeneration and stabilisation of the country thenceforth hinged on the introduction of law and order coupled with economic, employment, health and education programmes – the latter to include women. In addition to these major reforms lay the challenge to stamp out the drugs trade (at a UN meeting in April 2002 Britain undertook to take charge of counter-narcotics) and the attendant de-stabilising corruption, with 90% of the heroin entering Europe illegally (and 95% of the heroin entering UK) known to originate in Afghanistan. Unfortunately, and since the dispersal of the Taliban, drug production has progressively risen to unprecedented levels, notwithstanding efforts (largely unavailing) to induce farmers to grow alternative (but less lucrative) crops.

By 2001 – their final year in power – the Taliban had reputedly reduced Afghanistan's opium output to 185 tons, down from previous annual figures in excess of 3,000 tons; by year 2004 production had soared to a record 4,200 tons with a bumper harvest, and with the reaction of impoverished, debt-ridden farmers to the 'opium eradication programme' becoming increasingly militant. UN figures revealed that new record highs were achieved in 2006, production being assessed at 6,100 tonnes with 165,000 hectares under cultivation for opium poppies (104,000 hectares in 2005). Moreover, whereas previously the export was of raw opium, sophisticated laboratories now existed in-country for the processing of heroin and morphine (10kg of the opium paste converting to one kilogram of white heroin powder). All this in spite of the presence of 30,000 foreign troops in Afghanistan at that time and massive aid programmes.

UN figures for 2007 estimated an area of 193,000 hectares (i.e. six times the size of Malta) under poppy cultivation, with opium production having doubled in Afghanistan over the previous two years and 'the government having lost control because of the presence of insurgents'. Small wonder that the international community have debated – and are still considering – the possibility of buying out the entire crop at source as the most cost-efficient means not only of re-establishing control of the situation, but of effectively destroying the trafficking at a stroke. An alternative solution is wrapped in the observation made on behalf of the Afghan farmers: 'No demand, no supply'.

As for the pressing need to remove and destroy the mines and unexploded ordnance of past and present conflicts in Afghanistan, this remains (as in similarly war-ravaged countries elsewhere) an ongoing priority, and national and international mine clearance agencies continue working to this end. In September 1997 the Ottawa Convention banned the use and production of Anti-Personnel Mines (the Treaty was signed in December 1997 by 122 countries, and subsequently ratified and brought into force on 1st March 1999); notable non-signatories to the Agreement were the United States of America, Russia, China, India and Pakistan. It is known that much of the mine production technology formerly in possession of countries now subscribing to the APM ban has since passed to non-signatory countries in the developing world; certainly the previous hazards to the civilian population in Afghanistan are now being exacerbated and extended by the current fighting against the re-emergent Taliban. On the assumption that there are upwards of 10 million mines in Afghanistan, the UN has estimated that it will take 100 years to make the country completely safe for civilians; by 2008 the HALO Trust (UK-based international mine clearance NGO) alone had cleared upwards of 600,000 mines since 1988.

****

As indicated, the year 2004 was marked by a number of significant developments in Afghanistan: the signing of the new constitution; the holding of Presidential elections; the inauguration of the new President. However, whatever progress has been made since 2004 has been punctuated by a succession of indicators which are uniformly negative. For example, in July 2004, after an unbroken presence in the country of more than 20 years, Médecins sans Frontières announced their intention to leave Afghanistan in view of the deteriorating security situation. More than 40 aid workers, including five MSF staff, were reported as having been killed in the country in that year alone – this against a backdrop when not long afterwards aid agency field staff were declaring that 'up to 1,000 children may have died from malnutrition and hypothermia in western areas during severe winter weather', underscoring the prevailing requirement for external humanitarian aid in Afghanistan.

Typical of the earlier murders were the two Afghan relief workers shot dead in February 2005 by 'robbers or militants' in Helmand province (acknowledged Taliban and drug smuggling centre), and the drive-by shooting in March 2005 on a main road in the centre of Kabul of a British adviser working for the Afghan Government. At the subsequent coroner's inquest in UK in mid-June 2005 it was stated that 'the killers were still free because of the lack of skills of the local police in Kabul'.

These were not isolated incidents. Other examples of the deteriorating internal security situation were the nine Afghan policemen ambushed and killed whilst on patrol in Helmand province, and the 10 alleged Taliban killed in an attack on a

Government convoy in Khost province, both events in February 2005. In December 2004 a Turkish engineer was murdered in the eastern province of Kunar whilst working on a US-sponsored road project. In October 2004 an American women was killed in a suicide bomb attack on a busy Kabul street used mainly by foreigners, the same month as three UN workers were kidnapped; in August 2004 a vehicle loaded with explosives drove into the guesthouse of an American security firm, killing 10 people, the Taliban claiming responsibility. In May 2004 two Westerners were stabbed and stoned to death in Kabul.

The spiral of violence continued, much unreported. In early June 2005 a suicide bomber killed 14 in a mosque in Kandahar; the following day two US soldiers were killed by a roadside bomb attack on a convoy. On 12th June 2005 five US soldiers were killed in a suicide bomb attack on a military convoy near Kandahar. It was stated on 25th June 2005 that Afghan and US forces had killed 109 Taliban guerrillas but that their commanders had escaped across the border into Pakistan. Four days later a Chinook helicopter was brought down, allegedly by a Taliban missile, with the loss of 17 US servicemen en route to provide back-up for a four-man special forces team, two of whom were later also believed to have been killed.

In mid-July 2005 it was announced that Australia was committing more than 150 special forces personnel for service in Afghanistan, and on 19th July 2005 President Hamed Karzai arrived in UK for talks at Downing Street seeking further British aid and military support – Britain at that time having some 900 troops deployed in-country, stationed mainly around Kabul. As if to reinforce the President's request, on 21st August it was reported from Afghanistan that two US Embassy staff had been injured in a bomb attack and that in a separate incident four US soldiers had been killed by a roadside bomb. On 30th August a British employee working on road construction sites was kidnapped whilst travelling between the cities of Kandahar and Herat; his body was recovered a few days later. He had been murdered by the Taliban.

Parliamentary elections were held in Afghanistan on 18th September 2005, 'marking the formal end to a four-year process of international support launched in Bonn after US-led forces overthrew the Taliban'. The run-up was marred by outbreaks of violence ('the election candidate was relaxing at home after his last day of campaigning in the southern Helmand province of Afghanistan when masked men appeared at his door, dragged him outside and shot him through the head … hundreds of miles to the north a female candidate was fighting for her life after gunmen ambushed and shot her as she campaigned to represent her home province of Nuristan … in Kandahar another candidate woke to answer her telephone to be told: "if you run for parliament, your children will never wake again"'). On the eve of the event

12 people (three policemen and nine civilians) were killed in Taliban attacks, together with a French special forces officer blown up in a bomb attack. Naively, the electoral charter contained a clause allowing a losing candidate to take the place of a winning one, should the latter die before taking up his seat...

President Karzai took the opportunity to remind the international community that 'they should not immediately think Afghanistan's work has been done and it's over and let the Afghan people forge ahead with their work with their own resources' – a sentiment re-echoed by UN officials who said 'Afghanistan's political transition is far from secure and long-term international commitment is needed'. Concurrently, President Musharraf of Pakistan proposed the construction of a 1,500-mile long security fence along its border with Afghanistan, a suggestion welcomed by the United States at the same time as Coalition forces reportedly killed ten 'insurgents' in southern Afghanistan whilst attempting to arrest a leading Taliban commander.

At the end of September 2005 the British Government re-confirmed undertakings made at an earlier meeting of NATO Defence Ministers in Berlin that Britain 'would set up a military base in April 2006 in Helmand Province, southern Afghanistan, heartland of the opium poppy harvest and an area where the Taliban posed the most severe threat, followed in May 2006 by the deployment of the headquarters of NATO's British-led multi-national Allied Rapid Reaction Corps'. The estimated number of UK troops to be involved was put at 4,000, with a declared mission of 'countering terrorism, insurgency and narcotics' and an indefinite timescale of 'until the job is done'. Responsibility for planning and implementing the role of NATO's International Security Assistance Force (ISAF), namely 'peacekeeping, nation-building, and eradicating the poppy harvest by offering Afghan farmers and warlords an alternative' (described as 'huge tasks'), was to be assumed by Britain 'for the foreseeable future'.

As for the mid-September Parliamentary Elections, announcement of the outcome of Afghanistan's first democratic vote in more than three decades was twice postponed following a flood a allegations of fraud and 'minor problems', but the results were finally announced on 12th November 2005, confirming expectations of an assembly (249 seats in the lower house and 102 in the upper chamber) 'dominated by warlords and drug barons responsible for years of bloodshed together with a few members of the ousted Taliban regime also present'. The fledgling Afghan Parliament formally re-opened on 19th December 2005 when the newly elected members were sworn in at the inauguration ceremony in Kabul. 'We should stand bravely before the world to say we have emerged from war,' declared President Karzai, tears welling in his eyes. 'This homeland will live forever.' On the same day, US Vice-President Cheney told troops at

Bagram airbase not far from Kabul that the elections in Afghanistan (and Iraq) would be 'an inspiration to democratic reformers in other lands'.

Meanwhile, the 2005 catalogue of security incidents continued unabated. For example: 18th October – 'US troops kill four Afghan policemen mistaking them for militants'; 29th October – 'One British and one US soldier gunned down in a deadly series of attacks that claim 23 lives'; 3rd November – 'Afghan clash leaves five policemen dead'; 12th November – 'Taliban kill Afghan Deputy Governor, Nimroz province; 13th November – 'Taliban kidnap and kill three policemen, Helmand province'; 14th November – 'Four killed as Taliban attack NATO convoy in Kabul, including ISAF German soldier'; 15th November – 'US military completes probe of burning of Taliban bodies'; 19th November – 'Portuguese ISAF peacekeeper killed in Kabul explosion'; 19th November – 'Three killed in Helmand province roadside blast'; 20th November – 'Indian Engineer kidnapped by Taliban in Nimroz province and shot'; 6th December – 'Afghan general injured and one killed in Urgun road blast'.

Concurrent with the foregoing reports, political and other observations in the media included the following: 15th November 2005 – 'Taliban reject Karzai's peace offer in a year when unrelenting violence has claimed the lives of some 1,500 people, including more than 50 US military personnel and cast a shadow over Afghanistan's moves towards democracy'; 20th November – 'US plan to rebuild Afghanistan flawed, with corruption and inefficiency causing millions of dollars to be wasted on useless projects'; 1st December – 'Foreign fighters influence Afghan situation, pointing to an "Iraqisation" of the insurgency'; 12th December – 'NATO-led soldiers deploying next year to insurgency-hit southern Afghanistan will not take over counter-terrorist operations conducted by US-led forces … the mandate and the mission of the ISAF troops when they operate in the south will be that of providing security assistance to the government'; 13th December –'Taliban exploit drug trade to step up Afghan attacks, forging an alliance with smugglers in lawless Helmand province and underscoring a worrying slide in security just months before thousands of British troops are due to take control in the spring … undermining the fragile authority of President Hamid Karzai's Kabul-based government'. On 26th December 2005 details of US planned troop reductions were reported from Kabul, to the effect that 'the number would shrink by some 2,500 (from 19,000) under a routine troop rotation'.

****

Kandahar, 2nd January 2006: 'A suicide attacker drove a car bomb into a convoy of foreign troops in southern Afghanistan wounding a US soldier as well as an Afghan woman and a child'. Kandahar Jan 5: '"A suicide bomber killed at least 10 people and wounded 50 in an attack in an Afghan provincial capital during a visit by the US ambassador," officials said. The envoy was unhurt; "15 of the wounded were critically hurt in the incident in Tarin Kot, capital of the central province of Uruzgan," said Hajji Abdul Aziz, the deputy provincial governor. Qari Mohammad Yousuf, spokesman for the Taliban insurgents speaking by satellite phone from an undisclosed location said, "our intention was to kill the US ambassador".' Mons (Belgium) Jan 6: 'NATO's military chief stated that the Taliban and Al-Qaeda were not regrouping in Afghanistan. "There's a knee-jerk reaction that wants to say – oh, the Taliban is coming back or Al-Qaeda is coming back – I don't know of any commander or any estimate that can say that with certainty" US General James Jones said, adding that there was no new spike or trend evident concerning attacks in Afghanistan since ISAF began operating in late 2001'. Kandahar, Jan 16: 'Taliban suicide bombers killed at least 26 people in two attacks in southern Afghanistan, a day after a Canadian diplomat and two civilians were killed in another attack in the area'. Kabul, Jan 20: '"The suicide attacks that have struck Afghanistan in the past months are clearly the work of Al-Qaeda and Taliban fighters operating with foreign support," the Afghan foreign minister said'. London, Jan 22: '"Afghan suicide bombings worrying," said UK official, suggesting "a deliberate change of tactic by the Taliban from conventional confrontation with the coalition troops in which they have sustained a very large number of casualties"'.

Under an increasingly-used but apposite by-line of 'The forgotten war' (January 2006) The Guardian stated that: 'Afghanistan has always been a dangerous place … and it may be getting more dangerous. The suicide bombers who have killed 25 people in three days are an alarming novelty for President Hamid Karzai and for the NATO countries in the 9,000 strong International Security Assistance Force. … Now concerns are starting to be heard in Britain where Tony Blair has pledged some 3,000 more men, most for Helmand province in the volatile south, where the Taliban and drug traffickers are active. … There is a lot to be worried about. The shadow of Iraq hangs over Afghanistan … there is consensus across the 26-member [NATO] alliance that there must be no return to the failed state after the Soviet withdrawal …'

Seizing the moment, President Karzai presented an international donor conference in Lancaster House, London at the end of January 2006 with a $20 billion request for aid over the coming five years (he achieved pledges of $10.5 billion) to 'boost reconstruction of his country' the money to be paid directly to the Afghanistan government, rather than being channelled through the proliferation of *non-governmental organisations (NGOs). He went on to say that the soon-to-arrive additional 3,300 British troops being deployed to southern Afghanistan as part of the 'major new three-year mission of NATO peacekeepers' (bringing the total of UK military in country to 5,700), would 'need to tackle the opium business; narcotics are a problem that we have to face – narcotics money feeds terrorism'. London, Jan 28: 'The British government has positioned around 240 people in south Afghanistan to prepare for deployment of up to 5,700 British troops in May as part of NATO's expansion plans in areas bordering Pakistan … the troops would hunt Taliban and Al Qaeda fighters along the border as part of the Allied Rapid Reaction Corps … British officials would also take over command of the NATO International Security Assistance Force (ISAF) for a period of nine months from May 2006'.*

Kabul, Feb 2 (2006): 'Four killed in Afghan suicide attack … a suicide attacker rammed an explosives filled car into an army convoy in south eastern Afghanistan, killing three Afghan soldiers and a road worker … the attack in Khost province late Wednesday was the latest in a spate of more than 20 such blasts in the past four months, pointing to a change of tactics in the insurgency'. Kandahar, Feb 3: 'US-led coalition planes bombed an area of southern Afghanistan where a fierce battle had erupted between Taliban-linked militants and police … the coalition spokesman confirmed the provision of close air support to Afghan forces during an engagement'. Kandahar, Feb 4: Afghan governor killed … a district governor and two policemen were killed by Taliban rebels fleeing a battle that left 25 dead in southern Helmand province's Sangin district … a purported Taliban spokesman confirmed the fighting but said the clashes in Naw Zad and Musa Qala did not involve fleeing rebels but reinforcements'. Kabul, Feb 10: Eight Afghan soldiers were killed on Friday and four Canadian soldiers hurt in a series of roadside bomb attacks in the provinces of Kunar and Kandahar … two soldiers were killed when their vehicle hit a roadside bomb … a convoy sent to their aid was hit by another explosive device and six more soldiers were killed'. Kabul, Feb 13: 'Four US soldiers killed in a bomb blast in insurgency plagued Afghanistan as five militia troops contracted to the US-led coalition and an Afghan soldier also died whilst on patrol in their Humvee vehicle in Uruzgan province. In a separate incident five Afghan militiamen were ambushed and killed by the Taliban in Helmand's Girishk district. In Kunar an Afghan soldier was killed and five wounded when their vehicle was bombed'. Kabul, Feb 26: 'Inmates on the rampage in main Afghan jail … about 1,300 prisoners, many of them from Al Qaeda and the Taliban riot at the notorious Pul-ı-Charkhi prison'.

At the end of February 2006 the incoming commander of Canada's 2,000 troops based in Kandahar said that 'Afghanistan has huge problems' and NATO forces will be in the country for 'years and years – for decades'. However, he went on to state that there would be fewer suicide attacks as they were 'counter-cultural to Afghans, the vast majority of whom wanted peace and a better life'. Kandahar, March 4: 'A second French special forces officer died after clashes with the Taliban, while an Afghan intelligence agent and three guards were killed as more violence shook southern Afghanistan … a Canadian soldier was wounded when insurgents opened fire on a patrol in the volatile south'. Kabul, March 5: 'Attackers torched two World Food Programme trucks and destroyed 29 tons of food destined for needy people in Uruzgan province; meanwhile a motorcycle bomb attack in Faizabad, the capital of north eastern Badaskhstan wounded three but just missed the provincial governor's convoy'. Kabul, March 12: 'Former President Mujaddedi was slightly hurt in a suicide car bomb attack that killed four others, blaming Pakistan's Inter Services Intelligence (ISI). Meanwhile, four US soldiers were killed during a patrol in the eastern province of Kunar close to the border with Pakistan, and the Taliban kidnapped four Albanians and four Afghan colleagues working in Kandahar'.

And so on.

****

In April 2006, as forecast, Britain completed construction and establishment of a military base (Camp Bastion) in Helmand Province, Southern Afghanistan (four times the size of Wales), with a follow-on build-up (Operation Herrick 4) of an estimated 3,300-4,000 additional UK military personnel (of whom only 650 were designated as combat troops) being committed to in-country operations (already previously described as 'countering terrorism, insurgency and narcotics'). Concurrently Mr John Reid, the British Defence Minister speaking on the BBC Radio 4 'Today' programme stated: 'We would be perfectly happy to leave in three years and without firing one shot because our job is to protect the reconstruction.' This was followed in May 2006 by implementation of the planned deployment of the HQ of NATO's allied rapid reaction force (ARCC) to Afghanistan and the assumption of command of ISAF by Britain through to February 2007.

At the end of June/beginning of July 2006 the British contingent suffered 6 fatalities in three weeks in the course of fighting around isolated 'platoon-house' outposts in Helmand province (e.g. Sangin, Musa Qala, Naw Zad, Kajaki) far from their main base at Camp Bastion, with troop survival taking priority over earlier declared 'hearts and minds' aims of the mission. The UK Defence Secretary (Mr Des Browne) conceded that the British troop deployment had 'energised the Taliban' and that the scale and nature of the opposition had become apparent 'when we were deploying'. The officer in command of British troops in the region said: 'If we were honest, we didn't expect it to be quite so intense … we came here not wanting to take casualties, but were prepared for the fact that they were likely'. Announcing an expansion of the British mission and an increase in force numbers, Mr Browne stated: 'No one ever suggested it was going to be easy'.

****

In an ambush by 'militants' in Helmand on 30th July 2006 three British soldiers were reported killed and one seriously injured. On 2nd August a suicide bomber killed 21 in Kandahar; 4 NATO soldiers were amongst the dead. On 11th August a suicide bomber attacked a NATO convoy in Southern Afghanistan, killing one soldier. On 2nd September 2006 an RAF Nimrod reconnaissance aircraft exploded over Kandahar minutes after undergoing air-to-air refuelling, killing all 14 crew. Also in September, the NATO Supreme Allied Commander, Europe called for the 26 members of the alliance to make more men and weapons available to augment his force of over 20,000 troops. As for the civilian population, five years on from the end of the Taliban regime The Times (11 November 2006) reported that 'triumph and hope have given way to despair and disappointment; as the number of villagers bombed and killed in air strikes multiplies and the paradox of "re-construction with a gun" is exposed, the disillusionment grows'.

In October 2006, and mirroring the pattern established in Iraq, it was reported that Taliban suicide bombings for the year numbered 78, with 200 civilians, security force members and international troops dead. Statistics for the three previous years were given as: two attacks recorded in 2003; six in 2004; 21 in 2005. Also in September/October 2006, 3 Commando Brigade Royal Marines relieved 16 Air Assault Brigade as the UK task force in Helmand Province on six-monthly tour rotation.

****

In February 2007 came the announcement that 1,400 additional UK troops were to be deployed for 'operations against the re-emergent Taliban', bringing the total of British servicemen in Afghanistan to 7,700 – by the far the highest number since the inconclusive 3rd Afghan War of 1919, almost a century earlier. Speaking in the House of Commons, the Defence Secretary made it clear that Britain was sending more troops because of the failure of NATO allies such as France to fight on the frontline, saying:

'It is increasingly clear that, at present, when it comes to the most demanding tasks in Afghanistan, only we and a small number of key allies are prepared to step forward.'

On 8th March 2007 the UK passed the milestone of 50 combat deaths in Afghanistan since the start of operations in November 2001, with four British servicemen killed in less than a week as a result of the increasing tempo of activity taking the total to 52. By the same token and at the same time, Ministry of Defence UK statistics were released to the effect that '500 improvised explosive device attacks were encountered in Afghanistan in 2005, tripling to 1,525 in 2006. It was one of these improvised bombs that killed a Canadian soldier on joint patrol with Afghan troops near Kandahar on 25th May 2007 – the 55th death suffered by Canada since sending its troops (approximately 2,000) to Afghanistan in 2002.

In June 2007 the Red Cross director in Afghanistan stated that as a result of the intensification of the conflict between the Taliban and the combined Afghan, British and US forces there was a large rise in civilian casualties (e.g. Guardian 19th June 2007: 'Seven children die as US-led air strike hits Afghan school'; Times 23rd June 2007: '25 civilians killed in air strike after Britons attacked'; Metro 29th May 2007: '13 people were killed and 35 wounded in Afghanistan when police opened fire to break up a violent protest yesterday … more than 1,000 pro-militia supporters gathered in Shiberghan, capital of northern province Jowzjan, to demand the removal of governor Juma Kahn Hamdard') and the humanitarian situation in the country 'is worse now than a year ago'.

The UK Foreign Office said 'real, tangible progress had been made in the last five years in Afghanistan'. Meanwhile the British Ambassador in Kabul (Sir Sherard Cowper-Coles) said: 'The task of standing up a government of Afghanistan that is sustainable is going to take a very long time. We should be thinking in terms of decades. This country does matter to us in so many ways.' On 11th June 2007 the Independent reported the third Taliban assassination attempt on President Hamid Karzai in recent years: 'Afghan President is targeted by Taliban's rockets during speech … he was later taken away from the building in Ghazni, south-west of Kabul, under heavy security'.

British fatalities in Afghanistan since the start of operations in November 2001 reached 68 on 31st July 2007 (with four soldiers killed in the space of five days). On 6th August 2007 it was reported: 'Talks between US President George W. Bush and Afghan President Hamid Karzai today will focus on worsening violence in Afghanistan and the threat from military hideouts in Pakistan'. Following two further British deaths, the UK Defence Secretary (Mr Des Browne) said on 13th August 2007: 'I have never underestimated the degree of difficulty we face here but we are making progress. The fact of the matter is it is a long-term commitment and our people are doing an exceptionally good job there but it has to be complemented by the growth of governance from the Afghans themselves,' adding that the troops were fighting to ensure that Afghanistan has the 'best future' it can have. On 16th August 2007 it was reported that 'Mr Browne felt that British troops could be at a "turning point" in stabilising Afghanistan but he warned that the Taliban were being helped by Iran, saying he had "no doubt" that the Afghan extremists were being supplied with weapons from Tehran via drug routes'. On 23rd August 2007 the police chief in Helmand province was killed by a bomb.

By 31st August 2007 the number of British service personnel killed in Afghanistan since 2001 had advanced to a total of 74 (including three by a US 'friendly fire' bombing attack on 24th August) – rising to 78 by 10th September 2007. To recapitulate, the operational area for the bulk of the 7,700 UK service personnel currently in Afghanistan is Helmand Province (one of 34 such provinces). Approximately 450 km long and 150 km wide, Helmand is very roughly the same size as Scotland; Afghanistan (250,000 square miles) is larger than France (211,208 square miles) and one and a half times the size of Iraq (168,750 square miles). The total population of Afghanistan is assessed at 28 million – that of Helmand Province is 745,000 (principally derived from the strong-willed Pashto tribe). The overall International Security Assistance Force level is around 37,000 troops.

On 10th September 2007 is was reported that the number of suicide bombings in Afghanistan was set to reach a record level for 2007, with 103 attacks up to the end of August, compared with a total of 123 for 2006, and that 'suicide bombings were unheard of in Afghanistan prior to the September 2001 assassination of anti-Taliban warlord Ahmad Shah Masood'. Also on 10th September the UN envoy to Afghanistan warned that security forces had to 'avoid provoking an outraged population into volunteering for Jihad'. The same day, Mr Donald Rumsfeld (former US Defence Secretary until November 2006) described Afghanistan as a 'big success – 28 million people are free, they have their own president and their own parliament'. Almost simultaneously 28 people were killed and 60 hurt in a suicide attack in southern Afghanistan.

There are regular reports of substantial Taliban losses, e.g.: 29th October 2007 '80 Taliban fighters were killed when they tried to ambush US-led coalition soldiers in Helmand Province in a six-hour engagement'; 29th August 2007 '100 Taliban fighters were killed today in a battle with US-led troops in southern Afghanistan'; 16th August 2007: 'Nine militants were killed in clashes with US and Afghan troops'; 26th July 2007: 'American soldiers killed 50 Taliban insurgents in Afghanistan after targeting compounds in the southern province of Helmand. The 12-hour assault, with the help of Afghan troops did not claim any civilian or coalition lives'; 11th June 2007: 'In southern Zabul province, 27 militants died after NATO air strikes were called in following clashes with Afghan troops'; 15th May 2007: 'Sixty Taliban fighters including three commanders were killed in overnight air strikes on two rebel bases in southern Afghanistan … hundreds have died in fighting already this year after more than 4,000 were killed last year'. However, observers believe that, within reason, manpower is not a problem for the Taliban, particularly with the influx of fighters from outside the country e.g. the Tribal Areas of Pakistan (the Russians killed an estimated one million Afghans during the course of their ten year occupation, before they withdrew, having themselves suffered 14,000 dead).

On 1st June 2007 it was reported that: 'A helicopter crash which claimed the lives of a British soldier and six others in Afghanistan was caused by a Taliban rocket attack. The CH-47 Chinook came down in an area of the volatile Helmand province … a NATO spokesman said "initial indications are that enemy fire may have brought down the helicopter".' The acquisition by the Taliban of upgraded sophisticated surface to air missiles purchased from abroad funded by the narcotics trade (production at record levels, doubled in the space of two years, greater than Colombia, Bolivia and Peru combined) will pose increasing problems for thinly spread coalition forces, dependent as they are on helicopters for troop movements and re-supply over difficult terrain (for example, and reverting to the earlier Soviet occupation of Afghanistan, the Stinger shoulder-fired missiles obtained by the Mujahideen reputedly brought down 512 Russian fixed and rotary-wing aircraft in 1987).

Similarly, the Taliban are likewise engaged in re-equipping with improved night sights and night vision devices to enhance their fighting capability, together with longer range mortars for use against static bases (Camp Bastion and the detached 'platoon-houses') . These advances, coupled with the provision of further external training for Taliban riflemen to improve the overall standard of marksmanship (hitherto assessed as low) will present increasing challenges for the already hard-pressed coalition forces.

On 19th September 2007 British-led NATO forces 'launched a major operation against the Taliban in Helmand province, with some 2,500 troops moving into the southern region supported by armoured vehicles, helicopters and jets'. On 27th September it was reported that 'at least 165 Taliban fighters were killed by the US-led coalition force during a day of bloodshed'. Two days later the NATO commander in the region 'cautioned that although the alliance had made significant progress in Helmand province the Taliban could regroup in the winter and recapture territory and "we are likely to have to do some of this work again, simply because we haven't had a good holding force"'. On 1st October 2007 it was stated by the office of the

Afghan President that the Taliban militants were 'having a serious debate about laying down their arms and want to give up'. On 2nd October it was reported that 'a suicide bomber killed 12 Afghan police on a bus in Kabul, the second such attack in four days'.

On 8th October 2007, the Oxford Research Group think-tank said: 'The "war on terror" has been a disaster with the concept now wholly discredited' and that operations in Afghanistan should be scaled back, with 'the removal of the Taliban providing a major boost for al-Qaeda' (cf Report 'Towards Sustainable Security – Alternatives to the War on Terror'). On 9th October it was reported that the NATO Secretary General was calling for an increase in the number of NATO troops in Afghanistan (totalling 40,000, albeit with those from Germany, Italy and Spain deployed to 'stable' regions). He said that 'a shortage of men and equipment was hampering coalition forces and "the fact that we have not fully been able to live up to the promises that nations have made is a point of concern for me"'.

Speaking after talks in Downing Street with Afghanistan's President Hamid Karzai on 25th October 2007 the British Prime Minister Mr Gordon Brown said: "We have got the Taliban on the defensive … we are all determined that Afghanistan should never become a failed state again, and to support the democracy that has been created in that country"; he went on to call for greater "burden-sharing" from the international community'. Coinciding with the President's four-day state visit to UK, the Kabul based newspaper Daily Afghanistan said 'Britain leads international efforts against drug production and trafficking … but unfortunately, not only has there been no reduction, but it has gone up year after year, and that failure to address the problem had pushed the country to the brink of a "political and social crisis" with Afghanistan turned into a "permanent nest of international terrorists"'. On 17th November 2007 the UN 'told NATO to tackle the Afghan opium trade, saying that exports, which total £2 billion, aided the Taliban'.

On 7th November 2007 'Afghans began three days of mourning for 41 people, including five MPs and many children, killed in the country's worst suicide attack. The attack, in the relatively peaceful north of Afghanistan, shook further public confidence in the ability of the government and the 50,000 foreign troops in the country to provide security against Taliban rebels. Insurgents have carried out more than 130 suicide attacks so far this year, but mainly in the south and east of the country.' With a further British fatality during the battle to retake the town of Musa Qala from the Taliban (previously the subject of a ceasefire and British withdrawal on 17th October 2006, only to be re-occupied by the Taliban in February 2007) by 10th December 2007 the number of British service personnel killed in Afghanistan since 2001 had risen to 86. Estimates of the number of Afghan civilians (i.e. men, women and children) killed in the fighting in the year 2007 alone varied from 2,000 to 10,000.

On a more positive note, November 2007 saw the finalisation of an agreement with a Chinese mining company to develop the Aynak copper reserves near Kabul, giving potential employment to some 5,000 Afghans and income of $400 million p.a., which would serve to double existing government revenue. Previous surveys had already confirmed very substantial iron, gold and coal deposits in Afghanistan, in addition to precious stones and further copper reserves. Natural gas resources could be as high as 36.5 trillion cubic feet, whilst oil estimates are as much as 3.6 billion barrels.

On 12th December 2007 under the headlines of 'Brown wants talks with Taliban' and 'Brown's Afghan olive branch', it was variously reported in the press that 'Gordon Brown was set to unveil a radical new strategy on Afghanistan including plans to get the Taliban to lay down arms and take part in peace talks (with President Hamid Karzai taking the lead in opening discussions), with political and economic solutions getting as much emphasis as the military campaign, using British troops to support rather than lead Afghan fighters, political deals between local elders and government provincial leaders, and cash to persuade farmers to plant non-poppy crops'.

On 13th December 2007 it was reported that Mr Brown had said that the battle against the Taliban in Afghanistan was being won and that talks with the insurgency were ruled out, rejecting claims that senior Taliban figures might be consulted. Mr Brown told the House of Commons: 'We are winning the battle against the insurgency, isolating and eliminating the leadership of the Taliban, not negotiating with them'. (In October 2007 the British Chief of the Defence Staff advised that 'the Afghan conflict could be resolved only by a political deal after talks with Taliban leaders').

****

On 14th January 2008 the UK press reported 'Troops in for long haul – Britain could be engaged in Afghanistan for another generation; the Defence Secretary Des Browne admitted: "We cannot risk it again becoming an ungoverned training haven for terrorists who threaten UK; it is a commitment which could last for decades".' Simultaneously Prime Minister Gordon Brown warned 'British troops will have to stay in Afghanistan for the foreseeable future, stating; "It will take time to win the fight. We do not want al-Qaeda to have bases in Afghanistan. Without action we would be in danger of that happening".' In the heart of Kabul on the same day Taliban suicide attackers entered the Serena Hotel, killing six, including a journalist from Norway.

On 17th January 2008 US Defence Secretary Robert Gates was reported as having said that the 30,000 US troops were 'doing a terrific job' against the Taliban insurgency but complained that some allies (ie. NATO) were not properly trained and lacked experience tracking militants. The Americans also claimed that British plans to make use of untrained Afghan militias to fight the Taliban were 'doomed to failure'.

Four days after the British combat death toll rose to 87, the Afghan President (speaking at the World Economic Forum in Davos in January 2008) 'accused Britain of allowing the Taliban to gain a stronghold in his war-torn country' (referring inter alia to the Musa Qala debacle). 'The British are making matters worse, says Afghan President' stated The Times on 26th January 2008, reporting the same day that: 'Lord Ashdown's appointment as the UN special envoy [charged with overall coordination] in Afghanistan has been blocked by President Karzai ... the Afghan leader claimed that British forces had failed in their mission in Helmand province which had been under Kabul's control before the British troops arrived on the scene and that the province was now overrun with Taliban'. On 4th February 2008 it was reported that Britain had drawn up 'secret plans for a military training camp in Afghanistan for former Taliban fighters' and that as a result 'two diplomats (Mervyn Patterson, a UN political officer, and Michael Semple, deputy head of the EU mission in Afghanistan) were ordered to leave the country by President Karzai for "threatening national security".' It was further reported that 'the revelation had placed relations between Britain and President Hamid Karzai's government in Kabul at a new low'.

At the same time the press reported: 'Britain and US push for more NATO troops'; 'NATO allies "must share burden of Afghanistan"'; 'Europe told do more to stop Taliban'; simultaneously with: 'Berlin slaps down US demand to send troops to fight the Taliban'. On 7th February 2008 the 'think tank' of the Senlis Council (NGO) warned: 'NATO is failing in Afghanistan because its forces are overstretched and hampered by a lack of political will ... Coalition countries, including Germany and Italy, have not deployed enough troops to support President Hamid Karzai ... the failure of NATO allies to take action has left the country close to a precipice'.

On 18th February 2008 it was reported that a suicide bombing at a dog fight near Kandahar had killed 80 people. The following day another British soldier was killed at Kajaki (Helmand province), whilst in the town of Spin Boldak (Kandahar province) 38 people were killed when a suicide bomber targeted a Canadian patrol in a busy market. On 17th March 'a suicide bomber ripped into a NATO convoy killing four soldiers and three civilians in Girishk, Helmand province'. On 25th March 2008: 'At least 100 people were injured when 36 oil tankers exploded in two attacks on a convoy taking fuel to US and NATO Forces at Torkham, the main crossing point on the Afghan-Pakistani border'. On 31st March: 'Two Royal Marines serving with 40 Commando were killed by an explosion whilst on vehicle patrol near Kajaki,

Helmand province, bringing British military fatalities in Afghanistan since the start of operations in November 2001 to 91'.

Also in March 2008, the UN Secretary General said 'violence in Afghanistan was at its highest level since US forces invaded the country in 2001 and that there were 8,000 conflict related deaths in 2007 [other reports gave the figure as 'more than 6,500 people, mainly militants], with a rise in attacks on Afghan and international humanitarian workers, with 40 such people killed.' He went on to say 'the effectiveness of the 41,700-strong NATO force was hampered by insufficient troop strength and national caveats limiting the function of some troops' and expressed concern 'about the spread of rebel activity from the south and east to the previously calm north-west.' The death toll from land mines and other unexploded ordnance (e.g. "bomblets") in Afghanistan for the year 2007 was reported as being 'more than 600, with half of the victims being children'. (On 28th May 2008 in Dublin 109 countries passed a treaty in banning the use of cluster bombs around the world and agreed to destroy any stockpiles within eight years; the US, China and Russia were not at the Dublin talks).

At the end of February 2008 and again in mid-April, the commander of UK 52 Brigade said: 'British troops have worn down the Taliban and forced them to abandon many of their key strongholds in Helmand province ... the Taliban are suffering from a lack of manpower and having to rely on foreign troops, damaging relations with the Pashtu people living in the area ... I would argue that in Helmand, NATO works ... with a greater level of security ... signs of real progress ... of course, there is an awful long way to go'.

On 11th March 2008 it was stated that 'the cost of British operations in Afghanistan amounted to £742 million in 2007, increasing by 122% to a forecast £1.6 billion for 2008'. Details of the basis for assessment were not given.

On 14th April 2008 'four Afghan policemen died in Helmand province when their vehicle was ambushed by Taliban fighters'. On 17th April 'at least 17 people died when a suicide bomber blew himself up in the south-western province of Nimroz, including children and two policemen'; that same week 'two Indian road engineers were killed in a separate suicide attack in the province'. Concurrently it was reported that 'violence has been increasing recently in Afghanistan, an expected upsurge after the traditional winter lull'. On 28th April 2008: 'President Hamid Karzai survived an assassination attempt by Taliban fighters who attacked a ceremonial parade in Kabul yesterday marking the 16th anniversary of the end of Soviet-backed rule in the country'. On 19th May it was reported that 'an RAF Chinook helicopter carrying diplomats and the Governor of Helmand crash-landed at Musa Qala without casualties after its body and rear rotor were badly damaged by a Taliban rocket-propelled grenade'.

In mid-May 2008 the UK Ministry of Defence stated 'the armed forces are increasingly overstretched with fewer units available to be sent on military missions … the strain of overseas campaigns in Iraq and Afghanistan has not been met by extra cash and the forces are now too weak to meet the government's strategic objectives … having operated at or above planned levels for the best part of a decade'.

On 9th June 2008 an Afghan journalist working for the BBC was shot dead in Lashkar Gah, southern Helmand province and it was further reported: 'Three British soldiers were killed in Afghanistan yesterday, bringing the total who have lost their lives in the conflict to 100.' The UK Defence Secretary (Mr Des Browne) said: "They have transformed the heartland of the Taliban from an area of lawless oppression and terrorism to a place of democracy and development". Earlier (27th May) during a visit to Camp Bastion he said: "There is a real sense of progress and optimism in Helmand, and our troops are making a difference; I come away with a sense we are succeeding against the insurgents and that the Afghans' ability to deliver their own security is ever-increasing".

In a Ministry of Defence briefing on operations given on 9th June 2008 it was stated: 'British troops are primarily in the country to bring democracy to Afghanistan and to make sure it is never again a safe haven for terrorists … the armed forces are also ensuring that human rights and equality are in place, such as education for girls and involving women in politics … Britain has spent more than £500 million on reconstruction aid and has pledged £200 million more'. Meanwhile, in Paris on 12th June President Karzai 'appealed for £25 billion of aid over five years to repair his war-torn country and to revive the shattered economy, pledging to fight endemic corruption which the World Bank had warned crippled the legitimacy of the government'.

On 13th June 2008 'militants attacked Kandahar's main Sarposa Prison with a suicide car bomb and rockets, killing police and setting free hundreds of prisoners … the building held over 1,000 inmates, of whom 400 were Taliban'. On 20th June it was reported: 'NATO onslaught "routs Taliban" – a swift attack to drive Taliban fighters from ten villages seized in the Arghandab area was a success, officials said … NATO and Afghan troops stormed the area, killing at least 56 insurgents with the help of air strikes … the offensive would reassure Afghans appalled at the mass escape of Taliban prisoners from Kandahr's jail … confidence in allied control had been shaken with the mass jailbreak of 900 prisoners the previous week'.

On 18th June it was reported that four soldiers (including one female) had been killed in their vehicle by a Taliban roadside bomb, bringing UK casualties to a total of 106 (with nine over the past nine days). Two days previously Defence Secretary Mr Des Browne announced the deployment of a further 230 British troops to Afghanistan, stating on 16th June that the UK force level 'will increase from 7,800 to 8,030 by Spring 2009'. On 25th June 2008 it was reported that UK combat fatalities had advanced to 108 with two further British deaths in Helmand province – 'hours after the UK Chief of the Defence Staff commented that the Armed Forces were "stretched beyond the capabilities we have"'. Two days later it was reported 'the RAF could run short of transport aircraft as operations in Iraq and Afghanistan take their toll on the ageing C130 Hercules fleet, the National Audit Office warned'.

By the end of June 2008, UK deaths in Afghanistan numbered 13 for the month. In the House of Commons on 2nd July Prime Minister Gordon Brown 'refused to set an "artificial timetable" for the withdrawal of British troops from Afghanistan, saying that Afghan forces would take over "more and more responsibility for their own affairs" as their capability improved, stating that British forces must remain to "stop the Taliban taking over and al-Qaeda coming back"'. By 31st July 2008 the total of British armed forces deaths in-country had reached 114.

On 7th July 2008: 'About 40 people were killed when a suicide bomber targeted the Indian embassy in Kabul … the deadliest attack in the Afghan capital this year … six policemen were among the dead and more than 100 were wounded'. On 13th July US forces lost nine soldiers in a single incident – a rebel attack on a remote outpost in Wanat village in the northern province of Kunar. July also saw two 'friendly fire' incidents. On 11th July it was reported: 'Nine British paratroopers have been wounded … by a burst of 30mm cannon fire from an Apache helicopter as they fought the Taliban … three were seriously injured whilst six were described as "walking wounded".' On 21st July it was reported: 'Friendly fire may have killed more than 13 civilians and policemen in Afghanistan … wrongly targeted mortars fired by NATO troops are said to have killed at least four villagers in the Paktika province in the east of the country near the Pakistan border … while in the west nine police officers died after they clashed with NATO forces in the belief that they were Taliban insurgents and coalition forces called in air support'.

On 18th July 2008 'two French Action Against Hunger humanitarian workers were kidnapped in the central Afghan province of Day Kundi'. On 2nd August 2008 the BBC reported that 100 aid agencies in Afghanistan had declared the internal stability situation to be placing continuance of their operations in Afghanistan in jeopardy, 'with 19 relief workers killed so far in 2008 up to the month of July, more than the whole number killed in 2007'. On 14th August it was reported that three female aid volunteers (UK/US/Canadian) working with the International Rescue Committee had been shot and killed together with their Afghan driver whilst travelling in Logar province, just south of the capital. A Taliban spokesman was quoted as saying:

"We don't value their aid projects and we don't think they are working for the progress of our country".

Under the headline 'An Afghan lifeline, plagued by insurgents' the International Herald Tribune said on 14th August 2008 'today the highway [Kabul-Kandahar], once the showpiece of the US reconstruction effort in Afghanistan [completed end-2003 at a cost of $1 million a mile], is a dangerous gauntlet of mines and attacks from insurgents and criminals ... the road has become the site of excessive carnage, disrupting supply lines for US and NATO forces ... in one of the worst attacks in Salar on 24th June 50 fuel tankers and food trucks were ambushed and the convoy set afire; seven of the drivers were dragged out and beheaded ... two days later three US soldiers and their Afghan interpreter died as their vehicles were hit by mines and rocket-propelled grenades ... security in the provinces ringing Kabul has deteriorated rapidly in recent months; today it is as bad as at any time since the beginning of the war'.

On 8th August 2008 the British Defence Secretary (Des Browne) 'admitted that the war in Afghanistan had come at a "high price" in casualties – but insisted progress was being made in spite of British forces having suffered 17 fatalities in a bloody period of fighting since June'. On 11th August it was announced that 'Afghan forces are set to take control of security in the capital, Kabul, despite a surge in suicide bombings and roadside blasts ... NATO would not say when this would happen officially, although government forces are steadily growing in size'. On the same day 'a suicide bomber rammed his car into a NATO convoy in Kabul, killing three civilians and injuring at least 12 others including NATO soldiers; another bomb attack against a NATO convoy in the north-western Faryab province injured 14 people including two foreign soldiers'.

On 18th August 2008 under the heading 'Probe as British rocket kills four kids' it was reported that: 'An investigation was underway after civilians, including four children, were killed in Afghanistan in a rocket attack by British troops; women and children were among those "accidentally" killed in the Sangin district of Helmand province'. On 27th August it was reported 'Afghan leaders have reacted with outrage after an airstrike killed 90 civilians, including 60 children ... President Hamid Karzai's government demanded an end to bombing raids in civilian areas and ordered a review of the presence of US and NATO troops in the country ... the backlash follows an apparently disastrous attack in Herat province where the UN found "convincing evidence" of such casualties'. On 2nd September there were reports that 'more than 70 civilians died in operations against the Taliban which US officials said killed more than 220 militants'.

On 18th August 2008 the French contingent in Afghanistan (variously reported as numbering 1,670-2,600) lost 10 soldiers with 21 wounded in an ambush and two-day battle in the Sarobi district of Kabul province, 30 miles east of the capital, bringing the total number of French dead in Afghanistan to 24 (US 574; UK 116; Canadian 89). Under the headline 'Brown: We've got the Taliban on the run' the British Prime Minister was reported on 21st August as saying; "The troops that I have talked to on the ground and our commanders on the ground believe they are making substantial progress against the Taliban" and that 'coalition forces were gaining ground'. The Times leader on 23rd August 2008 stated: 'The Taliban noose is being drawn ever tighter around the capital. The tactics are identical to those used against the British in 1841 and against the Russians two decades ago … gradually the Taliban have edged closer, and now hold territory only 20 miles southwest of the capital. The supply lorries are still running. But fear is growing, casualties are rising and NATO is looking hard and long at ways to defy an ominous historical precedent … but that precedent does not point only to defeat; it points to the vital need to rescue a country from its history.'

In an operation at the beginning of September 2008 NATO forces successfully delivered a massive replacement turbine and associated generating equipment weighing 220 tonnes for use at the Kajaki dam (out of action since the Soviet withdrawal in 1989) giving the prospect of electricity supplies to one and a half million Afghans within two years (subject to the repair of a second turbine and the provision of power lines). On 4th September 2008 the number of British dead in the conflict since November 2001 moved to 117.

Taking advantage of troop reductions in Iraq, President George Bush announced on 9th September the redeployment of 4,500 US soldiers to Afghanistan as part of a 'quiet surge' to combat the Taliban and to counter the growing insurgency outside Kabul, the reinforcements to join the existing US force of 33,000 in the country by February 2009. On 11th September 2008, the Chairman of the US Joint Chiefs of Staff (Admiral Mike Mullen) 'claimed a new military strategy was vital if the Taliban was to be smashed, saying "Frankly we're running out of time. I'm not convinced we are winning it in Afghanistan" adding: "Until we work more closely with the Pakistani government to eliminate the safe havens, the enemy will keep coming".' The following day the 118th British casualty in the war was announced (bomb disposal expert Warrant Officer Gary O'Donnell, subsequently awarded a Bar to his previously awarded George Medal), shortly followed by two further deaths the same week (the last in defence of the Kajaki dam), taking the total to 120. On 15th September 2008 it was reported that 'six children were killed and 12 wounded when they set off a roadside bomb in Ghazni province, south of Kabul; in a separate attack, a suicide bomber rammed a car into a UN convoy in southern Afghanistan killing a driver and two local doctors who were working on polio vaccination'.

On 19th September 2008 it was reported that the 'US plans to deploy up to 30,000 extra troops to Afghanistan next year [2009], taking its total force to more than 60,000' and that 'US Defence Secretary Robert Gates said Washington expected Britain to match its growing commitment'. On 22nd September the UK Defence Secretary said that 'British soldiers in Afghanistan face a long uphill task' and that whilst 'making a positive difference, it is difficult and dangerous and will take us years to achieve'. At the same time that Canada gave notice of its intention to withdraw from Afghanistan by 2011, the French announced their intention 'to send out 100 extra troops to bolster its in-country force' following recent losses. On 27th September it was reported that: 'Britain will not increase troop numbers in Afghanistan, despite the escalation in violent attacks by the Taliban – there will be no transfer of soldiers from Iraq – the current total of [around] 8,000 troops in Afghanistan is the "absolute ceiling" for Britain's contribution to the NATO operation'. The same news item confirmed that: 'The Americans are sending another 3,500 troops to Afghanistan in January (2009) and have promised to provide a further two combat brigades in due course.'

At the end of September 2008 'Taliban insurgents abducted up to 156 local workers helping to build a military base – the men were seized whilst travelling in buses at Bala Boluk in western Farah province'. The report added that 'despite the presence of 71,000 foreign troops, the militants have intensified their attacks'. Following the suicide truck bombing of the Marriott hotel in Islamabad (killing 53 and injuring 250) 'believed to be the work of al Qaeda and Taliban militants based on the Afghan border' Pakistan stepped up military operations in the 'Tribal Areas' [The seven Federally Administered Tribal Areas: Bajaur; Mohmand; Khyber; Orakzai; Kurram; North Waziristan; South Waziristan] claiming to have killed '60 Islamic rebels' at the same time that US forces in Afghanistan engaged in increased cross-border 'hot pursuit' activities (including continued use of un-manned Predator missile drones), violating Pakistan sovereign territory to the detriment of US/Pakistan relations. Simultaneously Afghanistan's ambassador-elect to Pakistan was kidnapped at gunpoint in Peshawar, NWFP and his driver killed.

On 29th September 2008 it was reported that Lieutenant Colonel Malalai Kakar, the female head of crimes against women in Kandahar, had been shot dead by the Taliban and that a suicide attacker had killed six civilians near the town. The following day General David Petraeus (incoming head of US Central Command and architect of the successful counter-insurgency 'surge' and 'Anaconda' strategy in the Iraq conflict) called for NATO allies to deploy more troops to Afghanistan, 'admitting that Taliban fighters were gaining a foothold in parts of the country and warning that Pakistan's "very existence" is being threatened by fanatics'.

On 6th October 2008 the outgoing commander of British forces in Helmand province (Brigadier Mark Carleton-Smith of 16th Air Assault Brigade, being relieved by 3 Commando Brigade Royal Marines) said that a military victory over the Taliban was 'neither feasible nor supportable' and that 'we are not going to win this war – it's about reducing it to a manageable level of insurgency that's not a strategic threat and can be managed by the Afghan army', this being in contrast to his reported comment that 'the Taliban military effort is on the back foot' made on taking up his appointment in April 2008.

At a meeting of NATO defence ministers in Budapest agreement was reported on 11th October that 'on a temporary basis' it had been agreed that ISAF forces would pursue 'facilities and facilitators' of the drugs trade in Afghanistan, worth 'an estimated $80 million' annually to the insurgents (the monthly cost of the war in 2008 for coalition nations was assessed at $3.5 billion). According to figures issued by the UN at the end of October 2008, opium production was estimated to have dropped by 30% for the year compared with the previous harvest. Conversely, the UK Guardian said in early November 2008: 'A glut of opium, fuelled by a record Afghan harvest threatens a heroin crisis in Britain, the EU's drug agency warned'. At the end of November 2008 a UN report declared that the Taliban had 'earned up to £300 million from the opium trade in the preceding year alone and that the hardline movement's drug money was being used to fund its fight against coalition troops … even hoarding supplies to push up prices … but NATO efforts to cut opium production are working and need more aid, according to the office on drugs and crime'.

On 15th October the UK suffered its 121st military fatality, and on 20th October it was reported that the Taliban had killed 30 bus travellers near Kandahar, beheading six of them. On 20th October two Taliban gunmen on a motorbike executed a British woman aid worker in Kabul; with 28 aid workers (including five foreigners) having been killed in Afghanistan so far in 2008 it was reported that 'aid agencies may be forced to withdraw if attacks continue'. On 25th October a British man and a South African working for DHL were shot dead in Kabul. On 31st October 'Taliban commandos stormed an Afghan ministry in the heart of Kabul' killing five. It was reported on 3rd November that five Afghan soldiers were mistakenly injured by US forces who opened fire on them in Kunar province. At the same time gunmen in Peshawar (NWFP Pakistan) kidnapped the brother of the Afghan Finance Minister.

The UK registered its 122nd fatality in Afghanistan since 2001 in early November 2008 when a soldier of the Royal Gurkha Rifles was killed in an attack in the Musa

Qala area of Helmand province. It was reported on 13th November that two Royal Marines had been killed in Helmand province when their vehicle was blown up, taking the British combat total to 124. At the beginning of the month, a commander of the returning UK Parachute Battalion had said that 'British forces need to win over the hearts and minds of the Afghans if the war against the Taliban is to be won; the insurgents have the ability to regenerate their ranks quickly and British troops could not "just keep having slugging matches with them"'. Meanwhile, an air strike by US forces on an Afghan village left 23 children and 10 women dead amongst the 37 wedding guests killed (5th November); 14 private security guards working for a road building firm were killed by US troops in Khost province (9th November); six people were killed and 40 wounded by a suicide bomber in Kandahar, but President Karzai's brother (who was present in the compound) survived (12th November); a suicide attack in a market in Nangarhar province (14th November) killed at least 21 people and injured 74 – one US solider was killed in the explosion, bringing US troop fatalities for the current year to 148; US cross-border missile strikes on Pakistani villages close to the frontier with Afghanistan continued (at least 18 strikes inside north western Pakistan since August), with 20-30 people killed at the outset of the month and a further 14 'militants' killed in North Waziristan on 7th November by an unmanned Predator drone aircraft. It was also reported (13th November) that 'six schoolgirls were seriously hurt after two men on a motorbike threw acid at them' in Kandahar.

President Karzai had talks with the British Prime Minister (Mr Gordon Brown) in London on 13th November 2008, at the same time that a survey 'showed that more than two-thirds of the of the UK population believed that British troops should be withdrawn from Afghanistan in the next year'. The 125th British fatality was reported on 17th November from Musa Qala District (Colour Sergeant Krishna Dura, Royal Gurkha Rifles) in a bomb attack that, significantly, was the first to penetrate the armour of the 25-ton Warrior 'light' tank. The 126th British casualty (roadside bomb, Kajaki) was recorded on 24th November 2008, followed by two more Royal Marine deaths in an ambush near Lashkar Gar in Helmand province three days later(total 128), the same day that four people died in Kabul near the US Embassy when a suicide bomber targeted a military convoy. The British Foreign Secretary confirmed on 28th November 2008 that Britain was willing to send a further 2,000 troops to Afghanistan if requested to do so by the incoming US President Barack Obama, thus taking the UK military total in the country beyond 10,000.

On 3rd December 2008 a treaty banning cluster bombs (which scatter hundreds of 'bomblets' indiscriminately over a wide area where they can lie dormant for years, and which are a major hazard in Afghanistan) was 'signed by more than 100 countries in Oslo, Norway – but not by the US, Russia or China'.

On 8th December a report by the International Council on Security and Development stated that 'the Taliban now have an influential and permanent presence across approximately two-thirds of Afghanistan'. The report went on to say that only one road out of Kabul – to the north – was safe to use and that 'the Taliban insurgents are closing a noose around the city and establishing bases close by from which to launch attacks' (the British Ambassador to Afghanistan, Sir Sherard Cowper-Coles, described the report as 'a very thin piece of work with seriously flawed methodology'). At the end of the previous month President Hamid Karzai had offered talks with Mullah Mohammad Omar (the Taliban leader) but the suggestion was rejected. Concurrently, the British government undertook a review of UK strategy in Afghanistan following warnings that 'Western attempts to stabilise the country are failing in several key aspects, including crime and corruption'. Issues considered included 'Afghanistan's porous border with Pakistan and the need for more helicopters to support British troops'.

Also on 8th December 2008 it was reported that 'more than 160 military vehicles destined for US-led troops in Afghanistan' had been destroyed in logistics depots on the outskirts of Peshawar prior to being driven through the Khyber Pass. A US spokesman said that the losses were 'militarily insignificant'. The attack by 'about 300 insurgents using rocket-propelled grenades' followed earlier hijackings of Allied trucks and supplies, including 12 NATO trucks, 4 US helicopter engines, and 36 NATO fuel bowsers using the same re-supply route, 'mimicking tactics used against British invaders in the 19th century and Soviet troops in the 1980s'. Reportedly 'about 70 per cent of the fuel and other supplies for NATO and US forces in Afghanistan are shipped into the Pakistani port of Karachi and then driven over the Khyber Pass'.

Elsewhere in Afghanistan combat casualties continued to mount, with three Canadian troops being killed by a roadside bomb in Kandahar on 5th December 2008, and two Danish soldiers being killed the previous day. On 10th December 'American forces mistakenly killed six police and a civilian in the southern city of Qalat', whilst on 26th January 2009 it was reported that up to 16 civilians had been killed in a US air raid, leading to protests and demonstrations in the city of Mehtar Lam. By 22nd December British military deaths in Afghanistan totalled 135 since 2001, this figure rising to 141 by mid-January 2009, and 143 by the end of that month, concurrent with a statement by the UK Chief of the Defence Staff that 'the British Armed Forces had been "smug" and "complacent" about their ability to mount counter-insurgency operations in places such as Afghanistan … leading to friction with US forces'. Additionally 'he also warned that Britain could ill afford to send more troops to Afghanistan' – notwithstanding indications to the contrary given by the British

Defence Secretary on 25th January, particularly with respect to some 300 specialists to be deployed 'to deal with the threat of landmines and roadside bombs' – which have caused 80 per cent of British fatalities – as part of a new focus on 'thickening' UK forces which was also to include the movement of seven Merlin helicopters from Iraq to Afghanistan (subsequently delayed by 'at least four months for implementation of a £50 million modification programme') and as many as 1,500 additional support personnel.

****

The New Year and the Presidential change gave renewed impetus to the intended US troop 'surge' in Afghanistan, with forecast total numbers to be deployed in 2009/10 doubling from 30,000 to as much as 60,000 in Helmand, Kandahar and Uruzgan provinces, and in the eastern area, together with an acknowledgement that the US could not win the war by military means alone, and that NATO allies must do more in respect of training the national police, eradicating drugs [2008 production: '7,700 tonnes of opium, 90 per cent of the world's illegal supply, principally from Helmand province, worth about £2 billion with at least $100 million going to the Taliban], building the Afghan army, establishing governance and promoting civilian economic development.

The beginning of February 2009 saw the vital allied supply route through the Khyber Pass again disrupted, this time with the destruction of a strategic bridge, following a battle with Pakistan's security forces in the Swat Valley in which 'at least 35 Taliban insurgents were killed'. The Pakistani ground and air offensive to secure the area for trucks carrying NATO supplies claimed to have killed 52 militants in the northwest Khyber region by 7th February 2009. To compound the allied logistical problems, Kyrgyzstan announced at this time its intended closure (with six months notice) of the US airbase in Manas, a key part of the northern military supply route into Afghanistan.

On 11th February 2009 (the day before Mr Richard Holbrooke, the new US special envoy to Afghanistan and Pakistan, was due to visit) 'a Taliban suicide bomber killed nine people inside a justice ministry building in Kabul and a gun battle broke out near the presidential palace'. A week later 'President Barack Obama authorised the Pentagon to send an extra 17,000 troops to Afghanistan to fight the Taliban', taking US troop levels to 55,000 (plus 30,000 from 40 other countries, mostly NATO members) at the same time that Lord Ashdown (who at the outset of 2008 was the hotly-tipped nominee for the position of UN 'super-envoy' in Afghanistan – subsequently blocked by President Karzai, and with Norwegian diplomat Kai Eide appointed instead in

March 2008) 'warned that the strategic position in Afghanistan is getting "steadily worse", saying that military power alone would not be enough to turn things around, adding "Unless we act quickly we may find ourselves in the position where the tipping point has passed"'. This theme was re-iterated by the American commander of the coalition force two weeks later who said in a radio interview: 'There are large areas in the south [of the country] where we are not winning, and in these areas more has to happen'.

Meanwhile, and as 'the first wave of the US troop surge consisting of 3,000 soldiers commenced operations in the northern provinces' it was reported that 'the number of Afghan civilians killed by NATO forces rose by a third last year [2008] to 829', although The Sun newspaper stated: 'More than 2,000 civilians were killed in 2008, an increase of 40 per cent from the previous year'. The British Foreign Secretary visited Kabul on 18th February 2009 for 'talks with his counterpart in which he emphasised the substantial human and financial cost of Britain's contribution to the war in Afghanistan'. The same week the 145th British serviceman was killed in the country since the start of operations in 2001, a figure that had risen to 149 by 25th February 2009 with the deaths of three soldiers 'in a Land Rover vehicle when they were hit by the blast from an improvised explosive device' and a Royal Marine 'shot while on patrol in Helmand'.

On 7th March 2009 the press gave details of an interview with the former British SAS commander in Afghanistan (Major Sebastian Morley, who had previously resigned over the number of troops being killed in the UK's inadequately armoured 'snatch' Land Rovers) in which he said that 'operations in Afghanistan are "worthless"', before going on to say: '"We hold tiny areas of ground in Helmand and we are kidding ourselves if we think our influence goes beyond 500 metres of our security bases. We go out on operations, have a punch-up with the Taliban and then go back to camp for tea"'.

On 10th March 2009 it was reported: 'Nimrods grounded for safety update – the RAF surveillance planes are to be taken off overseas service until early summer for safety modifications; " the work was meant to finish by the end of this month but has been delayed," defence minister Bob Ainsworth said yesterday. An inquiry into the 2nd September 2006 crash in Afghanistan, which killed 14 servicemen, found fuel seals and hot-air ducts should be replaced'.

As stated above, in early March 2009 General McKiernan, the US commander of coalition forces in Afghanistan stated that 'in large areas in the south and parts of the east of the country we are not winning and more has to happen', whilst on 21st March the UK Foreign Secretary (Mr Miliband) said 'the Taliban have achieved a strategic stalemate in Afghanistan' and that 'there could not be a solution in the region brought about by military means alone'. Three days later it was reported that 'President Obama is searching for an exit strategy to pull tens of thousands of US troops out of Afghanistan, even though with violence rising ahead of the August elections he has already committed an extra 17,000 soldiers to the country'. On 28th March the US President 'unveiled a new regional strategy to win the war in South Asia with an additional 21,000 US troops to be sent to Afghanistan and a trebling of civilian aid to neighbouring Pakistan … he announced no grand vision of a democratic Afghanistan, nor a timeline for withdrawal … downgrading the mission "to disrupt, dismantle and defeat" al-Qaeda in Pakistan and Afghanistan, and recasting the war as a regional conflict involving Pakistan, Russia, Iran, India, China and the Central Asian states'. However, during a European tour at the outset of April 2009 President Obama failed to gain any increase in NATO troop numbers in Afghanistan, leading on 27th April to the US commander (General McKiernan) 'to launch a scathing attack on the "half-hearted" efforts of alliance countries to fight the Taliban'. On 12th May 2009 General McKiernan was replaced by President Obama after just 11 months in charge of NATO's International Security Assistance Force (ISAF), with Lt Gen McChrystal assuming 'control of the 45,000 US troops and 32,000 others from NATO allies in Afghanistan'.

By the middle of May 2009 the number of British servicemen and women killed in Afghanistan since the invasion in 2001 numbered 158; by October2009 the death toll for British forces in the war had reached 220. In the intervening months the press headlines followed a now familiar pattern: 'Marine killed by roadside bomb was in "vulnerable" vehicle due to be replaced' (16th May); '2 more Britons die on Afghan mission' (29th May); 'Sixth British death in Helmand in two weeks' (4th June); 'Demand for more British troops' (13th June); 'Bombing kills star officer' (22nd June); 'Operation "Panther's Claw" targets Taliban' (23rd June); 'More US troops head to Helmand' (26th June); '10 Afghan policemen killed in gunfight' (30th June); '4,000 US Marines move in to crush Taliban drugs trade' (2nd July); 'Taliban kill most senior officer so far' (3rd July); '3 British soldiers killed by Taliban in Helmand' (6th July); 'Grief for eight British soldiers killed in a day' (14th July); 'We "need boots on the ground" in Afghanistan' (16th July); 'Helicopter shortage in Afghanistan "a scandal"' (20th July); 'Hero dies defusing bomb' (22nd July); '2 more die as mission is declared a "success"' (28th July); '3 Paras die in Afghan road blast' (7th August); 'Afghanistan will take 40 years' (8th August); 'Afghan blast kills 3 British servicemen' (14th August); '100 soldiers are wounded in one month' (17th August); 'British casualties soar in Afghan bloodshed' (18th August); 'British Chinook helicopter is shot down in Taliban ambush'

(21st August); 'Nightmare of Taliban's road bombs' (28th August); 'Afghan strategy in doubt as two more soldiers die' (1st September); 'We'll bring back British soldiers early, vows PM' (4th September); 'Two dead as Afghan toll hits 216' (17th September); 'Send more troops or we'll lose' (Lt Gen McChrystal – 22nd September); 'Thousands pay tribute to 6 Italian war dead' (22nd September); 'No time limit on Afghan mission' (2nd October); '8 US soldiers die in Taliban ambush' (5th October); 'Brown vows to send 500 more troops to Afghanistan' (15th October 2009) – taking the UK total of in-country forces to 10,000. The 8th Anniversary of the War in Afghanistan passed on 7th October 2009.

****

A presidential election was held in Afghanistan on 20th August 2009. Related press headlines included: 'Suicide bomb kills 10 in pre-poll attack in Kabul' (19th August); 'Election "is move away from terror"' (20th August); 'Terror of Taliban keeps half Helmand's poll stations shut' (20th August); 'Violence erupts as Afghans vote' (20th August); 'Taliban fear as Afghans go to polls' (20th August); 'Karzai claims win in Afghan poll amid fraud allegations' (21st August); 'Afghan fraud may sway poll result' (24th August); 'Karzai noses into lead as scores die' (26th August); 'British soldiers die for just "150 Afghan votes"' (27th August); 'Obama's envoy [Holbrooke] and Karzai in "bust-up" over Afghan poll fraud' (28th August); 'Karzai "wins" but result is still in doubt' (17th September); 'Karzai run-off threat increases' (8th October); 'UN admits Karzai win was rigged' (12th October); 'Karzai caves in as West forces election run-off' (21st October); '200 Karzai poll fraud staff fired' (22nd October); 'History repeats itself as NATO loses faith in credibility of Afghan leader' (24th October); 'Karzai handed second term' (2nd November); 'Obama warns Karzai to sort out Afghan "mess"' (3rd November); 'Karzai "the puppet" in vow to fight corruption' (4th November 2009).

Meanwhile, by 8th November 2009 the number of British military personnel killed in Afghanistan since 2001 had climbed to 232, with nearly 1,000 wounded, prompting British 'military expert Lord Ashdown to warn that "the NATO mission is failing at an accelerating rate"', amid reports that 'calls for a pull-out grow stronger'. On 27th October 'eight coalition troops were killed in separate bomb blasts across southern Afghanistan; the following day 6 UN members were killed in a Kabul guest house by 'Taliban suicide attackers', leading to the 'relocation of 600 UN staff out of the line of fire'. On 4th November it was reported that: 'Five British soldiers were shot dead and six were wounded when a rogue Afghan policeman opened fire without warning in a military compound'.

At the outset of December 2009 President Barack Obama announced a 'surge' of 30,000 US troops to Afghanistan to join the 90,000 already deployed there. Additionally NATO pledged 7,000 extra service personnel in support. 'This is our fight together' declared US Secretary of State Hillary Clinton. On 14th December 'Taliban fighters attacked checkpoints in northern and southern Afghanistan killing 16 Afghan police'. The following day 'at least 8 people were killed when a suicide car bomb exploded outside a hotel in the Afghan capital, Kabul'. At the beginning of January 2010 seven CIA agents were killed by a suicide bomber in the town of Khost, reportedly an 'al-Qaeda double agent', with four US soldiers killed by a roadside bomb on 3rd January. The same day the first British casualty of the year 2010 in an explosion in Helmand province took the British death toll in operations in Afghanistan to 246, a figure which had advanced to 300 by 20th June 2010. (The American 'military death toll in Afghanistan passed 1,000' on 28th May 2010).

In Kabul on 18th January 2010 'Taliban militants and suicide bombers launched simultaneous attacks on the capital, causing explosions and sparking a fierce gun battle'. Ten days later in London at a conference to address the 'future of the war shattered country' President Karzai stated that 'British soldiers could be needed in Afghanistan for up to 15 more years'; at a joint interview with President Karzai, UK Prime Minister Gordon Brown said 'there was no timetable for bringing UK troops home but spoke of "turning the tide" against the Taliban and al Qaeda insurgents in mid-2011'. On 26th February 2010 'Taliban suicide bombers killed 17 civilians in a dawn attack on hotels used by foreigners in the heart of the Afghan capital'.

On 11th March 2010 it was reported that 'British forces are to pull out of the bitterly contested market town of Musa Qala and hand over to an American Marine battalion as part of "a readjustment of UK forces in Helmand" ...the town controls the approaches to the Kajaki dam and reservoir – which it is hoped will provide electricity soon to the whole region'. President Barack Obama visited Afghanistan on 28th March 2010, telling US troops they were helping " forge a hard-won peace", subsequently 'advising Afghan President Hamid Karzai that progress on fighting corruption should match military gains'. At the same time a military helicopter 'crashed in southern Afghanistan injuring 14 people ...the Taliban claimed responsibility'. Ten days later it was reported that 'three US troops and a civilian contractor died when their American Air Force tilt-rotor Osprey aircraft crashed in Zabul, south-eastern Afghanistan ... Taliban militants claimed they shot down the aircraft'. On 15th April 2010 'four German soldiers were killed in fighting in northern Afghanistan' whilst in the city of Kandahar 'up to seven people were killed – some British – in a blast at a compound shared by western companies'. A Taliban commander said 'if military pressure on the insurgents in Kandahar became too great, they would simply leave and then come back after the foreign forces had departed ... he added that "the Taliban's main goal in the war is to establish Islamic law in Afghanistan ... we want sharia, that is first"'. On 19th April 'President Karzai named a former judge to lead a clean-up of the electoral system after last year's fraud ... the US embassy welcomed the changes ahead of September 18's parliamentary election'.

On 23rd April 2010 'NATO announced that it would be handing control of Afghanistan to the Afghan Government this year'. In mid-May 2010 press reports stated: 'Barack Obama says the US is on course to start withdrawing from Afghanistan from July 2011 ... and that Allied forces had begun to "reverse the momentum of the insurgency" ... the US civil commitment to Afghanistan will be long term, he added ... the change of tone comes two months after the US criticised Mr Karzai for allowing corruption to spread through all levels of government'. On 18th May 2010 'a suicide car bomber targeted a NATO convoy caught in rush-hour traffic in Kabul leaving six soldiers (five of whom were Americans) and at least a dozen civilians dead'. The following day '20 insurgents attacked the US-run Bagram airfield 30 miles north of Kabul'. At the same time 'more than 40 people were feared dead (including three British security contractors) after a Pamir Airways (a private Afghan airline based in Kabul) passenger plane crashed in mountains in northern Afghanistan'. On the 21st May 2010 'the UK Ministry of Defence announced that 8,000 British troops in southern Afghanistan would come under the control of the US – a change that underlines Britain's diminished role in the region'.

On 2nd June 2010 'Taliban militants attacked a national peace conference in Afghanistan minutes after it was opened by the President ... the conference was aimed at bolstering Mr Karzai's strategy of offering incentives to Taliban troops to cease fighting'. On 9th June 2010 'more than 60 people were killed and a NATO convoy was set on fire in militant attacks in Pakistan ... the attack on the convoy, carrying military vehicles, equipment and fuel for US forces in Afghanistan was just six miles from the heavily fortified capital, Islamabad ... the US sends 75% of its supplies through or over Pakistan'. One day later new British PM David Cameron 'revealed his impatience to get Britain out of Afghanistan as he paid his first visit to meet troops on the front line', declaring that 2010 "was the vital year" for progress against the Taliban. "We should start talks with the Taliban in the very near future to sort out Britain's exit strategy from Afghanistan" said General Sir David Richards, head of the British Army on 27th June, 'a day after Prime Minister David Cameron said he hoped to bring British troops home for good by 2015'. A week previously it was reported that: 'Britain's most senior diplomat in Afghanistan is temporarily stepping down.

The Foreign Office said that Sir Sherard Cowper-Coles – the UK's special envoy to Afghanistan and Pakistan – was taking "extended leave". No reason was given for the move.' In the event, his permanent departure from this post was confirmed in September 2010. In Kabul at the beginning of June: 'Hamid Karzai ordered a review of all cases involving Taliban suspects held in jail to identify prisoners "who are in jails with not enough evidence" and to arrange for their release, after national talks recommended ways to end the nine-year insurgency.'

In the final week of June 2010 it was reported that 'the top US commander [General Stanley McChrystal] has been recalled to Washington after he insulted senior government officials and diplomats in a magazine article' and that 'President Obama has condemned his military commander in Afghanistan for "poor judgment"'. On 28th June 2010 it was stated in the press that: 'New NATO commander General David Petraeus will pursue the policies of his predecessor, US military command assured President Hamid Karzai, who had warmly praised ousted Gen Stanley McChrystal for reducing civilian casualties. There was concern that his dismissal could disrupt the counter-insurgency strategy'.

US General Petraeus arrived in Kabul on 2nd July 2010 to take command of the 130,000 NATO troops in Afghanistan 'admitting that the campaign was in a "critical moment" as tens of thousands more soldiers arrive in the country for a surge against the Taliban' and '48hrs after NATO marked the bloodiest month of the nine-year war (June 2010 saw the deaths of 103 international forces, including 60 Americans) and Congress suspended $4 billion in aid because of President Karzai's failure to tackle corruption ... the violence continued as four international aid workers – including a British national – were killed when a Taliban suicide squad stormed their fortified compound in Kunduz city ... an American was killed in the east of the country while a Royal Marine was killed in the south'. On 13th July 2010 'three British soldiers were killed and four were injured when a rogue Afghan soldier fired a rocket-propelled grenade at them in their base at a checkpoint ... it is the second time in nine months that British troops have been killed by members of the Afghan security forces they are training ... President Karzai apologised for today's attack in Nahr-e-Saraj' (near Lashkar Gah). On 20th July 2010 it was reported 'a rebel Afghan soldier killed two NATO civilian trainers (US citizens) today ... the attack came as President Hamid Karzai joined 70 foreign ministers for a landmark conference in Kabul on the future of his country and renewed calls for international forces to hand control for security to Afghans by 2014 saying "I remain determined that our Afghan national security forces will be responsible for all military and law enforcement operations throughout our country by 2014". British Foreign Secretary William Hague said NATO could still *"win" the war against the Taliban despite the timetable for withdrawal'.*

On 19th July it was reported that 'with four Britons killed in Afghanistan in the past three days, Britain, with nearly 10,000 troops in the country, has suffered 322 fatalities since 2001' and that 'more than 250 British soldiers have been wounded (70 suffering very serious or serious injuries) in less than six months this year'. At the same time 'Prime Minister David Cameron announced an extra £200million in aid for Afghanistan would help speed up the return of British troops'. He also said that '2010 was the "key year" for the mission in Afghanistan; "this is the time to get the job done and the plan we envisage makes sure that we won't be in Afghanistan in 2015"'. On 18th July 2010 'defence secretary Dr Liam Fox confirmed 2014 was the target pull-out date' (the same year that President Karzai has to be out of office under present rules). The same day it was announced 'British aid to Afghanistan is set to increase by 40 per cent … the UK international development minister said "it is an issue of national interest because many of the problems which make our world much less secure emanate from very poor developing countries often caught up in crisis and conflict" … the government has already committed £500 million to projects in Afghanistan over the next five years'.

It was reported on 18th July 2010 that 'a Gurkha soldier was removed from duty after beheading a dead Taliban commander … this is considered hugely offensive to Afghan Muslims'. On 21st July 2010 NATO revealed that 'six Afghan police officers have been beheaded by Taliban during a raid on government buildings in northern Afghanistan'. On 26th July it was reported thus: 'The war in Afghanistan has made Britain's streets less safe and the situation is getting worse, Pakistan cricket captain-turned-politician Imran Khan told a packed rally in Glasgow, saying "British lives continue to be lost and the situation continues to deteriorate and no objectives are being achieved" (despite the number of foreign forces rising to around 150,000)'. And on 3rd August 2010 Pakistan's President Asif Ali Zardari said: "Coalition forces are losing the battle against the Taliban in Afghanistan" adding that "the international community had under-estimated the situation on the ground and the war was being lost above all because we have lost the battle to win hearts and minds". However, on 23rd August 2010 'the head of NATO forces in Afghanistan said the tide was turning against the Taliban; General Petraeus added that the momentum built up by the insurgents had been and would be "reversed in many areas", speaking after intense violence in the country during the run-up to the second set of parliamentary elections'.

On 16th August 2010 it was reported that: 'One of the gunmen who killed 11 charity health workers including British doctor Karen Woo in Afghanistan hitched a ride with the medical team shortly before the murders; the group stopped on their way back to Kabul on 5th August to give three men a lift ... shortly after they were attacked by a gang and six Americans, three Afghans, and a German in the International Assistance Mission which gave medical aid to villagers in Nuristan were killed along with Dr Woo.' On 17th August 2010 President Hamid Karzai decreed that 'private security companies must leave Afghanistan within four months ... the 37 firms, which employ 40,000 people in the country, have faced criticism for being trigger-happy and operating outside Afghan law ... the move is likely to prove popular with voters ahead of next month's elections but will infuriate NATO leaders, said analysts'. On 21st August 2010 it was reported that 'British and Afghan officials are investigating an apparent Taliban massacre of 30 road crew workers and their guards on a flagship road development project in the south of the country ... the contractors were resurfacing the main north-south route through the Helmand valley, linking Gereshk, the commercial capital of the province, with the trouble hotspot of Sangin ... a military spokesman said that British Forces did not have a remit to protect civilian contractors whose security was handled by the Afghans'.

On 26th August 2010 is was reported: 'Coalition forces in Afghanistan have taken £712 million of heroin in what is the world's biggest seizure of the drug ... the haul of 5.7 tonnes was seized with 11.3 tonnes of opium and 841kg of hashish, along with 4.5 tonnes of ammonium chloride used to turn opium into heroin ...Helmand's former head of counter-narcotics, Philippa Brown, said the amount seized represented 25-30 per cent of Britain's annual consumption of heroin ... "we are making these seizures in conjunction with giving out alternative crops including wheat, grape and fruit trees to show that there is an alternative to poppy cultivation" she added ... bad weather, disease and insect damage have resulted in the cost of a kilgramme of raw opium rocketing from £29 to £142'.

Under the headline 'Soldiers killed as Afghan poll hit by deadly attacks' it was reported on 20th September 2010 that 'two British soldiers have been killed in Afghanistan as bomb and rocket attacks continue to disrupt the country's parliamentary elections ... they were part of a ground domination patrol when they were struck by an explosion ... the election has been marred by deadly violence and concerns over widespread fraud, including apparent use of fake voter cards at some polling stations ... yesterday the bodies of two poll workers who were kidnapped in Balkh province were discovered, adding to the 21 civilians and nine police officers already killed, many of which attacks were blamed on the Taliban ... a number of polling stations were closed because of security problems and turnout was estimated at just 24 per cent ... Britain's Foreign Secretary said the vote was an "important step towards a secure and stable Afghanistan" but the Free and Fair Elections Foundation of Afghanistan said it had "serious concerns" about the poll, adding that "ballot stuffing [multiple voting] was seen to varying extent in most provinces, as were proxy voting and underage voting" … the carnage continued in Kunduz province yesterday when six children died in an insurgent rocket attack and eight children were killed while playing with a rocket round left in a village'.

Also on 20th September 2010 'the withdrawal of UK forces from Sangin which began early this morning marks the end of a campaign in which 106 British service personnel were killed and hundreds more wounded in the area since they were deployed there four years ago …the handover of control to the US is part of a NATO deployment in which American forces will operate mainly in the north and south of Helmand, with British, Danish and Estonian troops in the heavily populated central areas … British commanders today rejected any suggestion of a retreat, insisting that the withdrawal was merely a logical reorganisation of coalition forces … the 106 deaths constitute nearly a third of the total 337 UK fatalities in Afghanistan since 2001'.

On 28th September 2010 'NATO helicopters in eastern Afghanistan launched rare airstrikes into Pakistan in an operation against the Taliban, killing more than 50 militants and prompting a protest from Islamabad'. At the same time British officials said 'they were in contact with the Afghan authorities about the disappearance of a British aid worker and three Afghan colleagues ambushed in north eastern Kunar province'. Subsequently it was reported that British aid worker Linda Norgrove had been killed during an attempted rescue, and that she 'had been supervising reconstruction programmes funded by the US government' at the time of her abduction, and that 'the three Afghans who were kidnapped with her' had been released.

****

The ninth anniversary of the war in Afghanistan passed on 7th October 2010. On 8th October 2010 'a bomb hidden in a mosque killed the governor of Kunduz province together with 19 worshippers … he was a former mujahideen commander and a close ally President Karzai'. At the same time 'in Khost, eastern Afghanistan, six community policemen, part of a new government-sanctioned militia, were killed by NATO airstrikes … a senior official said the men opened fire on US gunships, which bombed them'. On 14th November 2010 'the new head of Britain's Armed Forces, General Sir David Richards, admitted that Al-Qaeda and Islamist militancy can never be defeated by military power … although it will remain a threat for at least 30 years, extremism could be "contained" to allow Britons to lead secure lives, he believes … he underlined Britain's aim to end its combat role in Afghanistan by 2014/15 … Sir

David spoke as President Karzai called for a reduction in NATO military operations, saying "the time has come to reduce the presence of boots in Afghanistan … to reduce the intrusiveness into daily Afghan life"'.

It was announced on 18th November 2010 that 'one hundred members of the British armed forces have died in Afghanistan this year … in all 345 British military personnel have died since operations in Afghanistan began in 2001 … in another development, UN figures published showed this year has been the deadliest so far for ordinary Afghans since 2001, with 1,271 civilian deaths in the first six months of this year, up 21 per cent on last year'. On 20th November 2010 it was reported that: 'Britain has made it clear that it will withdraw combat troops from Afghanistan in 2015 whatever the state of the war-torn country amid growing pressure from NATO not to set binding timelines … Downing Street said that bringing home troops depended on handing over security control to the Afghan police and army, but denied that this meant its date would slip.' (On 7th September 2010 it was reported that 'the Henry Jackson Society think-tank warned that the Taliban will be boosted by the Afghanistan withdrawal dates set by the UK and US, saying "it emboldens insurgents to continue fighting and gives them a survival target"').

On 29th November 2010 'six NATO troops were shot dead by a man dressed as a member of the Afghan border police … the men – all American – were killed during a training mission in eastern Nangarhar province'. On 12th December 'six NATO and two Afghan soldiers were killed when a suicide bomber detonated a minibus packed with explosives at a military base just as vehicles were preparing to move out on patrol … the attack took place in Zhari district, where the US poured in troops this summer as part of a surge of forces to try to flush out the Taliban from its southern strongholds'. On 16th December 2010 'a minibus was destroyed by a roadside bomb killing at least 14 people thought to be on their way to a wedding in the relatively safe province of Herat … officials also announced four Afghan soldiers, mistaken for militants, were killed in a NATO airstrike in Helmand'.

On 16th February 2011 it was reported that 'more British soldiers have died in Afghanistan than troops from the other 26 EU nations put together … the UK military death toll is 356 compared with 298 for all other EU countries … France has the next highest fatality toll at 53, followed by Germany 46, Italy 35, Spain 30, Holland 25 and Poland 24 … some countries have suffered comparatively high fatality rates, including Denmark, Holland and Estonia, which have deployed 750, 196 and 159 troops to Afghanistan respectively … Britain has 9,500 troops in the country and the rest of the EU just over 23,000, with the contingent from Germany almost 5,000, France 4,000 and Italy 3,770 … the US has sent 90,000 troops and suffered 1,476 fatalities'. The same day, in response to conflicting forecasts 'the Pentagon said that US General David Petraeus will not leave his post as NATO commander in Afghanistan "any time soon"'.

On 22nd March 2011 President Karzai announced 'Afghan forces will soon take charge of securing seven areas … starting in July, when US troops are expected to start pulling out, local forces will take over in the provincial capitals of Lashkar Gah in the south [pivotal town in Helmand where more than 30 British servicemen have died – control passed from British troops to Afghan security forces on 20th July 2011], Herat in the west, Mazar-i-Sharif in the north, and Mehterlam in the east …"the Afghan nation doesn't want the defence of this country to be in the hands of others any more; this is our responsibility to raise our flag with honour and pride," Mr Karzai said'. At the same time it was stated 'at least 2,777 civilians were killed in Afghanistan last year, a 15 per cent increase on 2009'.

On 2nd April 2011 it was reported: 'The United Nations was on the brink of leaving Afghanistan last night after two of its staff were beheaded and four Gurkha security guards were shot when a mob overran its regional headquarters in Mazar-i-Sharif … hundreds of protesters met at the city's main mosque [the Blue Mosque, one of the holiest sites in Islam] for Friday prayers and then marched to the UN compound to demonstrate against the extremist American pastor, Terry Jones, who burnt a Koran last month [there is concern within the UN that the attack may be linked to a request from President Karzai to the security council to review the UN's mandate in Afghanistan … the attack in Kabul on a guesthouse full of staff working on the election followed a row between Mr Karzai and the UN over irregularities in his re-election … mobile phone footage showed Afghan police killing a UN worker who fled the building] … by the third day of violent protests [including a march on the UN office in Kandahar] the in-country death toll was 24'.

On 11th April 2011 'Afghan President Hamid Karzai blamed the West for playing a part in a corruption scandal at Kabulbank … he acknowledged negligence and recklessness at the country's biggest lender, which lost hundreds of millions of dollars through fraud, but said foreign advisers and institutions "with their wrong advice and possibly corruption" contributed'. On 16th April 2011 'a police chief and his two bodyguards have been killed in a suicide attack on police headquarters in the southern province of Kandahar … it is the second time in just over a month that the Taliban have murdered a police chief'. On 26th April 2011 'hundreds of Taliban fighters are on the run after tunnelling out of Sarposa prison in Kandahar … at least 480 militants escaped through a 300 metre passage dug over five months from a house close to prison guard towers … Sarposa prison has been part of a plan to strengthen the Afghan government's presence in Kandahar region, the Taliban's birthplace ... the 1,200 inmate facility underwent security upgrades and tightened procedures after a 2008 Taliban attack that freed 900 prisoners ... a spokesman for the President said "this is a blow"'.

On 28th April 2011: 'An Afghan air force officer shot dead eight American soldiers and an American contractor before being killed himself at Kabul airport yesterday ... it was the seventh incident this year in which members of the Afghan security forces, or insurgents impersonating them, have killed coalition soldiers or members of the Afghan security forces.' On 27th May 2011 'seven NATO troops killed in a bomb explosion in the Shorabak district of Kandahar province near the Pakistan border were all American ... two Afghan policemen also died in the attack ... another NATO service member was killed in a helicopter crash in eastern Afghanistan ... some 38 coalition troops have died in the country this month'. On 31st May 2011: 'NATO apologised yesterday for an air strike that killed nine civilians, including women and children in Afghanistan ... President Hamid Karzai condemned the attack and warned the coalition that such errors could not continue, saying "this will be the last warning to NATO and American forces, and American officials"'. It was also reported on 31st May that 'a suicide bomber blew up a car at the gates of an Italian NATO base, while a second explosion ripped through a busy street in Herat, killing at least four people and injuring more than 20 ... the attacks shook the normally secure city, the largest in western Afghanistan, which is one of seven areas to be handed over to Afghan control in July as the first step toward transferring the nation's security to Afghan forces by 2014'.

On 16th June 2011 'eight people, including police officers, were killed and four injured when a suicide bomber struck a governor's office in north-eastern Kapisa province ... at the same time, a mortar narrowly missed the country's second vice-president and NATO officials at the opening of a £65million police training centre in central Wardak province ... a bomb wounded four in Kandahar in the south'. On 29th June 2011 'a five-hour assault on the Intercontinental hotel in Kabul by Taliban militants left 11 civilians dead ... the raid came on the eve of a two-day conference about the transfer of security control to Afghans by the end of 2014'.

On 12th July 2011 it was reported that: 'The half-brother of the Afghan president has been killed, shot twice by one of his most trusted bodyguards ... Ahmed Wali Karzai, head of the Kandahar Provincial Council and one of the most powerful people in southern Afghanistan, was assassinated in his home by his long-time head of security who was killed immediately afterwards ... his death is likely to leave a power vacuum in Kandahar, focus of recent efforts by a "surge" of US troops to turn the tide against the insurgency … President Karzai said the assassination reflected the suffering of all Afghan people, adding "This is the way of life for the people of Afghanistan. Our hope is this violence will come to an end and peace and happiness come to our homes and will come to rule in our country".' On 14th July 'at a funeral service for the president's murdered half-brother, a suicide bomber who hid explosives in his turban killed four mourners and injured 15 at the entrance to Kandahar city's Red Mosque'. (On 27th July 2011 a suicide bomber who also had explosives in his turban killed the mayor of Kandahar in his office – the mayor was a possible successor to Ahmed Wali Karzai; the following day, 28th July, six Taliban suicide bombers killed at least 19 people, including 10 children, and injured 40 using explosives planted in vehicles outside a government compound in southern Afghanistan, while on 29th July the Taliban 'intensified its new offensive in southern Helmand, killing 18 people by blowing up a minibus … violence has been on the rise as the Taliban try to regain territory lost in the autumn and winter to the US-led coalition').

On 16th July 2011 it was reported: 'A year after arriving in Afghanistan with President Obama's assurance that he was the best man to defeat the Taliban, General David Petraeus is handing over command of the war with his mission incomplete to head the CIA [from which post he subsequently resigned in November 2012 for domestic reasons]… as planned American withdrawals gather pace, his successor (Lieutenant-General John Allen) will have 33,000 fewer American soldiers under his command by this time next year and probably several thousand fewer troops from the coalition partners … last year 711 International Security Assistance Force troops were killed, the highest of a decade-long involvement that has cost the lives of 2,590 allied troops, 375 of them British, and absorbed billions of dollars'.

On 16th August 2011 'a British officer killed by a Taliban bomb was leading a ten-man patrol to meet village elders in Helmand province as part of a community involvement project … five of his comrades were also injured in the blast, which took place just 150 metres from the front gate of their base'. Meanwhile, 'a French soldier was shot dead in eastern Kapisa province … the lieutenant was the 74th French soldier to die'. By the end of August 'US forces had suffered their worst ever month in Afghanistan, with 66 troops killed'. On 5th September 2011 'the bodies of two missing German hikers were found dumped in sacks 4km from the south end of the Salang Pass, where they began their day-long trek on August 19; the men died of gunshot wounds'.

On 15th September 2011 it was reported: 'A deadly attack on the US Embassy and NATO headquarters in Kabul which left 27 people dead, including 11 civilians, was carried out by the Pakistan-based Haqqani network, American officials said … the assault by the insurgent group, which has links with both the Taliban and al-

Qaeda, "will not stop the security handover from the US-led coalition to Afghan forces," said American Ambassador Ryan Crocker'. A subsequent press report on 24th September 2011 read: 'Pakistan warned the US yesterday that it would lose an ally if it continued to make humiliating accusations that the country supported insurgents in Afghanistan ... Islamabad has been taken aback in recent days by the claims of complicity including that the Haqqani branch of the Taliban "acts as a veritable arm" of Pakistan's Inter-Services Intelligence (ISI) spy agency ... the US has long pressed Pakistan to take military action against Sirajuddin Haqqani, an Afghan warlord said to command 15,000 troops and to have bases in the Pakistan province of North Waziristan ... the recriminations come at a crucial time for the Afghanistan peace process, with the burial of Burhanuddin Rabbani in Kabul yesterday ... the murder of the former Tajik warlord has created tensions in Afghanistan and new dangers for President Karzai.'

On 27th September 2011 'eleven children, four women and a man were killed in Herat province when a roadside bomb hit an estate car ... four others were wounded; all the passengers were related'. The same day 'a suicide attack on a police lorry in Lashkar Gar, southern Helmand province, killed a man and a boy ... and NATO supply tankers were attacked by armed Taliban fighters on motorbikes in the outskirts of Quetta in south-west Pakistan'. The following day 'eight policemen were shot dead at a checkpoint near Lashkar Gah, three others were wounded and one was missing after the attack by insurgents ... meanwhile, a NATO soldier was killed in Wardak province'. On 4th October 2011 'an Afghan soldier suspected of murdering a British soldier during a Taliban firefight in Helmand in July has been arrested and allegedly confessed to the killing'.

On 7th October 2011 the British Defence Secretary 'spoke of the "deep debt of gratitude" owed to British servicemen and women, ten years on from the start of the war in Afghanistan in which 382 of our service personnel have lost their lives ... he said "as we mark ten years since military operations began it is vital to remember the reasons why our armed forces were deployed to Afghanistan and continue to serve there today – to protect our national security at home in Britain; the UK, together with 49 other countries, is helping to create a stable Afghanistan, able to maintain its own security, to prevent it once again becoming a safe haven for terrorists" ... Britain has spent an estimated £18billion on the war and has committed to spend a further £510million on development in the country until 2015 ... thereafter "we will continue to have a very strong relationship based on trade, diplomacy, aid and development [Afghanistan's minister of mining claims that his country holds untapped minerals worth more than $3 trillion] and on developing the Afghan forces"'.

Also on 7th October 2011 on the tenth anniversary of US military involvement, General Stanley McChrystal in Washington was reported as saying that 'a decade after it embarked on an invasion of Afghanistan, the US still does not know how to bring the conflict to an end ... he said that America had held a "frighteningly simplistic" view of the country and even now was "only a little better" than halfway to achieving its war goals there ... he said that the most difficult outstanding task was the creation of a legitimate government that Afghans could trust and could counter-balance the influence of the Taliban before the US troop withdrawal, due by 2014 ... more than 2,750 foreign troops and at least 10,000 civilians have been killed there since the first US and British special forces went in to destroy al-Qaeda and overthrow the Taliban ...Afghanistan [current population approaching 30million] has been given £36billion in international aid since 2001 but agencies say most rural Afghans remain impoverished'.

****

The US Secretary of State, Hilary Clinton, confirmed on 21st October 2011 that 'American officials had contacted Haqqani militants in Pakistan to gauge interest in peace talks; the meeting was organised by Pakistan's intelligence service'. On 25th October 2011 it was reported that 'about 200 insurgents were killed or captured in NATO operations in the east; among the targets of two Afghan-led raids were the Taliban-linked Haqqani network'. 22nd October 2011: 'A Chinese state-owned company has become the first foreign oil explorer to secure a licence to drill in Afghanistan ... beating off competition from Britain, Pakistan, Australia and America to win the right to explore for oil in the northern province of Sar-e-Pol, close to the border with Turkmenistan ... a new refinery is critical for Afghanistan which imports almost all its fuels and is dependent on supplies from Pakistan and Iran'.

On 29th October 2011 it was reported that 'at least 30 insurgents were killed after attacking a convoy of Afghan and international troops in Shinwar district of Nangarhar province, eastern Afghanistan' while in the south, in Kandahar province, 'a NATO service member died in a roadside bombing, bringing to 480 the number of coalition forces killed in Afghanistan this year'. On 31st October 2011: 'Two British electricians were among 17 killed by a suicide bombing in Kabul, in the deadliest attack on coalition forces in the Afghanistan capital since the war began. The contractors were in a military convoy of mine-resistant transport when their heavily armoured Rhino bus was rammed by a vehicle laden with 700kg of explosives ... they were among 8 civilians killed on the bus along with four US soldiers and one from Canada ... three

Afghan civilians and a police officer were also killed in the blast'. The same day: 'Three Australian soliders died when a man wearing an Afghan Army uniform opened fire during a morning parade … violence across Afghanistan is at its worst since the start of the war ten years ago, according to the United Nations'. 5th November 2011: 'A British soldier was killed yesterday when his patrol was attacked in the Nahr-e-Saraj district of Helmand province – "he had only been in the Army for a few months" said his parents', and 'US Major General Peter Fuller, second in command of training Afghan security forces, was relieved of his duties after telling a newspaper that Afghan leaders were "isolated from reality".'

'A widow and her teenage daughter were dragged from their beds and shot dead by armed men in south-eastern Afghanistan after allegations that they had committed "moral crimes",' it was reported on 12th November 2011 – ' the deaths are seen as another grim indicator of the appalling state of women's rights in the country, ten years after the Taliban fled Kabul'.

On 21st November 2011 it was reported that: 'The Taliban in Pakistan is holding exploratory peace talks with the country's government … a Pakistani expert on the Taliban said "the US won't be happy; if there is less pressure from Pakistan on the militants then they (the Tehrik-e-Taliban Pakistan, the TTP) will turn their attention to Afghanistan"'. On 28th November 2011 the press stated: 'Afghan soldiers "asked for NATO planes to bomb" two frontier posts in a mission that left 24 Pakistani soldiers dead because they wrongly thought they were being attacked by Islamist militants … outraged by the strike, Islamabad closed its border to trucks delivering supplies to coalition troops in Afghanistan and demanded the US leaves a base used by American drones within 15 days … it has plunged Washington's troubled relationship with Pakistan to a new low'. With seven fatalities during the month, the number of British military personnel killed in Afghanistan since 2001 rose to 390 by the end of November 2011, and to 397 by January 2012.

At a conference in Bonn on 5th December 2011 on the future of Afghanistan attended by delegates from 100 countries (but boycotted by Pakistan in protest at the NATO attack on its border checkpoints) to discuss the withdrawal of foreign forces by 2014, future international aid and a possible settlement with the Taliban, President Hamid Karsai said 'We will need your steadfast support for at least another decade'. On 6th December 2011: 'More than a dozen children were among 60 killed and 180 injured in a double bomb atrocity in Afghanistan … at least 56 Shia Muslims celebrating Ashura were killed at the entrance to a shrine in Kabul and four more were killed and 21 injured in Mazar-i-Sharif …there have long been tensions between Shia and Afghanistan's Sunni Muslim majority … thousands of Shias, mostly ethnic

Hazaras have been massacred by the Taliban'.

On 21st January 2012 it was reported: 'Four unarmed French soldiers were shot dead yesterday by a member of the Afghan Army, with a further 15 soldiers injured, 8 seriously ...France, the fourth largest contributor to the coalition, with 4,000 troops in Kapisa province [east of Kabul], is expected to complete its withdrawal by 2013, but with the deaths of 82 soldiers in Afghanistan in the past decade, there is pressure to speed up the departure'. On the same day, 'a classified document leaked to the American press says that 58 coalition soldiers have been killed in 26 attacks by Afghan soldiers since 2007, including at least eight British lives'.

On 2nd February 2012: 'The Taliban are controlled and aided by Pakistan's secret service, a leaked NATO report claims ... Inter-Services Intelligence spies give fanatics advice on fighting British and other troops ... the report follows claims ISI agents sheltered Osama Bin Laden before US troops killed him in May ... Pakistan dismissed the allegations as "old wine in an even older bottle"'. A report on 20th February 2012 said: 'Afghanistan's coldest winter in 15 years has claimed the lives of 41 people, most of them children ... 24 of the deaths were in the capital Kabul in camps for people who have fled the fighting ... also, three Italian soldiers died today in a car accident in the western province of Herat'.

8th March 2012: 'Six British soldiers were killed when their Warrior armoured troop carrier [25 tonnes] was blown up in a massive explosion in Afghanistan, it was revealed yesterday ...the tragedy came just three weeks after the troops began their tour of duty ... it is believed their vehicle caught fire after the blast and ammunition on board exploded, causing a fierce blaze from which nobody escaped, taking the total number of deaths of UK service personnel to 404 ... the men died as they patrolled the border between Helmand and Kandahar provinces, at a junction of roads between Gereshk and Lashkar Gah ... it is believed the Warrior hit either a Taliban-planted IED or an anti-tank mine from the war with the Soviet Union in the 1980s ... Afghanistan is littered with large numbers of mines from that time when the Soviets fought the Mujahideen'. Also on 8th March 2012: 'David Cameron yesterday remained insistent that the occupation of Afghanistan was "vital to our national security" despite signalling that Britain will join the US in a full withdrawal of troops by 2014 ... analysts warned that the remaining years of occupation could bring many more British deaths without any guarantee that Afghanistan would not return to anarchy after their departure ... Afghan National Army numbers have risen to 184,000'.

11th March 2012: 'Sixteen Afghans, including women and children, were killed in their homes in Kandahar province by a rogue US soldier in a pre-dawn rampage, plunging relations between the two countries into a new crisis … Afghan President Hamid Karzai condemned the slaughter as unforgivable, saying "when Afghan people are killed deliberately by US forces it is murder and terror"'. On 17th March 2012 it was reported that 'a NATO helicopter has crashed into a house on the outskirts of Kabul, killing 12 Turkish soldiers on board and at least two Afghan civilians'. On 21st March 'David Cameron told the Commons that a hand-over of security can happen at the end of 2014 "even without a political settlement" adding that the Taliban had opportunities for a settlement if they "give up violence, renounce al-Qaeda and want to play a part in the future politics of Afghanistan"'. On 26th March 2012 'a Royal Marine and a British soldier were shot dead by an Afghan National Army gunman, who also injured a third British serviceman when he opened fire at the British military HQ in Lashkar Gah in Helmand province … so far this year 15 NATO service members have been killed by Afghan security officials or militants disguised in their uniforms'.

On 16th April 2012: 'Explosions and gunfire rocked Kabul yesterday as the Taliban launched one of the biggest assaults on the Afghan capital in more than a decade … dozens of heavily armed fighters and suicide bombers mounted a series of co-ordinated attacks on NATO bases, the national parliament and the embassies of Britain, the US and Germany … the start of the "spring offensive" being in retaliation for events including the alleged killing of 17 Afghan civilians by a US soldier … Afghan MPs who grabbed weapons and opened fire from the roof of the parliament building said the attack exposed the "poor training" of the police who had "no idea where they were firing" … apart from Kabul, the eastern capitals of Paktia, Logar and Nangarhar provinces also came under attack … the violence showed that the Taliban and their allies are far from beaten … an arrested militant said the attacks were the work of the Haqqani network which has ties to the Taliban and al-Qaeda … meanwhile, at least 380 prisoners – including at least 20 "very dangerous" insurgents – were freed when about 100 Taliban militants attacked a jail in the city of Bannu in north west Pakistan yesterday'. On 2nd May 2012 'under the cover of night, Barack Obama flew into Afghanistan yesterday to cement America's commitment to the country after the long and unpopular war ends … he was on the ground for about seven hours and his main objective was to sign the Strategic Partnership Agreement with president Hamid Karzai … it will govern America's role in Afghanistan after its combat mission ceases at the end of 2014'.

14th May 2012: 'Two traitor Afghan policemen shot dead a British soldier and an RAF officer at Patrol Base Attal near Lashkar Gah …one was killed in return fire, the other escaped'. On 21st May 2012 – 'Two NATO service members have been killed in an insurgent attack in southern Afghanistan …the deaths bring the number of foreign troops killed this month to 24 … a total of 156 have been killed this year … a suicide bomber also struck a checkpoint in Uruzgan province, injuring six'. The same day: 'British soldiers could remain in Afghanistan after the main withdrawal in 2014 … about 200 special forces may stay on to counter any attempt by al-Qaeda to re-establish a foothold in the country … Britain has pledged £63 million a year as part of a £2.8 billion international fund to prevent Afghanistan from becoming a "safe haven" for terrorists …but it is feared the absence of international troops could tempt al-Qaeda into shifting its efforts back to Afghanistan after recently focussing its activities on Yemen and Somalia'. 22nd May 2012: 'British soldiers will be out of Afghanistan on schedule, despite fears that the Taliban could regain control, David Cameron told a NATO summit in Chicago yesterday … "that is our deadline" he added, insisting the Taliban could never win back control through force after the international withdrawal of troops …"I am confident that our troops can leave with their heads held high having completed the combat task in 2014, because they will be handing over to fully capable Afghan National Security Forces"'. On 26th May 2012 it was reported that 'French combat troops will leave Afghanistan by the end of the year, 12 months earlier than planned, President Hollande said in Kabul; about 1,300 soldiers from a 3,300 force will stay to train the Afghan army and police, and return equipment to France'.

Reverting to 12th May 2012: 'Afghanistan may sue the British accountant PwC over the £560 million collapse of Kabul Bank … "They could easily have detected the problems," Finance Minister Omar Zakhilwal said … the P&C affiliate that audited the bank in 2009 said it knew of "no basis" for complaint … regulators seized Kabul Bank after it became exposed to huge loans, including to President Karzai's brother, Mahmoud'. On 7th June 2012 it was reported that 'Afghanistan has named as ambassador to London a close friend of President Hamid Karzai who had been accused of fraud in the US … raising fresh questions about corruption and nepotism at the heart of government … the London post has been vacant for a year as the Afghan government failed to find a candidate for one of its most prestigious diplomatic posts'. The same day: 'NATO has been accused of killing 18 members of a wedding party during an air strike in Afghanistan … the organisation's forces were targeting militants in Logar but instead killed a tribal elder and his family, it is claimed … NATO denies the reports … meanwhile three suicide bombers killed at least 22 and wounded another 50 in Kandahar, and two US service members died in a helicopter crash'.

2nd July 2012: 'Three British soldiers have been shot dead by an Afghan policeman at a military checkpoint in Helmand province in Afghanistan … the gunman was shot and captured … the three were part of an Afghan police advisory team attending a meeting of tribal elders … the fatalities will increase pressure on the Government to speed up the withdrawal of British troops … Mr Cameron said "these brave soldiers were demonstrating great courage to help prevent Afghanistan once again become a haven for terrorists and therefore to help keep us safe here in UK" … General Sir David Richards, Chief of the Defence Staff, added "attacks like this will not stop us from moving forward; I know that the resolve of those on operations will be unshaken" … he insisted that overall there remained a high level of trust between Afghan and British forces … the shootings bring the British military death toll to 422'.

On 4th July 2012 it was reported that 'Pakistan is to end a seven month blockade and re-open NATO supply routes to Afghanistan after the US apologised for killing 24 Pakistani troops [cf 28th November 2011] and agreed to pay $1.1 billion … the US has been forced to use lengthy routes through Russia and Central Asia … Washington has also offered road building projects to sweeten the deal … Qamar Zaman Kaira, Pakistan's information minister, said: "A superpower has acknowledged our principled stance; it was not the issue of money, it was the issue of our sovereignty"'. Also on 4th July 2012: 'Five NATO soldiers have been shot and wounded by a man in an Afghan Army uniform … it is the second "green-on-blue" attack in four days … 26 foreign personnel have died in 18 similar incidents this year alone, compared with 20 deaths last year'.

On 9th July 2012 it was reported that 'a video has emerged of the Taliban apparently executing a woman who was accused of cheating on her husband … the three-minute film shows a crowd watching as the wronged man shoots the kneeling woman five times at close range with an automatic weapon … when the woman falls sideways after being shot, the spectators chant: "Long live the Afghan mujahideen! (Islamist fighters)" … countries, including Britain, yesterday pledged to give £10.3 billion in civilian aid to Afghanistan to prevent it lapsing into chaos after NATO troops pull out in two years'. Also on 9th July 2012: 'The Taliban said today that they planted a roadside bomb that killed six US troops in eastern Afghanistan … the blast struck an armoured vehicle last night in Wardak province, south of Kabul … the deaths didn't stop there as three children were killed by suicide bombers … other militants attacked two police HQs, leaving two children and three policemen dead in Kandahar … meanwhile President Hamid Karzai said he was encouraged by pledges to provide Afghanistan with $16bn in aid after foreign troops leave in 2014'.

'An Afghan soldier who killed four French soldiers has been sentenced to death by hanging at a military court in Kabul' it was reported on 17th July 2012. On 20th July 2012: 'David Cameron yesterday warned Taliban fighters waiting for our troops

to leave that Britain will continue to support Afghanistan for years to come ... "The Taliban should be in no doubt that we will be handing over to a very large, very capable Afghan security force," he warned, speaking in Kabul alongside President Hamid Karzai and Pakistan's prime minister Raja Pervaiz Ashraf, adding that "the terrorists that are trying to wreck Afghanistan are the same terrorists that are trying to wreck Pakistan" ... Mr Cameron and Mr Karzai signed a memorandum of understanding on the planned "Sandhurst in the sand" training academy which will see 90 British military leaders train Afghan counterparts ... The US commander in Afghanistan, Gen John Allen, told Mr Cameron that the handover of security to Afghan forces was progressing well ... meanwhile, two NATO service members were killed by roadside bombs in Eastern Afghanistan, bringing the death toll among foreign troops to 27 this month and 242 this year ... a roadside bomb in north-western Faryab also killed eight minibus passengers'. On 23rd July 2012: 'Roadside bombings killed four NATO troops in Afghanistan yesterday ... three civilian contractors [one British, two US] working with the coalition forces were also killed when a man in an Afghan national security force uniform opened fire on them in the west of the country ... elsewhere, four civilians died when hundreds of rockets were fired into insurgent hot spots from neighbouring Pakistan ... a spokesman for President Hamid Karzai said "This will have a negative impact on the friendly relations between Afghanistan and Pakistan"'.

24th July 2012: 'An Afghan police commander and 13 officers have joined the Taliban in the western Afghan province of Farah, in what could be the biggest defection yet ... the men are said to have taken heavy weapons and US-made armoured Humvee vehicles'. On 26th July 2012 it was reported that 'seven children were killed when they triggered a booby-trapped spring ... they were grazing farm animals when a bomb went off near Taywara in western Ghor province'. Two days later: 'Attacks by insurgents in Afghanistan are at their highest level since 2010, NATO figures show ... "enemy-initiated attacks", such as roadside bombings, have also risen by 11 per cent in the past three months compared with the same period last year, ISAF said ... the rise is attributed to an early end to the opium poppy harvest, the insurgents' main source of income, which meant the fighting season began earlier'. A week before, on 20th July 2012, it had been reported that: 'Almost 850 stolen artefacts dating back to the Bronze Age have been returned to their rightful home in Afghanistan, travelling from RAF Brize Norton to the National Museum in Kabul ... "The transfer of these items is a step forward in Afghanistan's journey towards normalisation," said British defence secretary Philip Hammond'.

On 4th August 2012 it was reported: 'President Obama has chosen seasoned diplomat James Cunningham to fill one of the most difficult overseas posts as Ambassador to Afghanistan … Mr Cunningham succeeds Ryan Crocker who left his post after less than a year for health reasons'. Also on 4th August: 'Thousands of American troops from the surge force of 33,000 sent to Afghanistan by President Obama in 2010 will be leaving this month … US commanders are trying to ensure that the gaps left by the US Marines and Army in the south of the country are adequately filled by properly trained Afghan units … last month 40 US Marines and soldiers were killed, the majority by improvised explosive devices … on present planning, the size of the Afghan national security forces should reach 352,000 by October; by then US troop strength will have shrunk to 68,000 … about 900 members of the Afghan national security forces have been killed in four months'.

On 8th August 2012: 'Two Taliban suicide bombers killed three NATO troops today in Eastern Afghanistan … the attack targeted a patrol near the headquarters of the Kunar provincial government'. 10th August 2012: 'Three American special forces members were shot dead by a gunman wearing an Afghan security forces uniform after he lured them to a pre-dawn Ramadan breakfast in the Sangin district of Helmand province … three days previously a US soldier was killed by two gunmen wearing Afghan army uniform in eastern Afghanistan … more than 20 ISAF military personnel have been killed in green-on-blue attacks this year'. 11th August 2012: 'Two British soldiers have been killed in separate incidents in the Nad-e-Ali district of Helmand Province, the first UK fatalities in the country for more than a month … one died in a shooting while on foot patrol, the other was killed working on a construction task'. 15th August 2012: 'At least nine worshippers were wounded today when two grenades exploded at a mosque compound during morning prayers in Khost, eastern Afghanistan … a string of bombs across the country killed 50 people yesterday as the Taliban offensive intensifies amid international moves to hand over security to Afghan forces'.

On 16th August 2012 it was reported that: 'The Pakistani Minhas air force base in Kamra, about 25 miles north-west of Islamabad, with suspected links to the country's nuclear programme, was in flames today after being stormed by gunmen with automatic weapons and rocket-propelled grenades … the Pakistani Taliban claimed responsibility for the attack … Kamra houses fighter jets, including F-16s … some experts suspect it could also house part of Pakistan's nuclear arsenal … safety of the country's nuclear arms has been a major concern for Western nations'. The following day: 'Eleven people including seven US troops died when a UH-60 Black Hawk helicopter came down in Kandahar province … the Taliban claimed insurgents shot down the aircraft'. On 18th August 2012: 'An Afghan who signed up to join the police five days ago shot dead two US soldiers minutes after they handed him his weapon at an inauguration ceremony in Kinisk, Farah province … he was shot dead by coalition troops'. 20th August 2012: 'Martin Dempsey, the US military's top general, is to hold talks with senior officials in Afghanistan in a bid to stop "green-on-blue" attacks by Afghan soldiers and police against international forces … two policemen killed an American yesterday, taking the US toll to 10 in only two weeks … at least 37 foreign troops have died in green-on-blue attacks this year, seven of them British'.

28th August 2012: 'Taliban insurgents beheaded 17 people at a dance party in Helmand province's Musa Qala district to show their "disapproval" of the event … the killings were seen as a brutal reminder that insurgents are starting to recover control from international forces and are trying to re-establish draconian controls over people's behaviour … in separate incidents yesterday, ten Afghan soldiers were killed in a Taliban attack on a checkpoint in Helmand province and two American soldiers were shot dead by an Afghan colleague in Laghman province'. 30th August 2012: 'Worst day in Afghan war for Australia with five soldiers killed in two incidents … the first took place in Uruzgan province when three soldiers were resting at a base when a man in an Afghan army uniform opened fire at close range, killing the three and wounding two others … hours later two more soldiers died and a crew member was injured when their Black Hawk helicopter rolled over while landing in Helmand … the latest fatalities come as Afghan President Hamid Karzai moved to replace his intelligence chief and the ministers of defence in the first step of a planned wider Cabinet shake-up aimed at solidifying his power before foreign forces leave in 2014'.

1st September 2012: 'A boy aged 12 and a girl aged 6 have been beheaded in separate incidents … both murders were the work of Taliban fighters intent on intimidating the local population, police said … the boy, whose brother is a policeman, was kidnapped and killed in southern Kandahar and his severed head placed near his body to send a warning … the girl was killed in Kapisa province in a Taliban-controlled area … the local police chief said he dared not send detectives to the region'. The same day: 'Soldiers from the King's Royal Hussars are championing an Afghan government programme aimed at improving animal welfare in Lashkar Gah … an Afghan paramedic vet explained: "It is important to visit these remote areas and discuss with communities basic animal husbandry … many farmers have little understanding of animal care as their forefathers have not taught them"'. On 11th September 2012: 'Soldiers attended a ceremony in the eastern province of Parwan yesterday to mark the handover of the notorious Bagram prison from US forces to Afghan authorities'. While on 12th September 2012 it was reported: 'Eight people – nearly all children – were killed in a bomb blast in an attack on NATO headquarters in Kabul carried out by a teenage boy wearing a suicide vest'.

On the 15th September 2012 it was reported that: 'Insurgents attacked Britain's main base in Afghanistan last night, where Prince Harry is currently posted, killing two US Marines, destroying six AV8B Harrier jets worth about £100 million, and damaging two others, six aircraft hangars and three refuelling stations … Camp Bastion, a huge base shared with US, Estonian, Danish and Afghan troops in southern Helmand, was attacked on the north east side which houses the US base Camp Leatherneck … the Taliban have threatened to kidnap and kill Prince Harry … there are fears of a surge in violence before coalition forces withdraw in 2014 … the British Defence Secretary has made it clear that the British forces would maintain a steady withdrawal with the reduction of 500 men to 9,000 troops by the end of the year … Britain has closed 52 of its bases and checkpoints in the past six months, he said, leaving 34 operating … he concluded by saying "over the years we have contained the threat to UK security and we have built the Afghan security forces to the point that they can take over that burden … we are confident we will leave in place a solution that will not look perfect … but if it maintains the integrity of Afghanistan and stops the use of it for international terrorists, we have achieved our primary purpose"'.

17th September 2012: 'Hundreds of Afghans burned cars and threw rocks at a US military base today in protest at an anti-Islam film ridiculing the Prophet Mohammed … at least 20 police officers were injured in violent demonstrations outside the Camp Phoenix base and other parts of the capital Kabul … it was the fourth day of Afghan protests against the video, produced in the United States, which seeks to portray Mohammed as a fraud, a womaniser and a child molester'. On the same day it was reported: 'Eight women and girls were killed by a NATO airstrike on a remote village in Laghman province … the NATO coalition, which initially said only insurgents were killed in the strike, later took "full responsibility for the tragedy"'. Also on 17th September 2012: 'Two British soldiers gunned down in Afghanistan were lured to their death by a killer dressed as an Afghan policemen who was pretending to be wounded at a checkpoint in Nahr-e-Saraj, Helmand … Defence Secretary Philip Hammond said the military campaign in Afghanistan would not be derailed as he paid tribute to the soldiers … fifty-one allied soldiers, including nine Britons, have died in such "green on blue" incidents this year in which supposedly friendly Afghans turn on allied troops'.

On 18th September 2012 it was reported that 'Britain was today battling to stop a blunder by US-led military chiefs damaging the Afghan campaign following reports that partnering with Afghan troops will be scaled back and that joint operations with Afghans below battalion level will now need the consent of a two-star general … US general John Allen, the Isaf commander, issued a second statement to clarify the earlier announcement, stressing the new partnering arrangements were a "temporary" measure … a UK defence source said the original Isaf statement was "ill-judged" … Defence Secretary Philip Hammond acknowledged green on blue attacks were "sapping public opinion and morale" adding "that is why we are determined to solve this problem, to nip this trend in the bud and make sure we get on top of this"'. Also on 18th September 2012: 'Twelve people were killed when a suicide bomber's car rammed into a bus in Kabul carrying mainly foreign workers, including a British woman'. On 30th September 2012 'the American death toll in Afghanistan reached 2,000 after a checkpoint shooting left a soldier, a contractor, and three Afghan troops dead'. The following day: 'A suicide bomber riding a motorcycle packed with explosives rammed into a patrol of Afghan and international forces today, killing at least 14 people in Khost'.

7th October 2012: 'With virtually no fanfare, Sunday marked the 11th Anniversary of the US-led invasion of Afghanistan that was launched to destroy al-Qaeda training camps and oust the Taliban regime that supported the terrorist group behind the deadliest terrorist attacks on American soil … the Taliban has proved a resilient enemy, which has vowed to never surrender in its goal to destroy the still fragile democratic government, which remains beset by corruption and an unstable security force … the Taliban issued a statement on Sunday to say that "With the help of Allah, the valiant Afghans under the Jihadi leadership of Islamic Emirate defeated the military might and numerous strategies of American and NATO alliance, and now after 11 years of unceasing terror, tyranny and crimes and savagery, they are fleeing Afghanistan with such humiliation and disgrace that they are struggling to provide an explanation"'. Following a gathering in Trafalgar Square, London, marking the 433 British military lives lost in the conflict, Defence Secretary Philip Hammond said troops would be withdrawn in 'significant' numbers next year before combat operations end in 2014, adding, "to those who say get out of Afghanistan, I reply that is exactly what we are doing"'.

****

On 20th October 2012 it was reported that 'a minibus carrying guests to a wedding party was hit by a roadside bomb … 19 people were killed and 16 wounded in the attack, most of them women and children, in the northern province of Balkh, about 25 miles from Mazar-i-Sharif'. On 25th October 2012: 'The [UK] Commons Overseas Development Committee concluded that the international community's aim of creating a viable modern state in Afghanistan is no longer viable.' Also on 25th October 2012: 'A Royal Marine Commando and an Army medic (the third woman soldier to be killed in Afghanistan) were shot dead in a firefight with an of-duty Afghan policeman'. On 31st October 2012: 'Two Gurkhas were shot dead at a checkpoint in Nahr-e-Saraj, Helmand province yesterday by a rogue Afghan policeman'. On 12th November 2012: 'A British soldier was killed yesterday, Remembrance Day, by a member of the Afghan army as he played football at Patrol Base Shawqat in the Nad-e-Ali district of Helmand province ... the insider attack takes to 438 the number of UK service members to have lost their lives since operations in Afghanistan began in October 2001 ... the death brings the number of British servicemen killed by Afghan soldiers or police to 12 this year, compared with one in 2011, three in 2010, and five in 2009 ... at least 54 international troops have died this way'.

****

Two reports from neighbouring Pakistan. On 22nd November 2012: 'A Taliban suicide bomber killed at least 23 people including eight children today at a Shia Muslim procession in Rawalpindi'. 18th December 2012: 'Six anti-polio campaign workers, including four women, have been shot dead in Karachi by suspected Taliban gunmen'.

Returning to Afghanistan. 24th November 2012: 'The UK Ministry of Defence is to buy 51 extra Foxhound light patrol vehicles ... the first Foxhounds were deployed to Afghanistan this year, replacing the Army's Snatch Land Rover which proved vulnerable to roadside bombs, and are being used by soldiers mentoring the Afghan National Security Forces ... the new order, part of a £340 million investment, will take the Army's fleet to 376 vehicles'. 28th November 2012: 'Hundreds of millions of dollars were spirited out of Afghanistan – some hidden in airline food trays – in the huge fraud that led to the collapse of Kabul Bank, the nation's largest financial institution ... new details have been revealed about how fraudsters and their friends and relatives got rich using $861million (£538million) in fraudulent loans etc'.

3rd December 2012: 'Three Afghan soldiers and two civilians died yesterday after Taliban suicide bombers attacked the US air base at Jalalabad ... the nine attackers were killed'. 18th December 2012: 'Nine girls were killed when a landmine exploded as they gathered firewood outside their village yesterday ... the children, whose ages ranged from nine to 13, were in the eastern province of Nangarhar ... two more were in a critical condition in hospital ... meanwhile, at least two Afghan workers were killed and a dozen others injured when a car bomb targeted a US military contractor in Kabul'.

On 19th December 2012: 'David Cameron today announced a significant withdrawal of British troops from Afghanistan which could see 4,000 return home next year ... Downing Street said that progress by Afghan forces in taking charge of security was happening quicker than planned ... and Isaf commanders have been delivering optimistic reports ... but there have also been claims that investors are pulling out of the country over fears that Taliban insurgents will resurface when Western troops leave'. 21st December 2012: 'The Prime Minister flew to Camp Bastion yesterday ... he insisted that Afghan forces are ready to take over security, adding "This is a withdrawal based on success, not failure; we're confident it can be done while making sure Afghanistan does not return to being a haven of terrorism."

****

"For when death comes the brave are free
So in thy dreams remember me."

December 2012

BIBLIOGRAPHY

'Only the dead have seen the end of war.'

Arney, George, *Afghanistan (The definitive account of a country at crossroads)* (1990)

Danziger, Nick, *Danziger's Travels* (1987)

Edwards, Major T.F., MBE, (Somerset Light Infantry) *Military Customs* Gale & Polden (1948)

Fergusson, James, *A Million Bullets: The real story of the British army in Afghanistan* (2008)

Fraser, George MacDonald, *Flashman* (1969)

Heathcote, T.A., *The Afghan Wars 1839-1919* (1980)

Hensher, Philip, *The Mulberry Empire* (2002)

Hodson, Petegrine, *Under a Sickle Moon. A Journey through Afghanistan* (1986)

Hopkirk, Peter, *The Great Game. On service in high Asia* (1990)

Hosseini, Khaled, *The Kite Runner* (2003)

Isby, David C., *War in a Distant Country. Afghanistan, invasion and resistance* (1989)

Kipling, Rudyard, *Kim* (1901)

Kipling, Rudyard, *Selected Stories* (1972)

Newby, Eric, *A Short Walk in the Hindu Kush* (1958)

Rashid, Ahmed, *Descent into Chaos: The US and the disaster in Pakistan, Afghanistan and Central Asia* (2008)

Sale, Lady Florentia, *Journal of the Disasters in Afghanistan, 1841-2* (1843)

Schofield, Victoria, *Every Rock, Every Hill. The Plain Tale of the North West Frontier and Afghanistan* (1984)

Seierstad, Asne, *The Bookseller of Kabul* (2002)

Wragg, Sydney, *Far and Wide (Poems)* (2011)

****

Related titles published by Helion & Company and GG Books

Koevoet! Experiencing South Africa's Deadly Bush War
Jim Hooper
312pp Paperback
ISBN 978-0-957058-70-6

LZ Hot! Flying South Africa's Border War
Nick Lithgow
174pp Paperback
ISBN 978-1-908916-59-4

A Whisper in the Reeds. 'The Terrible Ones' – South Africa's 32 Battalion at War
Justin Taylor
172pp Paperback
ISBN 978-1-908916-58-7

Shadows of a Forgotten Past. To the Edge with the Rhodesian SAS and Selous Scouts
Paul French
228pp Paperback
ISBN 978-1-908916-60-0

HELION & COMPANY
26 Willow Road, Solihull, West Midlands B91 1UE, England
Telephone 0121 705 3393 Fax 0121 711 4075
Website: http://www.helion.co.uk